# TWO COOKS
# IN ONE
# KITCHEN

# TWO COOKS IN ONE KITCHEN

JINX AND JEFFERSON MORGAN

Doubleday & Company, Inc., Garden City, New York
1983

# ACKNOWLEDGMENTS

It would be impossible to thank everyone who deserves it, but we must express our special gratitude to all our editors at *Bon Appétit* magazine, whose help and comfort we have come to cherish.

Thanks also to Marie Comas, an imaginative, talented, and intrepid editor; Carl Brandt, whose advice is always sound and whose company is always amusing; Chaucy Bennetts, who did a heroic job of copy editing and, occasionally, saved us from ourselves; Alex Gotfryd, who helped name the baby, and Larry Alexander, who dressed it up so nicely.

DESIGNED BY LAURENCE ALEXANDER

Portions of this book appeared in different form in *Bon Appétit* in 1978, 1979, 1980, and 1981.

*Library of Congress Cataloging in Publication Data*

Morgan, Jinx.
Two cooks in one kitchen.

Includes index.
1. Cookery.   I. Morgan, Jefferson.   II. Title.
TX652.M668      641.5      AACR2
ISBN: 0-385-17462-4
*Library of Congress Catalog Card Number 81-43573*
Copyright © 1983 by Jinx Morgan and Jefferson Morgan

This book is dedicated to
Ruth Galindo
and
to the memories of
Helen Lum and Alma Couchman

We hope there are still teachers such as they

# CONTENTS

# ONE

# SURVIVAL TACTICS

Since long before the time of Noah, we've all been driven by the urge to pair off one way or another. As a species we have found that two is the ideal number for tea, the seesaw, the tango, and a number of other interesting pursuits. But when it comes to cooking, couples long have been the object of widespread discrimination. Most recipes, even today, are designed by people who think on a monumental scale, ignoring those of us who daily face the world in double harness.

This seems particularly shortsighted these days. It is true that a generation ago a book such as this would have languished on the shelf. That was the time when single people were expected to live in chaste studio apartments with Murphy beds and well-worn can openers until they landed acceptable mates and launched archetypical American families, thus guaranteeing the success of companies that manufactured station wagons, disposable diapers, and hamburger extenders. But, as we all know, things are different now. Boy, are they different.

Every year, it seems, more and more people find themselves living as duets. What formerly would have been frowned on as, let's say, untraditional relationships, now are generally accepted. People who are getting married are putting off having children. The number of older and retired couples is increasing as medical science is prolonging our active lives. At the same time all this has been happening there has been a tremendous upsurge in interest in and concern about good food. And those who set a table for two are unwilling to spend a lifetime either condemned to eating frozen dinners or wrestling with long division to try and make sense out of recipes that leave enough leftovers to feed the front line of the Dallas Cowboys.

"Cooking for two is easy," a friend once told us. "All you have to do is find recipes for one and double them." By way of explanation, we should tell you that the only recipe book he owns is devoted exclusively to directions for making things like the perfect martini. Although his advice is ridiculous on the face of it, you'd be surprised how many people think the reverse is true, that all you have to do with large recipes is cut them in half or quarter them. Some dishes, such as stews and many casseroles, are susceptible to this simple method, although seasoning them is trickier than just reducing spices in the same proportion as other ingredients. But others, especially things like cakes and soufflés, can become disasters if you try to cut them down without taking their basic chemistry into consideration.

This is not, however, a book simply about cooking for two. In recent years a few good cookbooks have been written addressing the unique problems of people who live alone or as couples. What makes this one different is the fact we have tried to come to grips with virtually every kind of situation involving food and drink that any couple might encounter, from dealing with diets to planning a weekend house party to feeding a dozen guests at a formal dinner. There are, naturally, also a lot of menus designed for just two people, in every situation from picnics to panicky last-minute meals. This is a book about cooking *by* two.

Because we came to each other with both a mutual passion for and a professional interest in cooking, we've had to run quite a few road tests over the years to learn how two people can work in the same kitchen without a live-in traffic cop. Curiously enough, as we have watched some of our friends take the first halting steps toward forming culinary partnerships, it became clear to us that some people take to cooking together with grace and ease, while others snap and snarl and never make the adjustment. We've watched in horror as normally mild-mannered and loving folk are transformed into temperamental tyrants when they put on aprons, much like the personality change that takes place when some people slip behind the wheel of a Porsche.

So be forewarned, but not frightened off. Sharing a sink and a range can be an experience you'll enjoy the rest of your lives, but it doesn't work for everyone. It's not necessarily true that the couple who sautées together stays together. For that reason be assured that all the recipes in this book, even those designed for large parties, can be prepared by a single cook. The non-cooking partner might offer to clean up, or be prepared for a little backchat.

If you want to cook together, though, you should have a plan. Who will do what first? Where's the knife to mince the onion? Why is the pepper grinder in the refrigerator? Why did you decide you could live together in the first place?

You see how things can escalate.

To ward off these problems, we've prepared, for most of the menus, step-by-step schedules which we've called "Plans of Attack" to guide two cooks through the wilderness. But they are just that—guides. One person (you'll notice how diplomatically we have avoided designations of gender—why ask for trouble?) might love to prepare salad but hate to make soup, for instance, so make whatever adjustments are appropriate. (After all, this is supposed to be relaxation, not close-order drill.) Some guides are more detailed than others, and in some cases we didn't think they were necessary at all.

Be flexible and remember that you're in the room where you probably keep most of your sharp implements. The same goes for the menus. Different recipes can cross the boundaries into other menus, or they can be taken out of the context of the book entirely for any appropriate meal. Be creative and don't be intimidated just because something is presented to you on a printed page. We both remember a letter we received once from someone who had read a magazine article we had written, asking whether it would be all right with us if she served green beans with the entrée, rather than the vegetable we had suggested. Now there's a person who would be a poor choice to put at our end of the Washington-Moscow hotline.

This book assumes that you have a basic knowledge of cooking, although the recipes, even the complicated ones, are written so that anyone who can read can prepare them on the first try. We also are assuming that this isn't the only cookbook you own and that you have at least one encyclopedic text to use for reference. More advanced techniques are carefully outlined throughout the book in the menus where they are needed, and are cross-referenced and indexed.

Although you already know this, we will repeat the most essential piece of advice for anyone using any cookbook: *Read the recipe through before starting and assemble all the ingredients in advance.* Nothing is more apt to ruin an evening than having to run out at cocktail time to find a quarter teaspoon of oregano.

A third assumption we have made is that you already have a furnished kitchen. Our advice is that you stock up on the basic utensils—stockpot, pans, good high-carbon steel knives, and so forth—before you get cute and start buying a lot of specialized gear. However, years of experience have taught us that with the right small pan it's possible to make a pie, for instance, and not have it left over for so long it becomes a host for penicillin. Here are some examples of special equipment called for occasionally in this book that facilitates cooking for two:

- Small bowls for mixing small amounts. Sometimes custard cups will do, especially for things like salad dressings.
- 8-inch skillets (in addition to your essential crêpe pan) and saucepans from 1 quart down to 2 cups are important to have when cooking small amounts. The food should be comfortable in them. And you'll be much happier if all your pans have lids.
- 1-cup ovenproof dishes for things like individual soufflés can double as soup servers. It's also handy to have a 2- or 3-cup mold for soufflés or molded desserts for two.
- You can never be too rich or too thin, or have too many dariole molds. In addition to timbales for two, these small cylindrical molds are wonderful for making custards and other dishes for company.
- A 7-inch tart pan with a removable bottom is perfect for making pies or tarts for two.
- An 8-inch quiche pan with scalloped edges works well for most quiche recipes for two.
- We have a whole stack of 3×6×2¼-inch loaf pans which we use for special breads, desserts, pâtés, and a lot of other things.
- In addition to a regular double boiler, a small, 2-cup, enameled double boiler or zabaglione pan is particularly helpful for making small amounts of custard or sauces.
- 1-quart casseroles are the right size for two people.
- Individual heatproof ramekins or *au gratin* dishes are good not only for individual servings—of poached fish, for instance—but it's nice to have enough to use when you have company.
- A small, oval copper serving dish makes for attractive presentations of many dishes for two (nothing looks as lonely as a small amount of food in an enormous container, no matter what the practitioners of *nouvelle cuisine* would have you believe).
- An undersized steamer, either to use with your wok or a small *couscoussier,* is very handy. There are examples of other improvised steamers in some of the recipes later in the book.
- Most automatic coffee makers that produce up to eight or a dozen cups do a miserable job on small amounts. A 4-cup drip coffee maker or a small *café filtre* infuser with a plunger works better.
- If you do a lot of deep frying for two, a small electric deep fryer is a good buy because you use less oil. For some foods for two—french-fried potatoes, for

example—we have found that an electric frying pan works well because you can control the temperature better.

• Another handy tool is a scale that can be used to weigh small amounts. As a matter of fact, a good kitchen scale is almost essential these days as we become more and more metric. And it's always been more accurate to weigh certain ingredients, such as flour for bread.

• Give some thought to putting a small TV on the kitchen counter. Aha, you cry, they are Philistines after all. Abide a moment. We make this suggestion because some people who don't cook like to use the excuse with a partner who does that he or she would be bereft without catching the evening news. It not only solves that problem for news junkies, it can have other benefits as well. The night before we wrote this, for example, we spent the entire evening in the kitchen stocking the refrigerator and freezer for a party later in the week. We also caught the uncut version of *Dial M for Murder* on an obscure UHF channel that isn't successful enough to attract many commercials. We love it when the Scotland Yard inspector combs his mustache at the end.

• Finally, although we are not advocating that you run out and buy one, you might want to consider one of the new small countertop convection ovens (*not*, we implore you, one of those little toaster ovens that everyone puts in garage sales after a couple of uses). Working on the same principle as the large commercial convection ovens by constantly moving the heat around, they cook in less time and use conventional household current (and less of it). Their manufacturers advertise that they can cook anything up to a large turkey, but that's a copywriter's pipe dream. They are, however, perfect for small roasts, chicken, and small baking jobs. We have a friend, a very talented cook who lives by himself, who designed his new kitchen around a full-scale restaurant range. He decided he had to have it when the salesman demonstrated its durability by opening the oven door and jumping up and down on it. Although he's still glad he has it, he has augmented it with a small convection oven. "I realized how silly it was," he explained, "burning a couple of cubic feet of gas to heat the oven to warm my croissant in the morning." If you do use a convection oven for any of the recipes in this book, by the way, consult the owner's manual to adjust cooking times. These recipes were developed for conventional ovens.

You may have noticed that a couple of big-ticket items are not on the list. Both the food processor and the microwave oven can be invaluable when it comes to saving time. Whether they are worth the expense is up to you.

When the first food processors went on the market, Jeff insisted they were just the root of another French plot to separate gullible Americans from the old whipout. After all, he argued, they did nothing that couldn't be accomplished with a knife or a KitchenAid, which we already had and which was made by honest American labor. Then one day we were teaching a cooking class in a laboratory kitchen. Naturally, it had a food processor. Among the advance preparations for the demonstration was chopping 15 pounds of yellow onions. "What would it hurt," Jinx asked, "to try it out?" Grumbling, Jeff found the instructions for the machine. When Jinx was finished with the onions she turned, dry-eyed, and pointed wordlessly to a kitchen shop across the street. Humbled, he went over and bought one before the students even showed up. Neither of us has ever regretted it.

Oddly enough, we have never felt compelled to own a microwave oven, even though we know many couples who insist they couldn't live without one. In addition to the routine cooking chores which they do so quickly, they also defrost frozen food in minutes, something that makes it possible for busy couples to decide what they want for dinner when they come home at night.

Both of these tools have many pluses and no real disadvantages, provided you don't expect them to perform miracles beyond their design capabilities. In many of the recipes in this book we give instructions with and without a food processor. Since microwave cooking is fairly specialized, we have not included microwave directions. If you do have one, the manual that came with it will convert cooking times.

When it comes to shopping for two, it's really a matter of common sense. A number of helpful hints about buying particular ingredients are scattered throughout the book, but the main thing you should do is assess your needs. Larger quantities tend to be cheaper, but not if you find that you're throwing things away. Eggs can be purchased by the half dozen, and dairy products do come in smaller containers than a half gallon. (Contrary to popular opinion, ice cream, which can be kept for several months in a deep freeze, loses its freshness after three or four days in the freezer of a refrigerator.)

Some things are much less expensive purchased in larger containers—oil, for instance. The simple answer is to keep it in the refrigerator to prevent it from becoming rancid. A lot of people who have done that mistakenly throw it away when it becomes cloudy, which it does under cold storage. Don't worry about it—it clears when you reheat it. Other basic ingredients such as flour, sugar, and spices will keep for months provided they are stored in *airtight* containers.

If you grind your own coffee beans, make sure you buy them the day they were roasted. At the risk of insulting an entire industry, the bags of beans you grind yourself at the supermarket are a rip-off. The problem is that coffee beans store well while they are unroasted, but begin to deteriorate the minute they come out of the roaster. Thus, unless you can get yours at a specialty store that roasts every day, you're better off buying canned ground coffee, which was vacuum-packed immediately after it was processed. Since you're likely not to be using coffee in great quantities, keep it, beans or ground, in the freezer of your refrigerator.

Bread, whether you buy it at the supermarket or bakery or make it yourself (a very satisfactory way for two people to spend a Saturday or Sunday, by the way), tends to go stale in bipartite households. That's OK if you eat a lot of *pain perdu* or use a couple of pints of bread crumbs every week, but we find it's easier to just keep it in the freezer, taking out slices as we need them or cutting baguettes in half before wrapping and freezing them.

Although we stress the use of fresh ingredients, you will occasionally find recipes in which we suggest prepared foods, such as canned *marrons glacés*, chestnuts in syrup. Purists may cry out, but in certain cases it's silly to attempt to do something yourself that's better and cheaper handled commercially. About *marrons glacés,* for example, Prosper Montagné wrote in his *Larousse Gastronomique,* "This is a long and intricate process and is therefore seldom undertaken in the home." That's jake with us.

In a few instances we also call for brand names, such as Tabasco sauce. These reflect our own prejudices based on experience, but if you disagree, feel free to substitute. You will also find that we have occasionally called for instant-blending flour. In those cases we have found it preferable, but regular all-purpose flour will work.

What follows is organized into six sections:

**A Table for Two** is divided into twelve menus designed primarily for people who lead busy lives and want to tuck into dinner not long after crossing the threshold at night. They are divided by the seasons.

**Private Celebrations** covers those magic moments when two people have the time, the inclination, and a reason to do something a little more ambitious.

**The Pleasure of Company** makes the point that having two cooks really pays off when it comes to entertaining. Four hands make for lighter work and, with proper planning, no one gets stuck in the kitchen for a whole evening while the guests are laying waste to the liquor supply. Of course, not all entertaining is done at night, or even at home for that matter, so we'll suggest a broad range of menus for different occasions.

**Two for the Road** is so named not only because it was the title of one of Jinx's favorite movies but also because it includes international dishes, many adapted for two, that have traditionally been the exclusive province of cooks with a lot of mouths to feed.

The next section, **Instant Elegance,** flows fairly logically from the last. There are those times when all systems have broken down and only swift improvisations or a call to the local purveyor of peripatetic food can save the day. Since our closest takeout emporium, known in the neighborhood as "The Flying Prawn," heads its list of gourmet specials with chop suey, we prefer to live by our wits and take our chances at home. So can you with omelets, pastas, and a host of other speedy dishes, provided you've stocked the larder properly.

Which brings us to the last part of the book, **Back to Basics.** Cooking, no matter whether for two or for a regiment, is made easier by the artful use of modern technology. For example, even our compact household would be considerably less efficient without a freezer. This section concerns itself with, among other things, the care and feeding of this treasure chest. While our recipes do not insist on the use of homemade stocks and basic sauces, these improve the final results immeasurably, are better for you because they contain no preservatives or other additives, and save money in the bargain. Weekends are the time to simmer several quarts of chicken broth from the bones and scraps you've been saving in the freezer, for instance, and then freeze the stock in usable portions. Throughout the book certain basic ingredients, such as *crème fraîche,* stocks, and mayonnaise, are cross-referenced to master recipes found here. In addition there are formulas for a lot of other goodies that are better homemade, such as your own tomato sauce and mustard. Stockpiling against the future always gives one a comforting sense of being at least one step ahead of the game.

Which is, after all, what life's all about.

# TWO

# A TABLE FOR TWO

If your life is anything like ours, the prospect of slaving in the kitchen for several hours after a long day is about as appealing as having the Hell's Angels crash your birthday party. Some people, it is rumored, solve the problem by sneaking off to fast-food emporiums or resorting to frozen prepared dinners. But dining on a steady diet of greaseburgers or pre-stuffed chicken breasts that taste like and cost only slightly less than a Gucci wallet can quickly pall.

It is to these busy people that this chapter is directed. This is the practice ground for dual entertaining. These are the menus to use when perfecting the patterns of your own kitchen choreography. This is the daily grind.

In working out these menus, we've taken several factors into consideration. In most cases, we've tried to keep the preparation time under an hour or have selected dishes that can be made well ahead of time and that profit from reheating. The menus are arranged seasonally so you can take advantage of the freshest and cheapest ingredients on the market. And we've suggested a timetable to divide the work equitably. Remember, this is just a guide, friends. We don't want to be hauled into court if you start slinging pots and pans at each other. These plans of attack are intended only as the most general of guides.

So get out your aprons and slip into the kitchen. Pour some wine and have a swallow for courage. Don't forget to set the table before you begin. Make it pretty and make it for two—after all, what guest could be more important than you?

# *Spring*

## MENU

*Avocado Consommé*
*Turban of Sole Mousse*
*Curried Tomato Salad*
*Golden Popovers*
*Praline Parfait*

For cooks on the run, any finny fillet can be a friend indeed. Fish is best when swiftly cooked, whether broiled, sautéed, fried, or poached. Flavorings can be simple: lemon, parsley, dill, chives, tarragon, or a little white wine often adds just the right touch when stronger seasonings would overpower.

Broiled fish is always a swift route to dinner. However, as in all fish preparations, the brief cooking time requires careful observation. If the fillets are very thin, they should be broiled on one side only, thereby eliminating the tricky maneuver of turning them over. Be sure to cover your broiler pan with well-oiled aluminum foil so you can remove the fish when it is cooked by sliding it directly onto the plate from the foil. Thicker cuts of fish will have to be turned halfway through cooking.

Poaching is a splendid way of preparing fish, since none of the natural flavor is masked. Generally speaking, poached fish is low in calories (until you add that irresistible sauce, that is) and doesn't require split-second timing. To poach a small whole fish, form a sling from a piece of aluminum foil, lower the fish into the poaching liquid with it and then fold the foil over it. Simmer for the proper length of time, using the Canadian rule of 10 minutes cooking for each inch of the fish at its thickest point.

If sautéeing is your style, use a mixture of butter and oil or clarified butter in the skillet so there's no risk of burning. Lightly flour the fish or leave it quite nude—it's up to you. But cook the fish just before serving so it will be fresh and hot and retain all its good savor of the sea. Frozen fillets are best sautéed without thawing, but they will need to be cooked almost twice as long as fresh.

To make one round of cooking do for two meals (always a good idea when you're pressed for time), double the quantity of fish you usually sauté and cook it in olive oil rather than butter. Cool the extra fish and marinate in layers with chopped green onion, chopped green pepper, and thin slices of lemon. Add olive oil to cover and sprinkle with oregano or basil (fresh, if possible). Cover and refrigerate overnight and serve the next day, perhaps with hot French bread grilled with butter and Parmesan cheese and a spinach and bacon salad.

## *Avocado Consommé*

½ avocado
½ lemon
2 cups well-seasoned chicken broth

2 tablespoons Sherry
2 teaspoons minced fresh parsley

Since you'll need only half an avocado and half a lemon for this soup, cut the whole avocado in two lengthwise leaving the seed in one side. Sprinkle the cut side with the juice from the half of the lemon you're not using in the soup. Wrap the half avocado with its seed in plastic wrap and refrigerate for tomorrow night's salad.

Heat the chicken broth to just under boiling. Peel and slice the avocado half thinly, dividing the slices between two soup bowls. Place 2 to 3 lemon slices on top of the avocado and ladle in the hot chicken broth. Add 1 tablespoon Sherry to each bowl and sprinkle with parsley.

## *Turban of Sole Mousse*

A more elaborate fish dish than the ones we've just discussed, this is just the thing for any special occasion. The delicate flavor of sole calls for a white wine such as a California Chardonnay. The wines made from the same grape in the Burgundy region of France, though sometimes richer than their American cousins, also would be ideal companions.

3 fillets of sole (about ¾ pound)
1 egg white
¼ cup heavy cream
½ teaspoon salt
1 tablespoon chopped fresh parsley
1 drop Tabasco sauce
¾ cup dry white wine
¼ cup water

4 thin slices onion
2 thin slices lemon
1 bay leaf
2 whole black peppercorns
½ teaspoon salt
1 teaspoon fresh or ¼ teaspoon dried
   tarragon leaves

Cut one fish fillet into chunks and place in the container of a blender or food processor with the egg white, cream, salt, parsley, and Tabasco sauce. Blend or process until the mixture is smooth and a nice pale green color.

Place the two remaining fillets on a flat surface and spoon half of the fish mixture on each. Spread to make an even layer and, starting at the narrow end, roll up the fillets and secure the ends with toothpicks.

Place the fillets upright in a small saucepan. Add the wine, water, the onion, lemon, bay leaf, peppercorns, salt, and tarragon. Bring just to the boiling point and cover. Lower the heat and simmer for 10 to 15 minutes, or until the fish is cooked and filling is firm.

Remove the rolls with a slotted spoon, draining well. Place on a heated serving platter. Reserve the poaching liquid for the sauce.

**SAUCE**

½ cup poaching liquid  
¼ cup heavy cream

1 teaspoon tomato paste  
1 tablespoon brandy

Bring the poaching liquid to a boil and continue boiling until reduced by half. Add cream, tomato paste, and brandy and cook over low heat until thickened (it should be about the consistency of heavy cream). Spoon over sole. Garnish with sprigs of fresh tarragon, if available.

## Curried Tomato Salad

2 tomatoes, peeled, seeded, and diced  
½ red onion, chopped  
Salt and pepper  
¼ cup mayonnaise

1 tablespoon minced parsley  
1 teaspoon curry powder  
Lettuce

Combine the tomatoes and onions in a bowl. Add salt and pepper to taste and refrigerate until ready to serve.

In a small bowl, mix together the mayonnaise, parsley, and curry powder. To serve, spoon the tomato-onion mixture onto lettuce leaves and top with the curry dressing.

## Golden Popovers

⅔ cup unsifted flour  
¼ teaspoon salt  
⅓ cup milk  
⅓ cup water

2 eggs  
¼ cup Cheddar cheese  
2–3 tablespoons shortening

Mix together the flour and salt and slowly stir in the milk and water. Beat the eggs into the batter until well blended and fold in the cheese.

Heavily grease 3 or 4 6-ounce custard cups with shortening. Fill each cup half full. Place cups on a baking sheet and slide into a *cold* oven. Set the temperature for 425 degrees F. Turn on the oven and bake popovers 35–45 minutes. Serve immediately.

## Praline Parfait

1 cup dark brown sugar
2 teaspoons butter
3 tablespoons boiling water

½ cup chopped pecans
Coffee or vanilla ice cream

Combine the sugar, butter, boiling water, and pecans in a saucepan and bring to a rolling boil. Remove from the heat and cool. Refrigerate. Layer praline sauce with ice cream in parfait or wine glasses.

# PLAN OF ATTACK

## Cook Number One

**1 hour before**
Make popover batter and place in prepared custard cups.
**45 minutes before**
Put popovers in to bake.
**40 minutes before**
1. Prepare fish mousse and spread on fillets. 2. Roll into turbans, cover, and refrigerate.
**25 minutes before**
1. Prepare avocado and lemon for soup. 2. Place chicken broth in pot to be heated. 3. Arrange avocado and lemon slices in bowls.
**10 minutes before**
1. Heat broth for soup. 2. Begin poaching fish.
**just before**
1. Make sauce for fish. 2. Serve soup.

## Cook Number Two

**1 hour before**
1. Chill wine. 2. Make praline sauce and refrigerate.
**40 minutes before**
Peel, seed, and chop tomatoes for salad. Chop onions and add to tomatoes. Season with salt and pepper and refrigerate.
**20 minutes before**
1. Set the table. 2. Prepare salad dressing and refrigerate. 3. Layer praline sauce with ice cream and place parfaits in the freezer.
**just before**
1. Arrange salad on plates. 2. Remove popovers from the oven.

# MENU

Lamb, asparagus, and a lighter-than-air soufflé—all are as reliable signs of spring as daffodils and robins. No problem with the lamb or asparagus—they practically cook themselves. But to some, a soufflé is arrogant, unreliable, and difficult—the diva of the dining room. Its reputation for being too delicate to survive in a world of slamming doors and fickle ovens has driven it from the repertoire of many cooks. Yet this ethereal creation is not as temperamental as is reputed, and its dramatic arrival at the table can turn an ordinary meal into an event.

By carefully observing a few simple rules, you can make all your soufflés successes. First, be sure to choose the correct size dish. Our recipe fills two 1-cup dishes. This is perfect for a pair of individual servings of either a savory or a dessert soufflé. Our filling is fresh tomato with a whisper of Crème de Cassis, but the same base can be used with any number of marvelous things to create your own masterpieces. We'll give you some ideas at the end of the recipe.

But back to the rules. The soufflé base (that is, the mixture before the beaten egg whites have been added) should have a soft consistency and drop easily from a spoon. Be sure to overseason it slightly to compensate for the addition of the unseasoned egg whites. The base can be prepared a few hours ahead, but the whites must be beaten and folded in at the last minute.

Try to get as much volume as possible into the egg whites, since it is the air incorporated into the whites that makes the soufflé rise. The traditional method is to use a copper bowl and whisk, but in the absence of the perfect tools a pinch of cream of tartar will help the whites reach their full potential.

The basic mixture should be warm when the whites are folded in. With a rubber spatula, fold them into the base gently by moving the spatula downward through the center, along the bottom and up the near side of the bowl, rotating the bowl as you fold. Take care not to overfold. Place the soufflé in the center of a preheated oven with no rack above. Now restrain the urge to peek, and you'll have a spectacular soufflé.

Half a rack of lamb is just the right size for two, we find, and any lamb pairs well with a red wine such as a full, dry Petite Sirah from California or a French Saint-Emilion.

# Prosciutto-Wrapped Asparagus

The fine, delicate flavor of Italy's air-cured ham is a nice contrast with asparagus. A fine country ham from Kentucky or Virginia would be equally delicious. Or substitute any thinly sliced baked ham.

*16 asparagus spears*
*Melted butter (optional)*
*2 slices prosciutto or other ham*

Snap off the tough ends of asparagus and discard. Rinse spears well. With a sharp knife, peel stalks. Tie into a bundle with kitchen twine. If you don't have an asparagus cooker, arrange spears upright in the bottom of a double boiler. Pour 3 inches of boiling water into bottom. Invert top section of double boiler over asparagus to trap steam. Cook until stalks are tender, about 8 minutes. Drain. Drizzle with melted butter if you wish. Divide spears into 2 bundles and wrap each with a slice of ham.

# Rack of Lamb Battuto

In Italy, meat often is flavored with battuto—a mixture of oil, seasonings, and lemon juice or vinegar. The ingredients are worked into a paste that is spread over the meat as much as 24 hours ahead of the cooking time. We like this particular battuto combination with lamb. The zesty freshness of lemon juice makes the lamb more succulent and the juniper berries add their own special flavor.

If your butcher won't cut a 4-rib rack of lamb for you, buy a conventional 8-rib rack and cut it in half, freezing the remainder for a later meal. Be sure the butcher cracks the chine between the ribs for easier carving.

*4 juniper berries*
*1 clove garlic, minced*
*½ teaspoon grated lemon peel*
*¼ teaspoon freshly ground pepper*

*2 tablespoons olive oil*
*1 teaspoon fresh lemon juice*
*1 rack of lamb (4 ribs), trimmed*

Combine the juniper berries, garlic, lemon peel, and pepper in a mortar and work with pestle until the mixture is smooth. Gradually add the oil, drop by drop, mixing constantly until thoroughly blended. Slowly blend in the lemon juice. Spread the mixture over the lamb. Wrap loosely in waxed paper and refrigerate for at least 8 hours, or up to 24.

*Preheat the oven to 475 degrees F.* Roast lamb meaty side down for 10 minutes. Turn lamb over, reduce oven temperature to 400 degrees F. and continue roasting to desired doneness (but be sure it's underdone to your taste because it will continue to cook after it leaves the oven).

For rare: 25 to 30 minutes, or 140 degrees F. on a meat thermometer.

For medium: 30 to 45 minutes, or 160 degrees F. on a meat thermometer.

For well done: 40 to 50 minutes, or 170 to 180 degrees F. on a meat thermometer.

# Tomato Soufflé Cassis

If you have only one oven, cook the lamb first. Remove it from the oven and tent it with foil to keep warm. It will continue cooking and the juices will be well set when you carve it. Reduce the oven temperature and cook the soufflé.

*2 tablespoons (¼ stick) butter*
*2 tablespoons minced onion*
*½ medium tomato, peeled, seeded, and chopped*
*½ teaspoon tomato paste*
*2 teaspoons Crème de Cassis*

*1 tablespoon flour*
*⅓ cup milk*
*Salt and freshly ground pepper*
*1 egg yolk*
*2 egg whites*
*Pinch cream of tartar*

Melt 1 tablespoon butter in a small skillet over low heat. Add onion and cook until very tender. Add tomato, tomato paste, and Cassis and cook gently until all liquid has been absorbed. Set aside.

Melt remaining butter in a saucepan. Remove from heat and stir in flour. Blend in milk and season with salt and pepper. Bring to a boil, reduce heat and simmer, stirring constantly until mixture thickens. Remove from heat and beat in egg yolk. Stir in tomato mixture.

Generously butter two 1-cup soufflé dishes. Position rack in lower third of the oven and preheat oven to 375 degrees F. Beat egg whites with cream of tartar until stiff but not dry. Using a rubber spatula, fold about one fourth of the whites into the tomato mixture to loosen. Quickly fold in remaining whites but do not overfold; there should be some white streaks. Pour into prepared dishes and bake until puffed and lightly browned—about 20–30 minutes, depending on how firm you like the center.

This basic recipe can incorporate any number of items you might have on hand. Use the same proportions, but vary the ⅓ cup filling according to your fancy or what happens to be hanging around the refrigerator. A soufflé is one of the classiest forms of recycling.

*For Example:*

Creamed spinach and Gruyère cheese
Sautéed onions with fennel seeds
Creamed corn and chopped chilies
Sautéed grated zucchini and Cheddar cheese served with a tomato sauce

Puréed cooked asparagus
Puréed cauliflower and watercress
Chopped cooked broccoli with chervil

---

# Artichoke and Watercress Salad

1 bunch watercress
1 jar (6 ounces) marinated artichoke
 hearts
2 tablespoons capers

Wash and dry the watercress. Drain the artichoke hearts, reserving the marinade. Rinse and drain the capers.

Divide watercress between two salad plates. Top each with half the artichoke hearts and sprinkle with capers. Dress with some of the reserved marinade.

# Walnut Torte

1 egg
⅓ cup sugar
⅓ cup graham cracker crumbs

3 tablespoons finely chopped walnuts or
 pecans
Vanilla ice cream or rum-flavored
 whipped cream

Preheat oven to 350 degrees F. Butter two 3-inch tart pans, or custard cups or gelatin molds with ⅔ cup capacity. Beat egg in small bowl. Blend in sugar, crumbs, and nuts and mix well. Divide between pans. Bake until set, 20–25 minutes. Let cool. Turn onto dessert plates and top with ice cream or whipped cream.

# PLAN OF ATTACK

## Cook Number One

**ahead of time**
Make walnut tortes.
**1 hour before**
Clean and scrape asparagus spears.
**½ hour before**
Set table.
**15 minutes before**
Cook asparagus and wrap in ham for serving.

## Cook Number Two

**ahead of time**
Make battuto, spread on lamb, refrigerate.
**1 hour before**
1. Make soufflé filling.  2. Make soufflé base.
**½ hour before**
1. Beat egg whites for soufflé, fold in and put soufflé in to bake.  2. Put lamb in to roast.  3. Open wine.
**15 minutes before**
Make salad.

# MENU

---

*Shrimp-Filled Avocado Shells*
*Veal Chops Duxelles en Papillote*
*Zucchini with Pesto*
*Strawberry Mousse*

---

Although cooking *en papillote* might seem to be an esoteric kitchen conceit requiring the combined talents of a multi-starred chef and an origami master, in truth even fumble-fingered types whose idea of wrapping a gift is to take it to a wrapping desk and say, "I'll take number 7, please," can master the skill with almost no effort. In this menu the main course—veal chops smothered with walnut-punctuated duxelles and flanked by thin slices of ham—arrive at the table in the whimsical paper shells in which they were cooked. When the paper is slit, a cloud of mushroom-scented steam escapes, previewing the flavors to come.

For cooking *en papillote* we like to use parchment paper because it puffs up and crisps so nicely, but foil is a perfectly acceptable substitute. Since it's easy assembly-line work to prepare the chops *en papillote,* we often make about a bushel of the little packets to freeze (if you're using parchment, wrap in paper first and then in foil for freezing). It's a great comfort to know you have a number of elegant main courses on ice just waiting to be popped into the oven.

When folding the paper around the chops, be sure the edges are crimped shut so the *papillotes* will puff as they should, and for a little extra lift, blow some air into the package through a straw just before twisting the tip closed. If you become a fan of paper cooking, you can go on to adapt the veal recipe to small loin lamb chops, chicken breasts, fish fillets, or whatever your imagination suggests.

Like Nicolas Soyer, a devotee of paper-case cooking in the early years of this century, we find it an ideal way to prepare all manner of good things, but we have to agree with his reluctant admission: "It is evident that tea must still be made in a teapot."

As for wine, the delicate flavor of veal with duxelles wouldn't be overpowered by a well-chilled Vouvray or a light, dry California Chenin Blanc.

## Shrimp-Filled Avocado Shells

1 avocado, halved and seeded
Fresh lemon or lime juice
½ cup cooked small shrimp
¼ cup minced water chestnuts
2 green onions, minced

2–3 tablespoons mayonnaise
½–1 teaspoon curry powder (or to taste)
Salt and freshly ground pepper
Lettuce leaves

Sprinkle cut edges of avocado with lemon or lime juice. Combine all remaining ingredients except lettuce and toss lightly. Mound in avocado halves. Set each on lettuce-lined plate. Cover and chill until ready to serve.

## Veal Chops Duxelles en Papillote

¼ cup minced walnuts
½ pound mushrooms, minced
¼ cup butter
Salt and freshly ground pepper

1 tablespoon oil
2 veal loin chops
4 thin slices ham (about the same size as chops)

*Preheat oven to 350 degrees F.* Place walnuts on baking sheet and toast in the oven for 15 to 20 minutes. To make duxelles, squeeze minced mushrooms in kitchen towel to remove excess liquid. Melt butter in medium skillet over low heat. Add mushrooms and cook very slowly until all liquid evaporates. Stir in walnuts and salt and pepper to taste.

Heat oil in large skillet over medium-high heat. Add chops and sauté about 2 minutes on each side. Set aside to cool.

*Preheat oven to 450 degrees F.* Generously oil a baking sheet. Cut two 11×13-inch heart-shaped pieces of parchment paper or heavy foil. Place one slice of ham lengthwise on one side; spread with ¼ of the mushroom mixture. Set veal chop on top and spread with another ¼ of the duxelles. Top with another thin slice of ham. Fold paper in half lengthwise and crimp edges closed. Repeat with remaining chop. Transfer to prepared baking sheet. If you are using parchment, brush packages with oil. Bake about 12–15 minutes or until parchment is puffed and golden. Serve in paper, opening packets with sharp knife.

## Zucchini with Pesto

2 tablespoons pine nuts
1 medium zucchini
1 tablespoon olive oil

1 tablespoon pesto sauce
Salt and pepper

*Preheat oven to 350 degrees F.* Place pine nuts on baking sheet and toast in the oven for 5 minutes, stirring occasionally, until golden. Cut the zucchini into julienne strips on a mandoline or by hand. Lightly salt and drain. Heat olive oil in a skillet and sauté zucchini until just tender. Stir in 1 tablespoon pesto sauce and toss well. Season to taste with salt and pepper and sprinkle with toasted pine nuts.

**PESTO SAUCE**

Pesto sauce is now available year round in frozen form, but to make your own you'll need fresh basil, which can often be found in markets in late summer. Make a large batch and freeze it in an ice-cube tray, then store cubes in plastic bags. Pesto is not only marvelous with vegetables and pasta, it also can be stirred into minestrone or other bean or vegetable soups for extra flavor, and it does wonderful things for rice.

Pesto can be made in a food processor if you use great care not to let it turn into a smooth, unidentifiable mush. Mortar and pestle, the traditional tools for making pesto, give a wonderful result in which all the ingredients blend together magically but still retain their individual character.

*¼ cup pine nuts or walnuts*
*2–3 garlic cloves, chopped*
*2 cups fresh basil leaves, shredded*
*½ cup freshly grated Parmesan cheese*
*2 tablespoons freshly grated Pecorino Romano cheese*

*½–¾ cup olive oil*
*2–3 tablespoons heavy cream*
*Salt and pepper*

Grind the nuts and garlic in a food processor or with a mortar and pestle. Add basil and cheese and continue to grind until puréed. Add olive oil in a thin stream. When mixture is thick, stir in the cream and, if necessary, a little water to make it the consistency you like. Season to taste with salt and pepper.

# *Strawberry Mousse*

*½ pint strawberries*
*1 egg*
*1 egg yolk*
*3 tablespoons sugar*
*2 tablespoons fresh lemon juice*

*1 ½ teaspoons gelatin*
*⅓ cup heavy cream, whipped*
**GARNISH**
*Fresh strawberries*
*Minced pistachio nuts or fresh mint leaves*

Wash and hull the strawberries. Mash or chop in food processor.

Combine the egg and the egg yolk with the sugar in a bowl and beat until well mixed. Using an electric mixer, beat until the mixture is thick and forms a ribbon when lifted.

Combine lemon juice and gelatin and allow to stand until gelatin is softened. Dissolve gelatin over a pan of hot water and stir into the egg mixture. Stir in strawberry purée. Place bowl in a pan of ice water and stir until mixture is almost at the point of setting. Lightly fold in the whipped cream and pour immediately into an oiled 2-cup mold. Chill for at least 2 hours. When ready to serve, unmold the mousse onto a platter and garnish, if you like, with fresh strawberries, and pistachio nuts or mint leaves.

# PLAN OF ATTACK

---

## Cook Number One

*ahead of time*
Make pesto.
**45 minutes before**
Prepare avocado salad and refrigerate.
**½ hour before**
Cut zucchini, lightly salt and drain.
**15 minutes before**
Prepare zucchini.

## Cook Number Two

*ahead of time*
Make strawberry mousse and chill.
**45 minutes before**
Prepare mushroom-and-walnut duxelles.
**½ hour before**
1. Sauté veal chops and arrange with ham and duxelles in foil or paper packages.  2. Chill wine.
**15 minutes before**
Set the table.
*just before*
Unmold mousse and garnish.

---

# Summer

---

# MENU

---

*Chicken-Walnut Salad*
*Wine Lover's Salad Dressing*
*Cottage Dill Bread*
*Glace au Sauternes*

---

Some people find the months of summer a time more to be endured than enjoyed. For those who live in areas where the humidity readings are in the numerical range of a Rhodes scholar's I.Q., July, August, and September can be long months indeed. The French, with their gift for practicality, solve the problem by skipping the month of August entirely. Shopkeepers, secretaries, and corporate presidents all retreat to the cool comfort of the countryside as Paris swelters to a halt.

We are not always so foresighted. When we find ourselves panting through the dog days and a turn in the kitchen holds all the appeal of a brisk walk through Death Valley, we usually find solace in a cold main-dish salad.

The salad we suggest here is ideally suited for two people, and for the summer season. It would be well matched with fresh-flavored cottage cheese and dill bread. A delicious ice flavored with Sauternes ends the meal on a properly chilly note.

As a rule, we don't serve wine with any salad dressed with vinegar. But as we hate to give up wine in favor of greens, we've come up with a wine lover's salad dressing that works well as an alternative with this salad or with your favorite selection of lettuces.

The wines of summer are those that should be drunk while they're young and fresh. With any of these salads we might open a Vouvray from the Loire Valley, a Chenin Blanc, a Folle Blanche or a Gewürztraminer from Alsace or California. For the Palm Springs Salad, an alternative might be a Beaujolais or California Gamay chilled for about 15 minutes to bring it down to "cellar temperature"—50–55 degrees F.

## Chicken-Walnut Salad

1 whole chicken breast, boned, skinned,
   and slightly flattened
2 tablespoons butter
1 tablespoon oil
1 teaspoon fresh lemon juice
Salt and pepper

**DRESSING**
6 tablespoons olive oil
3 tablespoons cider vinegar
½ teaspoon dry mustard
Salt and pepper

**SALAD**
2 stalks celery
¼ head romaine lettuce
¼ pound Gruyère cheese
¼ cup coarsely chopped walnuts

**GARNISH**
Walnut halves
Pimiento strips
Minced parsley

To poach the chicken breast, melt butter and oil in a small skillet. Add the chicken and turn to coat with the butter-oil mixture. Sprinkle with lemon juice and salt and pepper. Cover with a round of waxed paper and the lid. Poach over low heat for 12 minutes or until cooked through. Allow to cool, covered, in the pan.

Combine dressing ingredients in a small bowl and whisk to blend thoroughly.

Cut the celery in julienne strips and the lettuce in thin crosswise strips. Cut the cheese in julienne strips. Combine celery, lettuce, cheese and nuts and toss with half of the dressing.

When the chicken is cool, cut each half into 5 crosswise slices. Moisten with cooking liquid. Gently toss with the remaining dressing.

Place a bed of the lettuce mixture on two plates. Arrange the chicken slices on top. Place a walnut half on each slice, crisscross pimiento strips, and sprinkle with minced parsley.

## Wine Lover's Salad Dressing

This is a very gentle, subtle dressing without the aggressive zing of those made with vinegar. However, you may find you like its austere charm, especially if you are serving something special from your cellar.

| | |
|---|---|
| *3 tablespoons peanut oil* | *1 teaspoon minced shallots* |
| *1 tablespoon dry red or white wine* | *Salt and pepper* |

Combine all ingredients in a bowl and whisk until well blended.

## Cottage Dill Bread

| | |
|---|---|
| *¼ cup likewarm water (105°–115°F.)* | *1 teaspoon salt* |
| *1 package dry yeast (¼ ounce)* | *1 egg* |
| *1 tablespoon sugar* | *1 tablespoon dried dill weed* |
| *1 cup creamed cottage cheese* | *2¼ cups flour* |
| *2 tablespoons chopped onions* | *¼ cup wheat germ* |
| *2 tablespoons melted butter* | *1 egg beaten with 1 tablespoon water* |

Pour the water into the container of a blender or food processor. Add the yeast, stir, and let stand 5 minutes. Blend or process for 10 seconds. Add the cottage cheese, onions, melted butter, salt, and egg and blend for 20 seconds. Stir together the dill, flour, and wheat germ in a mixing bowl. Using a wooden spoon, stir in the cottage cheese mixture until the dough pulls away from the sides of the bowl.

Turn out onto a floured surface and knead about 5 minutes or until the dough is smooth and elastic. Place in a greased bowl. Cover and let rise in a warm, draft-free place 1 hour or until doubled. Punch dough down and divide in half. Form into loaves and place in 2 greased 6×3×2¼-inch loaf pans. Allow to rise in a warm, draft-free place until doubled, about 35–45 minutes. *Preheat oven to 350 degrees F.* Brush loaves with the egg wash and bake 35–40 minutes.

## Glace au Sauternes

2 cups water  
¾ cup sugar  

1 teaspoon lemon rind, grated  
½ cup sweet Sauternes  

Combine the water and sugar in a heavy-bottomed saucepan. Bring to a boil and continue boiling for 6 minutes. Cool. Add grated lemon rind and Sauternes. Freeze in a refrigerator tray, stirring once or twice during the freezing process or churn-freeze according to your machine's directions.

# PLAN OF ATTACK

## Cook Number One

*ahead of time*  
1. In the cool of the morning, poach chicken breasts or cook and cool salmon.   2. Make Sauternes Ice.  
*1 hour before*  
Prepare lettuce, wrap in clean dish-towel to absorb moisture, and chill.  
*½ hour before*  
1. Chop and prepare any vegetables for salad of your choice.   2. Chill wine.

## Cook Number Two

*ahead of time*  
Bake the bread, preferably the day before after the sun goes down.  
*15 minutes before*  
Cook and crumble bacon if making Palm Springs Salad.  
*just before*  
1. Make salad dressing of choice.   2. Arrange and toss salad with dressing.

# MENU

*Orange Barbecued Spareribs*  
*Curried Rice*  
*Watercress Walnut Salad*  
*Lemon Meringue Tarts*

For some atavistic reason, probably harking back to the time one of our prehistoric ancestors accidentally dropped a mastodon haunch into the campfire, meat prepared over a grill seems to taste better than protein fixed any other way.

Most people, certainly those who live there, will tell you that barbecuing originated in the American Southwest. The word itself, however, comes from *barbacoa,* the Spanish name for a frame made of sticks that the Indians of the Greater Antilles and the Bahamas set over deep pits to roast meat or fish. All of this lore, of course, ignores the fact the Chinese were barbecuing for centuries before Columbus convinced Queen Isabella that she should finance his Caribbean vacation.

Wherever it came from, the barbecue grill has become a popular household tool from coast to coast. But what of the growing number of urbanites who occupy apartments without gardens or even a tiny balcony upon which to fire a hibachi? Are they to be denied what has become an American culinary tradition?

It is our contention that nobody should have to forgo the joys and mess of barbecuing, so we've devised an entrée that can be grilled on a patio or cooked in the kitchen. In fact, there even are advantages to the indoor method, since summer is the rainy season in vast areas of North America.

The ginger and soy in the orange marinade give it a whiff of the trade winds and the faint flavor of the South Pacific. The ribs are accompanied by curried rice and a spinach salad with mushrooms, water chestnuts, and sesame seeds. A light, refreshing dessert is called for here and lemon meringue tarts fill the bill beautifully.

Although we generally serve white wine with pork, we think the hearty flavor of barbecued ribs is better complemented by one of the lighter reds, such as a Beaujolais or California Gamay lightly chilled to about 50–55 degrees F.

The secret of barbecuing ribs, no matter where it's done, is parboiling them first. Otherwise you have to cook them for at least an hour to make sure they're done. That is guaranteed to give them the taste and texture of a slightly charred running shoe.

## *Orange Barbecued Spareribs*

*2 pounds spareribs*
*Water to cover*
*¼ cup soy sauce*
*2 slices fresh ginger*
*2 green onions including tops, cut into*
*   ½-inch pieces*
*2 pieces star anise (or 2 drops anise*
*   extract)*

**BASTING SAUCE**
*½ cup chicken broth*
*½ cup sugar*
*2 tablespoons soy sauce*
*1 teaspoon finely chopped fresh orange*
*   peel*

Cut ribs apart into individual pieces. Place them in a pan and cover with cold water. Add ¼ cup soy sauce, ginger, onions, and anise to the water. Bring to a boil and simmer, uncovered, for 20 minutes. Drain, discarding liquid. This may be done in advance and ribs allowed to cool. If they are refrigerated, let them come back to room temperature before broiling. For other recipes, ribs may be parboiled in plain water.

Combine ingredients for basting sauce in a small pan. Bring to a boil and simmer, stirring occasionally, for 15 minutes.

Preheat broiler or prepare barbecue grill. Grill the parboiled ribs slowly in the oven broiler (5–6 inches from the heat) or on a barbecued grill, turning and basting often with orange sauce, for 30 minutes.

# Curried Rice

| | |
|---|---|
| *1 tablespoon butter* | *1 ½ teaspoons curry powder* |
| *1 medium onion, chopped* | *2 cups chicken broth* |
| *1 cup uncooked long-grain rice* | *Parsley* |

Melt butter in a skillet over medium heat. Add onion and sauté until translucent. Add rice and curry and sauté until rice is lightly toasted. Bring broth to a boil and add. Cover and cook until rice is tender and all liquid is absorbed, about 20–25 minutes. Sprinkle with parsley just before serving.

# Watercress Walnut Salad

This tangy salad will counter the richness of the ribs and can be served with them or as a separate course afterward.

| | |
|---|---|
| *1 bunch watercress, washed and dried* | **DRESSING** |
| *½ cup walnut halves* | *4 teaspoons walnut oil* |
| *1 tablespoon minced green onion* | *1 teaspoon wine vinegar* |
| | *¼ teaspoon Dijon mustard* |
| | *Salt and pepper to taste* |

Combine the watercress, walnut halves, and onions in a bowl. To make the dressing, whisk together the walnut oil, vinegar, mustard, and salt and pepper to taste. Toss the watercress mixture with the dressing and serve.

# Lemon Meringue Tarts

**CRUST**
½ cup flour
1 tablespoon confectioners' sugar
¼ cup butter
**MERINGUE**
2 egg whites
Pinch cream of tartar
Pinch salt
3 tablespoons sugar
¾ teaspoon fresh lemon juice

**FILLING**
2 egg yolks
⅓ cup sugar
2 tablespoons fresh lemon juice
1 teaspoon finely shredded lemon zest
Pinch salt
1 egg white

**FOR THE CRUST** *Preheat oven to 425 degrees F.* Sift flour with confectioners' sugar into bowl. Cut in butter until mixture resembles coarse meal. Chill 15 minutes. Divide evenly and press into bottoms and sides of two 4½-inch tart pans with removable bottoms. Bake 10–12 minutes. Cool.

**FOR THE FILLING** Place yolks in top of small double boiler. Beat in sugar, lemon juice, lemon zest, and salt. Set pan over simmering water and cook, stirring constantly, until thick and smooth, about 10 minutes. Remove from heat and cool slightly. Beat egg white until stiff peaks form. Gently fold into custard. Divide between cooled tart shells.

**FOR THE MERINGUE** *Preheat oven to 350 degrees F.* Beat egg whites until foamy. Add cream of tartar and salt and continue beating, gradually adding sugar, until whites are stiff and glossy. Stir in lemon juice. Gently spoon meringue over tarts, spreading to edges to seal completely. Swirl tops, using knife or spatula. Bake until meringue is lightly golden, about 15 minutes. Let cool before removing from pans. Serve chilled.

# PLAN OF ATTACK

## Cook Number One

*ahead of time*
1. Make barbecue sauce of choice.  2. Parboil and refrigerate ribs.
*1 hour before*
Wash spinach, wrap in a clean dish-towel, and refrigerate to crisp.
*½ hour before*
Make salad dressing
*just before*
Toss salad

## Cook Number Two

*ahead of time*
1. Make tart crust and bake.  2. Make tart filling and meringue.  3. Finish tarts.
*½ hour before*
1. Make curried rice.  2. Chill wine.
*just before*
Broil or grill ribs.

# MENU

---

*Fresh Tomato Soup*
*Polpettone di Pollo e Tonnato*
(Chicken and Tuna Terrine)
*Trattoria Eggs*
*Espresso Nut Cookies*

---

Summertime and the living is easy . . . or at least it was when folks spent long, languid afternoons sipping lemonade while swinging in hammocks. But today the busy world continues to spin winter and summer alike. Only our appetites and our interest in spending time in the kitchen pall as the season grows warm. This menu is designed to appeal to both listless eaters and spiritless cooks. It is a cold meal that would be perfect for a starlit dinner served al fresco on a terrace or balcony, if romance is your quest, or it makes a perfectly good portable meal for a picnic. Moreover, everything can be made in advance.

We begin with a fresh soup that captures the sunny brilliance of summer's vine-ripened tomatoes. It can be served hot or cold as the weather dictates.

One of our favorite Italian dishes is Vitello Tonnato, the classic cold veal preparation with tuna and anchovy sauce. With this in mind, we developed a terrine that marries the subtlety of chicken (you can, of course, use veal if your Ecuadorian bonds have just matured) with anchovies, tuna, and capers. It slices beautifully and is lighter and more refreshing than many of the more wintery pâtés.

Although English food rarely inspires, our Trattoria Eggs began life as the simple Scotch eggs served in British pubs. We like the spicy kick that Italian sausage gives this variation.

A loaf of crusty bread, some crunchy fresh vegetables or a big green salad, and fresh fruit would round out the menu with Espresso Nut Cookies to add the perfect finishing touch. We like to make refrigerator cookies like these and keep them in the freezer. That way we can cut off just what our demanding little sweet teeth desire at the moment.

With this menu either a bright Frascati, the wine that is gulped by the gallon in Rome, or a dry California Chenin Blanc would be a good choice.

---

# Fresh Tomato Soup

1 stalk celery, chopped
1 carrot, peeled and diced
1 onion, peeled and diced
1 clove garlic, crushed
2 tablespoons olive oil
¾ pound tomatoes, peeled, seeded, and
  chopped

1 tablespoon chopped fresh basil
1½ cups chicken broth
1 tablespoon fresh lemon juice
Pinch sugar (optional)
Salt and pepper

Sauté the celery, carrot, onion, and garlic in olive oil over low heat until the onions are limp. Add the tomatoes, basil, and chicken broth. Bring to the boiling point, then reduce heat and simmer for 15 minutes. Strain and season to taste with fresh lemon juice, a pinch of sugar if desired, salt, and pepper.


# Polpettone di Pollo e Tonnato
## (CHICKEN AND TUNA TERRINE)

1 slice firm-textured white bread, crusts
  removed
½ cup milk
1 whole chicken breast, boned and cut in
  chunks (about 10 ounces boneless meat)
1 3¼-ounce can tuna
1 1-ounce can anchovy fillets

1 egg
Juice and zest of 1 lemon
1 tablespoon capers
¼ cup parsley, chopped
½ onion, diced
1 clove garlic, minced

*Preheat oven to 350 degrees F.* Soak the bread in milk for 5 minutes. Squeeze dry and discard milk. Place damp bread, chicken, tuna, 2 anchovy fillets, egg, lemon, capers, parsley, onion, and garlic in the container of a blender or food processor and whirl until smooth, scraping down the sides several times (if using a blender, you may find it necessary to purée the mixture in several batches). Butter a small (6×3×2¼-inch) loaf pan and make a lattice pattern in the bottom of the pan with the remaining anchovies. Spoon mixture into the pan and smooth top. Place in another pan containing 1 inch of boiling water and bake 40–50 minutes. Remove and cool. Wrap and refrigerate overnight. Slice and garnish with lemon slices and black olives. Serve with French bread and caper-laced mayonnaise. This makes a handsome first course too, and the recipe doubles easily when you have guests.

# Trattoria Eggs

2 hard-cooked eggs
¼ pound Italian sausage (either hot or
   sweet, to your taste)
1 egg, beaten
Flour

½ cup fine dry bread crumbs from Italian
   or French bread
¼ cup finely grated Parmesan cheese
Fat for deep frying

*Preheat oven to 400 degrees F.* Shell the hard-cooked eggs. Remove sausage meat from casings and divide in two. Pat each portion of meat into a round on a dampened board. Lightly dip the hard-cooked eggs in beaten eggs. Roll them in flour and wrap completely in a thin layer of sausage meat. Paint the sausage with additional egg. Combine bread crumbs and cheese and roll eggs in the mixture. Fry in deep fat heated to 370 degrees F. for 2 to 3 minutes, or until the bread crumbs are golden brown and the sausage is firm. Place in a baking dish and bake, uncovered, 10 minutes. Refrigerate and serve cold.

# Espresso Nut Cookies

2 cups flour
1 teaspoon baking powder
⅛ teaspoon salt
½ cup butter
1 cup sugar

1 egg
1 tablespoon instant espresso coffee dissolved in 1 tablespoon hot water and
   allowed to cool
½ cup finely chopped walnuts

Sift together the flour, baking powder, and salt. Cream the butter and add sugar gradually, beating until fluffy. Add egg and cooled instant coffee and beat well. Beat in flour mixture and stir in nuts. Shape the dough into 2-inch rolls, wrap in waxed paper and chill. (If you're going to freeze the rolls, wrap them in foil or put them into plastic bags and seal tightly.) When ready to bake, preheat oven to 375 degrees F., slice dough into ¼-inch rounds, and place on greased baking sheets. Bake for 8 to 10 minutes.

# PLAN OF ATTACK

Since all of the dishes for this meal can be made ahead, there's no need for a timetable for this meal. Just decide which will be the coolest hours of the day or night and plunge ahead. You'll have a lovely cool evening meal to greet you at the end of the sweltering day.

• Soup can be made the night before and chilled.
• Terrine can be made 2 to 3 days in advance.
• Make Trattoria Eggs the night before and refrigerate.
• Espresso Nut Cookies can be made weeks ahead and frozen. (Before cooking, move them to the refrigerator long enough to facilitate slicing.)

## *Autumn*

# MENU

*Emerald Consommé*
*Spinach-Stuffed Trout*
*Almond Potato Puffs*
*French Green Bean and Tomato Salad*
*Chocolate Kahlúa Soufflé*

It was one of those crisp autumn mornings that make you wonder if early risers haven't been right all along. The sun had been up a depressingly short time, but some Samaritan already had put the battered old coffeepot on the campfire. We lumbered into half-frozen waders and tried to look knowledgeable and eager as our companions discussed the relative merits of Royal Coachman and Rat-Faced MacDougall flies. They were there for the sport. But we were there for the fish—the legendary trout we hoped to whisk from stream to skillet in the shortest possible time.

We returned from our adventure with enough fish for breakfast and cooked them in accepted camper fashion, rolled in cornmeal and fried with bacon. It's still one of the best breakfasts in memory.

But as good as trout is, done up with no embellishments but the elusive flavor of woodsmoke, it also is wonderful boned, stuffed, and turned out in fancy-dress regalia, as in this, a sophisticated treatment in which the fish is boned and filled with a mixture of sautéed spinach, mushrooms, and shallots, glossed with a citrus-flavored butter sauce and garnished with golden orange slices. The prelude to the elegant fish dish is a cool, light jellied consommé flecked with the pungent freshness of watercress. The trout is accompanied by crunchy puffs of potato studded with chopped almonds. A salad of green beans and tomatoes adds color, and dessert is the crowning achievement—individual chocolate soufflés.

As with all fish, it's important when choosing trout at the market to be alert for all the signs of freshness. The eyes should be bright and clear and the gills reddish, clean, and fresh-smelling. The flesh, when you press it (and you should), must be firm to the touch and the fish shouldn't have any unpleasant odor. Since fish spoils easily, it should be wrapped in moistureproof paper as soon as you bring it home from the market and then refrigerated. If we are able to buy fish the morning of the day we're going to cook it, we often bring it home and place it in a pan filled with water and ice cubes. This chilly bath firms the fish and keeps it quite fresh.

An excellent wine with this menu would be a chilled Sauvignon Blanc, either one of the Fumé Blancs from California or a Sancerre from the Loire Valley.

## *Emerald Consommé*

2 cups jellied chicken consommé
1 cup watercress leaves, washed and dried
2 teaspoons lemon juice

**GARNISH**
Sour cream
Minced chives or parsley

In the morning, place 1 cup of the consommé in the container of a blender or food processor, add the watercress, and blend or process until well mixed. Stir in the remaining consommé and lemon juice. Spoon into two soup bowls or wine glasses and place in the regrigerator to firm. When ready to serve, garnish with a dollop of sour cream and a sprinkle of minced chives or parsley.

# Spinach-Stuffed Trout

2 small trout (about ½ pound each)
6 tablespoons butter
2 shallots, minced
½ cup sliced mushrooms
½ bunch (6–7 ounces) fresh spinach,
   coarsely chopped
4 tablespoons minced parsley

1 teaspoon fresh or ¼ teaspoon dried
   tarragon
Salt and pepper
1 orange
½ teaspoon fresh lemon juice
Parsley for garnish

Bone the trout, leaving on the heads and tails. First, use kitchen shears to cut off the dorsal and other fins, clipping them close to the body. With a small boning knife, split the lower half of the fish below the abdominal cavity to the backbone. Starting nearest the head, insert the knife between the flesh and the tiny rib bones, separating the bones from the meat and working toward the tail until the rib bones are free. Repeat on the other side. With the shears, clip the backbone just behind the head and just ahead of the tail. Pull the backbone out of the fish, and the rib and dorsal bones behind the backbone will come out.

Melt 2 tablespoons of butter in a skillet over high heat. Quickly sauté the shallots and mushrooms, add the spinach, 2 tablespoons of minced parsley and the tarragon, and reduce the heat. Stew the spinach, stirring, until most of the moisture has evaporated. Season to taste with salt and pepper. Stuff each trout with half the spinach mixture. In another skillet, melt the other 4 tablespoons of butter over medium heat and sauté the trout until golden brown, about 5 minutes on each side. Place the fish on a warm platter.

Cut the orange in half and slice three thin rounds off one side. Cut the rounds in half and set aside for garnish. Squeeze 2 tablespoons of fresh orange juice into the butter remaining in the pan; add the lemon juice and the remaining 2 tablespoons of minced parsley and reduce, stirring over high heat until slightly thickened. Pour the sauce over the fish and garnish with the orange slices and parsley.

# Almond Potato Puffs

¼ cup water
2 tablespoons butter
3 tablespoons flour
1 egg
1¹/₂ cups cooked potatoes, mashed or riced

Salt and pepper
Dash nutmeg
½ cup blanched almonds, chopped
Oil for deep frying

Place water and butter in a small saucepan and heat until butter melts and water comes to a boil. Remove from heat and add flour all at once. Beat until smooth. Beat in egg and cool. Add the flour and egg mixture to the mashed or riced potatoes. Season to taste with salt, pepper, and nutmeg. Flour your hands and shape the mixture into balls, using 1 tablespoon of the mixture for each. Roll them in the chopped almonds. Heat oil to 375 degrees and fry several balls at a time until golden. Drain on paper towels.

## French Green Bean and Tomato Salad

½ pound fresh green beans, trimmed
2 tomatoes, peeled and quartered
**DRESSING**
1 tablespoon Sherry vinegar or white wine
  vinegar
3 tablespoons olive oil

Salt and pepper
¼ teaspoon Dijon mustard
1 teaspoon chopped fresh dill or ¼ teaspoon dried dill weed
1 teaspoon minced parsley
1 garlic clove, minced or pressed

Cook the beans in salted simmering water for 5 to 15 minutes depending on their size and youth. They should be crisp and not limp. Drain, rinse under cold water, and arrange in the middle of two salad plates. Place the quartered tomatoes around the beans.

Combine all the dressing ingredients in a small bowl and whisk until thoroughly combined. Pour over the beans and tomatoes. The salad may be made ahead and chilled for up to an hour before serving.

## Chocolate Kahlúa Soufflé

2 tablespoons butter
¼ cup sugar
1 tablespoon flour
⅓ cup milk, scalded
1 square unsweetened chocolate

1 tablespoon Kahlúa
¼ teaspoon vanilla
1 egg yolk
2 egg whites
Confectioners' sugar

Butter interiors of two 1½-cup soufflé dishes with 1 tablespoon butter. Sprinkle with 1 tablespoon of the sugar. In a saucepan melt remaining 1 tablespoon butter, add the flour, and stir until blended. Add the hot milk to the roux and stir over medium heat until thickened.

Melt the chocolate with the Kahlúa and remaining 3 tablespoons sugar in a double boiler over simmering water. Stir chocolate mixture into sauce and add vanilla. Beat in egg yolk. This much can be done ahead.

*Preheat oven to 375 degrees F.* Beat egg whites and fold into soufflé mixture, taking care not to overblend. Pour into prepared soufflé dishes. Bake for 15 to 20 minutes, then sprinkle with confectioners' sugar and serve immediately.

# PLAN OF ATTACK

## Cook Number One

*ahead of time*
1. Prepare consommé and chill.  2. Make salad dressing.
*1 hour before*
Make salad and chill.
*½ hour before*
1. Prepare potato mixture.  2. Set table.  3. Chill wine.
*15 minutes before*
Deep-fry potatoes and keep warm.
*just before*
Garnish soup and serve.

## Cook Number Two

*ahead of time*
Bone trout.
*1 hour before*
Prepare soufflé base up to the point of adding egg whites.
*½ hour before*
1. Make spinach stuffing for trout.  2. Cut oranges for fish garnish.
*15 minutes before*
1. Cook trout.  2. Preheat oven for soufflé.
*just before*
1. Beat egg whites and fold into soufflé mixture.  2. Place soufflé in oven.

# MENU

*Smoked Salmon in Artichokes*
*Choucroute Garnie*
*Caraway Potatoes*
*Green Salad with Mustard Vinaigrette*
*Pear Tart*

Most people think of choucroute garnie, the hearty Alsatian dish of smoked meats and sauerkraut, as something to serve masses of people. We always did too until we realized that this brasserie-style dinner is easily scaled down and even provides a delicious disguise for leftovers. Since there are few rules about what meats go with the sauerkraut, we like to make a choucroute garnie when we have leftover roast pork, ham, or duck. A choucroute garnie also provides an unimpeachable excuse for exploring untried territory in the sausage kingdom.

We like kielbasa with its slight edge of garlic. Kosher franks are good too, and easy to find. The gentle flavor of bockwurst, an unsmoked veal sausage, is a nice addition. Spicy Swiss bratwurst, knockwurst, and thuringer cervelat also are good choices. This is a dish that adjusts easily to personal interpretations. We usually buy two or three sausages of different types and cut them in chunks to share the tasting pleasure without overdoing the calorie count.

The sauerkraut question is one we feel should be met head on. The fact is, lots of people hate the stuff or at least think they do. But most of the antipathy toward this innocent pickled cabbage is due to the fact that it requires careful grooming before it's presented and some cooks don't take the trouble. You can begin with fresh sauerkraut, the canned variety or that which comes in plastic bags. Although fresh is best, any will taste delicious and delicate if it's thoroughly rinsed to remove all but a hint of the pungent brine and then braised in flavorful stock and wine.

A chilled Alsatian wine such as Gewürztraminer or Riesling, a domestic white wine of a similar type, or a sturdy beer all go well with this meal which is ideally eaten just prior to curling up in front of the fire to follow the footsteps of Inspector Maigret through Paris.

## *Smoked Salmon in Artichokes*

2 large artichokes
½ lemon
**FILLING**
2 tablespoons mayonnaise (see p. 221)
2 tablespoons sour cream
2 ounces smoked salmon, minced

1 teaspoon minced onion
1 teaspoon minced capers
1 tablespoon minced parsley
**GARNISH**
Lettuce
Cherry tomatoes or pimiento strips

Cut off artichoke stems at base with a stainless steel knife. Trim away tough outer leaves. Rub cut edges with lemon. Slice off tops of artichokes so pink tips of chokes are visible. With kitchen scissors, cut off tips of leaves. Place upright in pot and add water until it comes one quarter of the way up the artichokes. Stir in juice from ½ lemon. Bring water to a boil, cover and simmer 35–40 minutes or until tender. Drain. When cool enough to handle, scoop out prickly choke with teaspoon to form cup.

Mix together all filling ingredients and mound in chilled artichokes. Serve on lettuce leaves and garnish each artichoke with a slice of cherry tomato or crossed pimiento strips.

# Choucroute Garnie

1 pound sauerkraut
2 thick slices bacon
1 tablespoon butter
½ onion, chopped
¼ cup chopped carrot
½ apple, peeled and diced

Salt and pepper
Bouquet garni of 6 juniper berries
    (optional), ½ bay leaf, 2 cloves, and 2
    parsley sprigs tied in cheesecloth
¼ cup white wine
½ cup rich chicken broth

For the meat, include two or three choices from the following:

thinly cut smoked pork chops
smoked baked ham slices
ham hock
cooked sausages

roast goose, duck, or pheasant
sliced cooked smoked pork butt
cooked pork roast

*Preheat oven to 300 degrees F.* Drain sauerkraut. Place in a bowl and cover with cold water. Soak for 20 minutes, changing water twice. Drain again and squeeze dry with your hands. Chop bacon and simmer in water 5 minutes. Melt butter in skillet. Add bacon, onions, carrots, and apple and sauté for 2 minutes. Cover and cook over low heat for 5 minutes. Place half of mixture in bottom of casserole. Cover with half of sauerkraut. Place whatever meats you have selected on top of sauerkraut. Top with remaining vegetables and sauerkraut. Season with salt and pepper. Add *bouquet garni*, white wine, and broth. Bring to a boil on top of the range, cover, and then place in preheated oven. Cook for about 3 hours or until liquid is absorbed.

# Caraway Potatoes

4 new potatoes, scrubbed
2 tablespoons butter, melted

Salt and pepper
1–2 tablespoons caraway seeds

Place the potatoes in boiling water to cover and cook, covered, until tender, about 20 to 30 minutes. Drain and then shake over heat until dry. Toss with melted butter, salt and pepper, and caraway seeds.

# Green Salad with Mustard Vinaigrette

Wash and crisp your favorite combination of salad greens—perhaps butter or Boston lettuce, watercress, spinach, and romaine—and toss with the following dressing:

1 tablespoon fresh lemon juice
1 teaspoon stone-ground mustard such as
  moutarde de Meaux

¼ cup olive oil
Salt and pepper

Whisk together all ingredients before tossing with salad greens. *Moutarde de Meaux,* which was described by Brillat-Savarin as "the gourmet's mustard," is an interesting mixture of coarsely and finely ground seeds that give the mustard a pleasant texture and earthy flavor. It has a nice bite that comes through in the dressing.

# Pear Tart

**SHORT CRUST DOUGH**
1 cup flour
2 teaspoons sugar
¼ teaspoon salt
5 tablespoons sweet butter, cut in pieces
2–3 tablespoons ice water

**FRUIT FILLING**
2 pears
1 cup sugar
½ cup water

**PASTRY CREAM**
2 tablespoons sugar
1 egg yolk
1 tablespoon flour
½ cup milk
½-inch section of vanilla bean

**GLAZE**
¼ cup apricot jam or apple jelly
1 tablespoon grated walnuts

To make the pastry, place flour, sugar, and salt in bowl. Add butter and cut in until mixture has a coarse, sandy texture. Sprinkle with water and mix with fork until mixture can be gathered into a ball. Wrap in foil or plastic wrap and chill at least 1 hour.

*Preheat oven to 350 degrees F.* Roll out dough on floured board into a rectangle about 8×11 inches. Trim edges. Place on a baking sheet. Cut off a ¾-inch strip from each edge. Paint sides of remaining rectangle with water and place strips on edges of rectangle to form rim. Trim excess from ends. Crimp with fork. Prick all over with a fork. Bake for 30 minutes or until golden brown. Cool.

To make pastry cream, whisk together sugar and egg yolk until thick and creamy. Gradually whisk in flour. Combine milk and vanilla bean in small saucepan and bring to a boil. Remove vanilla. Pour hot milk in a thin stream into sugar mixture, stirring with a wooden spoon. Strain into saucepan and bring to a boil, stirring constantly. Boil until thick. Cool.

To poach pears, combine sugar and water in a small skillet and boil for about 10 minutes. Meanwhile, peel and core pears and cut into thin slices. Poach pears in syrup over low heat for about 5 minutes or until tender. Drain and cool.

Heat jam or jelly and strain if necessary.

To assemble tart, spread pastry shell with pastry cream. Arrange pears on top. Brush with jam or jelly and sprinkle with chopped nuts.

# PLAN OF ATTACK

The Choucroute Garnie requires 4 hours from start to finish, so save this menu for an occasion when you have time to spend in the kitchen—we like to serve it on Sunday nights.

## Cook Number One

**4 hours before**
Prepare Choucroute Garnie.
**3 hours before**
Place choucroute in oven.
**1 hour before**
1. Wash and crisp lettuce. 2. Make salad dressing and refrigerate.
**½ hour before**
Prepare caraway potatoes.
**just before**
Toss salad.

## Cook Number Two

**ahead of time**
1. Prepare and cook artichokes, remove chokes, and chill cups. 2. Prepare smoked salmon mayonnaise. 3. Prepare pastry crust and bake.
**1 hour before**
1. Make pastry cream and film with melted butter or cover closely with plastic wrap to prevent skin from forming. 2. Chill wine.
**½ hour before**
Poach pears and drain.
**15 minutes before**
Assemble tart.

# MENU

---

*Herb-Steamed Clams*
*Oxtail Stew*
*Fennel Salad*
*French Bread*
*Apple-Apricot Soufflé*

---

The day we liberate our tweeds from their cozy hideout among the mothballs, we know it is well and truly autumn. And the brisk, bracing days of the season bring a renewed appetite for heartier meals with soups and stews that bubble invitingly on the back of the stove. Happily, stews are at their best when made ahead and allowed to sit around and gather strength for a day or two, so even cooks who can't spend all day tending a burbling pot can still enjoy them by preparing them in advance and refrigerating them until the time comes for the unveiling.

We've selected oxtails because they make a particularly delicious stew. Now, we all know people who will gorge themselves on lobster tails but blanch when the same part of the beef is mentioned. Yet, prepared correctly, oxtails can be an equally delectable meal: succulent meat in a glistening fragrant sauce. Oxtails do require long, slow cooking to develop their wonderful gelatinous texture, but the result is well worth the effort. Choose an oxtail with as much lean meat as possible and with fresh, creamy-looking fat, and plan on a whole oxtail for two people.

We like to begin this meal with the fresh piquancy of herb-steamed clams. The fennel salad is a very simple one, but its distinctive anise flavor is a wonderful palate cleanser after a rich dish like the oxtail stew. With the oxtails we like the sturdy character of a well-aged California Zinfandel or one of the flavorful Riojas from Spain.

For dessert, an apple soufflé celebrates one of the finest fruits of the season.

## Herb-Steamed Clams

*2 dozen fresh clams in their shells*
*½ cup Vermouth*
*1 tablespoon parsley*
*1 clove garlic, minced*

*1 tablespoon olive oil*
*½ teaspoon oregano*
*Dash Tabasco*

Pick your clams carefully, choosing only those with tightly closed shells. Wash them thoroughly under cold running water, using a stiff brush to scrub them. Then let clams soak for about 20 minutes in salted water to release any sand they may still contain.

Put the washed and soaked clams in a kettle with the remaining ingredients. Place over very low heat so the liquid will just provide steam for cooking and not boil. Cook until the shells open, about 10 to 12 minutes. Strain the juice through several thicknesses of cheesecloth and reheat. Serve clams with the juice and some melted butter for dipping. Be sure to have plenty of good French bread on hand.

# Oxtail Stew

Oxtails are inexpensive and delicious, but some people who have never tried them shy away. This dish should change their minds. Make the oxtails a day or two before you plan to serve them so the flavors will have an opportunity to blend.

*2 pounds oxtails, cut into 2-inch pieces*
*Salt and pepper*
*Flour*
*2 tablespoons olive oil*
*2 tablespoons butter*
*1 carrot, minced*
*1 stalk celery, minced*
*1 onion, chopped*
*1 clove garlic, pressed*
*¼ cup minced parsley*
*½ bay leaf*
*½ teaspoon thyme*

*3 crushed juniper berries (optional)*
*1 tablespoon tomato paste*
*1 cup dry red wine*
*2 cups beef broth or stock*
**VEGETABLES**
*1 cup carrots, peeled and cut into matchstick slices*
*1 cup tiny new potatoes, peeled*
*¼ pound mushrooms, quartered*
*2 tablespoons butter*
*2 small zucchini cut in chunks*

*Preheat oven to 350 degrees F.* Trim oxtails of excess fat and dry them on paper towels. Sprinkle with salt and pepper and dredge in flour, shaking off the excess. Heat the oil in a flameproof casserole and brown the oxtail pieces a few at a time. Remove the oxtails and set aside.

Add the butter to the casserole and sauté the chopped carrots, celery, onions, and garlic until golden brown. Place the browned oxtails on top of the vegetables in the casserole and add parsley, bay leaf, thyme, and juniper berries. Combine the tomato paste, wine, and broth and add to the casserole. Bring the mixture to a boil, cover and place in the oven for 2½ to 3 hours or until oxtails are almost tender. Add the carrots and potatoes to the casserole and continue cooking for another 20 minutes while you sauté the mushrooms in butter. Add mushrooms and zucchini to the casserole and return it to the oven for another 15 minutes. You may need to add additional water or broth during the cooking time.

If possible, cool and refrigerate the casserole for a day or two, reserving the zucchini to add while rewarming. This will facilitate removing the fat from the sauce and allow the flavors to blend. Skim fat from sauce and, using a slotted spoon, remove oxtails and vegetables. Reduce sauce over high heat until thickened. Return meat and vegetables to the sauce and season to taste with salt and pepper. If oxtails are made ahead, reheat and cook until zucchini is tender. Serve in shallow soup plates with lots of crusty bread.

## Fennel Salad

1 head fresh fennel
2 tablespoons olive oil
Salt and pepper

Remove any discolored or shriveled parts from the fennel. Slice as thin as possible across the bulb. Arrange the fennel on a plate and sprinkle with the olive oil, salt, and freshly ground black pepper. No lemon juice or vinegar is needed as the sweet, nutty flavor of fennel shines brightest with just a little oil.

## Apple-Apricot Soufflé

Butter Sugar
1 tart apple, peeled, cored, and sliced
1 tablespoon apricot jam
Dash cinnamon
1 teaspoon water
1 egg yolk
1 tablespoon flour
2 tablespoons sugar

¼ cup milk, scalded
2 teaspoons butter
1 teaspoon vanilla
1 tablespoon Calvados, applejack, or dark rum
2 egg whites
Confectioners' sugar

Preheat oven to 375 degrees F. Prepare two 1-cup soufflé dishes by rubbing generously with butter, then sprinkling with sugar and discarding the excess.

Combine the apple slices, apricot jam, cinnamon, and water in a small heavy saucepan. Cover and place over medium-low heat, stirring occasionally, until the mixture is a thick purée. Cool.

Whisk together the egg yolk and flour and sugar. Stir in the hot milk. Pour the mixture into another saucepan and bring to a boil, stirring constantly. Continue to stir and cook the mixture gently for 2 minutes. Stir in butter, vanilla, and liquor.

Fold the apple purée into the soufflé base and check for sweetness, adding more sugar if necessary.

Beat the egg whites until stiff. Using a rubber spatula, fold ¼ of the whites into the yolk mixture. Fold in the remaining egg whites as gently as possible.

Pour the soufflé mixture into the prepared soufflé dishes and bake at once for 10 to 20 minutes or until the soufflé is puffed and brown. Sprinkle with confectioners' sugar and serve at once.

# PLAN OF ATTACK

---

## Cook Number One

### ahead of time
Prepare Oxtail Stew and refrigerate.
### 1 hour before
Skim fat from stew and reheat slowly.
### ½ hour before
1. Prepare apple purée for soufflé. 2. Open wine.
### 15 minutes before
Prepare soufflé base and stir in purée.
### about 20 minutes before dessert
1. Beat egg whites and fold into soufflé base. 2. Bake the soufflé.

## Cook Number Two

### 1 hour before
Scrub clams.
### ½·hour before
1. Soak clams. 2. Prepare fennel salad.
### 15 minutes before
Steam clams and serve.

---

# *Winter*

---

# MENU

---

*Gene's Borscht*
*Swiss Cheese Salad*
*Herb Loaf*
*Pears Cardamom*

---

No matter how dreary the weather or our spirits, a tureen of steaming soup always warms our innards and cheers our wintery souls. Great soup cooks, we have learned, are generous, inventive types who work with handfuls of this and that, tasting as they go. Not for them the prim, mathematical formulas that leave little or no room for creativity. Their satisfaction is in the sometimes unpredictable brews that keep the kettle crooning on the back of the stove.

If you are a born improviser, this recipe will be just a rough blueprint. Replace the beets in the borscht with other vegetables and you have a whole new soup. Occasionally, however, even the most gifted cook can run into problems with an extemporaneous production. If that should ever happen to you, try a rescue with one of the following:

- Garlic can give an instant lift to a dull soup.
- Fresh lemon juice can save a soup if the flavors have become somewhat muddled.
- A raw potato cooked with a too salty soup helps absorb the excess salt.
- Add some raw onion for bite, or sautéed onion for subtle sweetness.
- Used with discretion, curry powder can introduce an exotic undertone to any soup.
- Nutmeg is a nutty and fragrant addition to any cream soup that lacks character.
- Sometimes stirring in sour cream or *crème fraîche* (see p. 226) smooths and blends otherwise discordant flavors.
- Any single herb or combination (especially fresh ones) is a great boost to a soup and puts a personal stamp on your masterpiece.

## Gene's Borscht

| | |
|---|---|
| *1 pound lean beef, cubed* | *½ teaspoon sugar* |
| *5 cups water or beef broth* | *1 tablespoon butter* |
| *1½ teaspoons salt* | *1 can (16 ounces) sliced or shredded beets* |
| *1 cup shredded raw beets* | *1 cup shredded cabbage* |
| *½ cup grated carrots* | *1 bay leaf* |
| *½ cup coarsely grated turnip* | *Black pepper* |
| *1 small onion, chopped* | *Sour cream* |
| *1 tablespoon tomato paste* | *Dill sprigs or dried dill weed* |
| *2 tablespoons vinegar or to taste* | |

Place the beef cubes in a large pot with enough water or broth to cover, add salt, and simmer until the meat is tender, about 1½ to 2 hours.

While the meat is cooking, combine the raw beets, carrots, turnips, onion, tomato paste, vinegar, sugar, and butter together and cook over very low heat for about 15 minutes, covered. Be sure to keep the heat low and stir the mixture occasionally so it won't scorch. Add the cabbage and juice from the canned beets and cook the mixture 10 minutes longer.

Skim fat from meat and broth and add the vegetable mixture, canned beets, bay leaf, and a few grinds of black pepper. Cook until the vegetables are tender. Adjust salt and vinegar to taste. Serve in deep bowls with dollops of sour cream and sprinkling of dill on top.

## Swiss Cheese Salad

¼ cup sour cream or plain yogurt
½ teaspoon Dijon mustard
½ teaspoon prepared horseradish
Pinch ground cuminseed
Salt and pepper
¼ pound Swiss cheese, cut in julienne
   strips

1 raw zucchini, grated
4 mushrooms, washed and thinly sliced
½ cup sliced celery
2 radishes, grated

To make the dressing, combine the sour cream or yogurt, mustard, horseradish, and cuminseed and mix well. Add salt and pepper to taste.

Place the cheese, zucchini, mushrooms, and celery in a bowl and toss gently with the dressing. Spoon onto lettuce leaves and sprinkle with grated radishes.

## Herb Loaf

1½ cups flour
1 tablespoon sugar
1 teaspoon salt
½ teaspoon dried dill weed
Pinch rubbed sage

Pinch marjoram
2 teaspoons active dry yeast
⅓ cup milk
⅓ cup water
2 teaspoons butter

Mix ½ cup of the flour with the sugar, salt, dill, sage, marjoram, and undissolved yeast in a large bowl.

Combine milk, water, and butter in a small saucepan and heat slowly until warm. Add to dry ingredients and beat 2 minutes at medium speed. Add enough of the remaining flour to make a stiff batter and beat until well blended. Cover with greased waxed paper and let rise in a warm, draft-free place until doubled in bulk, about 45 minutes.

Fifteen minutes before baking, *preheat oven to 375 degrees F.* Grease a 6×3×2-inch loaf pan. Stir batter down and beat vigorously for about 1 minute. Turn into pan; bake until brown, 30–40 minutes. Remove from pan; cool on rack.

# Pears Cardamom

2 pears, peeled, cored, and cut in 8 lengthwise slices each
1½ tablespoons brown sugar

¼ cup orange liqueur (or orange juice)
½ teaspoon ground cardamom
½ cup slightly sweetened whipped cream

*Preheat oven to 375 degrees F.* Arrange the pears in a shallow baking dish and sprinkle with the sugar. Pour liqueur over the pears and sprinkle with cardamom. Bake 20–30 minutes or until the pears are tender. Cool and then chill for at least 15 minutes or serve warm. Top with whipped cream.

# PLAN OF ATTACK

*2–3 hours before dinner* Cook peas 10 minutes, drain, cover with fresh water, and simmer with other ingredients until done.

**OR**

*ahead of time* Cook meat for borscht.

## Cook Number One

*1½ hours before*
Make bread dough and cover for rising.
*45 minutes before*
1. Punch down bread, place in pan and bake.  2. Prepare ingredients for salad.
*20 minutes before*
Combine vegetables and meat for borscht and continue cooking until done.
*just before serving*
1. Reheat soup if necessary.  2. Garnish borscht with sour cream and dill.

## Cook Number Two

*1 hour before*
Prepare pears and place in the oven to bake.
*45 minutes before*
1. Cook vegetable mixture for borscht.  2. Remove pears from the oven and cool.
*20 minutes before*
1. Make salad dressing.  2. Place pears in the refrigerator.
*just before serving*
Slice bread

**NOTE**   Either soup can be made two or three days in advance and reheated.

# MENU

---

*Celery and Almond Soup*
*Stuffed Turkey Thigh*
*Sweet Potatoes Duchesse*
*Broccoli with Lemon Butter Sauce*
*Grand Marnier Soufflé in Orange Cups*

---

Turkey for two. Impossible, you say. There aren't enough curries or hashes in the world to accommodate the amount of meat left on a carcass when two people are finished with the first round. It's a fact of life that turkeys, like Zeppelins and opera stars, are built on the grand scale.

For years we've tried to resolve this dilemma, experimenting with different appendages of the bird or seeking out turkeys of extraordinary petiteness. Alas, tiny turkeys are as bony as *Vogue* models—all frame and little meat.

But at last we have an answer. The humble thigh. Boned, flattened, and stuffed with your favorite dressing or one of the three given here, rolled and roasted to a golden turn and then sliced to reveal a mosaic of dressing pinwheeled inside, a single turkey thigh is a perfectly beautiful main course for two. The juicy meat remains moist as it cooks, and any leftovers will be just enough to satisfy the late-night lusts of midnight snackers. Although diminutive, this roast produces plenty of drippings for old-fashioned gravy if that's your secret passion.

To fill out the menu, we suggest beginning with a lush celery and almond soup that showcases an often overlooked vegetable and enhances it with just a breath of curry. Handsome golden drifts of sweet potatoes duchesse make a fine companion for the turkey. Broccoli simply dressed in lemon butter sauce offers contrasting color and texture. And for dessert, Grand Marnier soufflé appears in pretty orange cups.

Contrary to the popular myth that white wine should be served with fowl, turkey is best matched with a sturdy red. Either a modest Bordeaux (save the great growths for a slightly more sumptuous menu) or a California Cabernet Sauvignon would be perfect.

# Celery and Almond Soup

2 tablespoons butter
¼ teaspoon curry powder
½ pound celery (about 3 large stalks),
   chopped
1 cup chicken broth (see p. 220)

2 teaspoons minced parsley
1 cup milk
Salt and pepper
2 tablespoons cream
2 tablespoons toasted slivered almonds

Melt the butter in a saucepan and add the curry powder and celery. Cook over low heat for about 10 minutes, stirring from time to time. Pour in the broth and add parsley. Bring to a boil. Reduce heat to low, cover, and simmer 20 minutes. Add milk and salt and pepper to taste.

   Whirl soup in blender until almost smooth (there will be tiny crunchy bits of celery that give the soup a pleasing texture). Reheat and garnish by swirling in a little cream and sprinkling with slivered almonds.


# Stuffed Turkey Thigh

1 turkey thigh (about 1 pound)
Stuffing of your choice or John's Dressing (below)
2 tablespoons melted butter

*Preheat oven to 350 degrees F.* To bone the thigh, cut it lengthwise down the bone on the inside. Pressing knife against the bone, cut until it's released. Pound meat to flatten as much as possible. Spoon stuffing down center. Bring skin together to enclose filling and tie with string, fastening ends with toothpicks or skewers. Wrap loosely in foil and place in a shallow baking pan. Bake 1 hour. Open foil and bake 1 hour longer, basting often with butter and juices until meat is nicely browned. Remove skewers and string and cut into slices.


# John's Dressing

This apple and nut combination is a specialty of Jinx's brother. It's on permanent loan to our house now. This amount will stuff one turkey thigh.

⅛ pound bulk sausage or 2 sausage links
  (casings removed)
¼ cup chopped onions
3 large mushrooms, chopped
½ cup toasted bread crumbs or small bread
  cubes
¼ cup peeled, chopped tart apple
2 tablespoons chopped walnuts
1 tablespoon minced fresh parsley

Pinch dried sage
Pinch dried thyme
Salt and pepper
½ beaten egg (in each of these dressing
  recipes, beat a whole egg, divide it
  roughly in half, and add the unused
  half to tomorrow's scrambled eggs or
  omelet)

Cook the sausage in a skillet until no pink remains. Remove from the pan. Add
the onions and mushrooms and cook until the onions are limp and the
mushrooms are just beginning to brown. Toss together the sausage, onions,
mushrooms, bread crumbs, apple, walnuts, and parsley. Season to taste with
sage, thyme, and salt and pepper. Stir in the egg and mix well. This mixture will
stuff one turkey thigh.

## Sweet Potatoes Duchesse

2 small to medium sweet potatoes, peeled
  and quartered
2 tablespoons butter
1 egg yolk

⅛ teaspoon mace
⅛ teaspoon nutmeg
Salt

Boil sweet potatoes in salted water until tender. Drain, return to pan and shake
over heat for a few seconds to evaporate any residual water. Beat with butter at
medium speed until smooth. With the mixer running, add the egg yolk and
spices and whip at high speed until fluffy. Salt to taste.

Using an open star tube in a pastry bag, pipe the potato mixture around the
edge of an ovenproof platter. Set aside, cover loosely when cool, and
refrigerate.

About 30 minutes before serving, remove platter from refrigerator and bring
to room temperature. *Preheat broiler.* Five minutes before serving, run platter
under broiler until peaks and ridges of mixture are lightly browned. Watch it
carefully.

## Broccoli with Lemon Butter Sauce

½ pound broccoli
2 tablespoons butter

1 teaspoon lemon juice
1 hard-cooked egg yolk

Wash the broccoli well and cut off the tough bottom part of the stems. Pull off any excess outer leaves. If the stalks are very large, cut gashes up through the bottom to allow them to cook more evenly. Steam the broccoli spears or cook them upright in a tall pan (coffeepot, asparagus cooker, etc.) in an inch of boiling salted water. When the stalks can be easily pierced with a knife (8–10 minutes), drain and keep warm.

Melt the butter and add the lemon juice. Pour over the broccoli. Garnish with a hard-cooked egg yolk rubbed through a sieve.


## Grand Marnier Soufflé in Orange Cups

*2 nicely shaped oranges*  
*1 tablespoon sugar*  
*1 tablespoon flour*  
*2 tablespoons milk*

*1 egg yolk*  
*2 tablespoons finely grated coconut*  
*2 egg whites*  
*2 teaspoons Grand Marnier*

Cut the tops off the oranges and scoop out the pulp. Clean out the inside of the shell, taking care not to puncture the skin. Drain pulp, reserving 2 teaspoons of juice. Chop and reserve 2 tablespoons of pulp.

*Preheat oven to 375 degrees F.* Combine the sugar, flour, milk, and 1 tablespoon of orange juice in a small saucepan. Cook over low heat, stirring constantly until thick. Remove from heat and stir in the egg yolk and coconut. Beat the egg whites until they form peaks; fold into the coconut mixture. Put one tablespoon of orange pulp in each orange shell and drizzle on 1 teaspoon of Grand Marnier. Spoon the soufflé mixture on top.

Place the filled shells on a baking sheet and bake for 15 minutes or until puffed and golden on top. Serve at once. If you've had a bad day at the barricades and don't feel up to scooping and scraping orange shells, the soufflé is equally delicious cooked in individual soufflé dishes.

# PLAN OF ATTACK

## Cook Number One

*ahead of time*
1. Make soup and refrigerate.
2. Scoop out orange shells.

*½ hour before*
1. Place orange pulp and Grand Marnier in orange shells.   2. Open wine.

*15 minutes before*
Prepare soufflé base up to the point of adding egg whites.

*just before*
1. Reheat soup.   2. Beat egg whites and fold into soufflé base. Fill orange shells and bake.

## Cook Number Two

*ahead of time*
1. Bone turkey thigh and refrigerate.
2. Hard-cook egg for broccoli garnish; sieve yolk and refrigerate.
3. Prepare stuffing and refrigerate.

*2–3 hours before*
Stuff turkey thigh. Place in oven to roast.

*1 hour before*
1. Prepare Sweet Potatoes Duchesse up to broiling point; refrigerate.
2. Wash and trim broccoli.

*15 minutes before*
Cook broccoli and make sauce.

*just before*
Brown sweet potatoes under broiler.

# MENU

*Pimiento Soup with Vermouth*
*Pork Medallions in Madeira*
*Cream-Glazed Corn*
*Chocolate Crêpes*

When confronted with the vast selection in most butchers' cases, it's often easy to overlook interesting cuts of meat that would be ideal for twosomes and settle into the old chop and steak rut. Unsmoked boneless pork tenderloin is one of our favorite meats and we find that if we buy one and cut it into individual ½-inch-thick medallions, freezing those not earmarked for immediate use, we usually can make several meals from one tenderloin. The medallions can be prepared with such a variety of sauces that if we didn't have a freezer we wouldn't mind having them several nights running.

Almost any sauce you might use with veal or chicken breasts works equally well with pork; you may find that you like the flavor of the sauce even better against the delicate, mildly sweet flavor of this meat.

The opening salvo for this meal is a sunset-hued cold pimiento soup. Cream-glazed corn is just fine made with frozen corn in the winter, but don't fail to try it with fresh when the kernels come just from the cob in summer. For dessert, chocolate crêpes make a grand finale.

Choosing a wine to serve with pork leaves a good deal of room for indulging personal preferences. If you are in the white wine camp, try one with an undercurrent of fruit, such as a Gewürztraminer. The herbal quality of Fumé Blanc also partners well with pork. If you prefer a red wine, a young, fresh Gamay or Gamay Beaujolais is a good choice.

## Pimiento Soup with Vermouth

¼ cup chopped onion
1 tablespoon butter
1 tablespoon flour
1¹/2 cups chicken broth (see p. 220)

1 jar pimientos (2 ounces)
½ cup cream
2 tablespoons dry white Vermouth
Salt and white pepper

Sauté onions in butter until soft. Stir in flour and cook over low heat for 2 minutes. Add chicken broth and pimientos and continue cooking until the soup has thickened. Whirl in a blender or food processor until smooth. Return the soup to the pan and stir in the cream, Vermouth, and salt and pepper to taste. This soup can be served hot or cold.

## Pork Medallions in Madeira

6 thin pork medallions
Salt and pepper
Flour
2 tablespoons butter
3 tablespoons olive oil

2 tablespoons warm brandy
½ cup Madeira
½ cup rich chicken broth (see p. 220)
2 tablespoons soft butter

Sprinkle the pork with salt and pepper and dust with flour. Heat butter and oil in a skillet. Sauté pork until brown on both sides. Remove meat from the pan and pour off fat. Deglaze the pan with the Madeira and flame by touching the edge of the pan with a long match. Stir in ¼ cup of the broth and scrape up any brown bits on the bottom of the pan. Return the meat to the pan and cook, covered, for 30 minutes, turning the meat occasionally. Remove the meat to warm plates, add the remaining ¼ cup of broth, and reduce sauce until thick and syrupy. Enrich the sauce by stirring in 2 tablespoons soft butter and spoon over the pork.

## Cream-Glazed Corn

*1 tablespoon butter*
*2 cups uncooked fresh corn kernels cut from the cob or frozen whole kernel corn, thawed and drained*

*2 tablespoons water*
*Pinch ground cloves*
*2 tablespoons heavy cream*
*Salt and pepper*

Melt the butter in a small skillet over high heat. Add the corn, water, and cloves. Cover and cook, stirring occasionally, for 3 to 4 minutes. Remove cover and add the cream. Cook, stirring constantly, until cream is almost absorbed. Add salt and pepper to taste.

## Chocolate Crêpes

This recipe makes enough batter to achieve 4 perfect crêpes, allowing for 1 or 2 that might have to be thrown away.

**CRÊPES**
*1 egg*
*⅓ cup flour*
*1 tablespoon sugar*

*2 teaspoons cocoa*
*6 tablespoons buttermilk*
*2 teaspoons melted butter*

Whirl all ingredients in a blender or food processor for about 1 minute or until smooth, or beat the egg in a bowl, add the remaining ingredients, and beat until smooth. Refrigerate for 1 hour.

To cook crêpes, brush a crêpe pan with a bit of oil. When it sizzles, pour in just enough batter to cover the bottom of the pan, tipping the pan to spread the batter. When the crêpe is firm on the underside, after about 1 minute, turn it and cook on the other side for 5 seconds. Repeat with the remaining batter.

**FILLING**
*3 ounces Petit Suisse or cream cheese*
*1½ tablespoons white Crème de Cacao*

Whip the cheese with an electric mixer and gradually beat in the Crème de Cacao until the mixture is the consistency of cake frosting.

**TO ASSEMBLE**
*4 tablespoons raspberry jam, strained*
*2 tablespoons granulated sugar (optional)*
*1 tablespoon Cognac*

Spread each crêpe with one tablespoon of the jam, and then carefully spread ¼ of the cheese mixture over the jam on each crêpe. Roll the crêpes jelly-roll fashion and arrange on an attractive heatproof platter or put two each lengthwise in ovenproof oval ramekins. If you aren't going to serve them immediately, place the crêpes in the refrigerator, but take them out well before dinner to allow them to come up to room temperature.

To serve, sprinkle sugar over the crêpes, heat the Cognac slightly in a very small pan, ignite it and pour the flaming brandy over the crêpes. Serve at once.

# PLAN OF ATTACK

## Cook Number One

*ahead of time*
Make soup and refrigerate.
*1 hour before*
Prepare and cook pork medallions.
*just before*
Cook Cream-Glazed Corn.

## Cook Number Two

*ahead of time*
1. Make crêpes.  2. Make crêpe filling.  3. Assemble crêpes and refrigerate.
*1 hour before*
Remove crêpes from the refrigerator.
*just before*
Heat soup if serving it warm.

# THREE

# PRIVATE CELEBRATIONS

At the risk of sounding like greeting-card poets, we believe that cooking together, or for each other, is in itself an act of celebration. Nothing—well, almost nothing—gives us as much of a charge as the prospect of getting into the kitchen and rustling those old pots and pans in tandem. We find the kitchen as romantic as any other room in the house (you can make of that what you will), and, although we haven't brought it up before, you may have guessed by now that we enjoy eating what we cook as much as we do cooking it. For us, any celebration worth the name has to involve food and drink.

There are celebrations, and there are celebrations. There are those that demand large numbers of people, such as weddings and birthdays, and then there are the more intimate moments. Some of our happiest memories stem from meals we have prepared and consumed alone on special occasions, including traditional holidays when we couldn't join our families.

Of course, you don't have to wait for some seminal occurrence. We have been known to celebrate the fact that it's Saturday, or that the car's odometer cranked another 10,000 miles withour requiring major surgery. However, for all of us—at least those of us who remember dates—there are the obvious times, such as anniversaries, when we know for months in advance that a celebration is in the offing.

Happily, life isn't always a mad dash from a job to the kitchen, and the menus in this chapter tend to be more elaborate and require more time for preparation than those in the previous one. We've pegged them to particular festivals, such as Valentine's Day and the holidays, but don't let that limit you. Only you know when it's time to celebrate.

This chapter, which deals extensively with candlelight and wine *à deux,* is probably as good a place as any to put to rest a number of fables about aphrodisiacs, a subject that still seems to fascinate people. Some years ago, as part of a journalistic investigation, Jeff researched the subject thoroughly. Since Jinx was an innocent bystander, we'll let him tell you about it.

When I was a youth, back in the days when the mythology current among males of my generation held (with no solid proof to back it up, believe me) that blowing on a girl's neck or gently stroking the small of her back on a darkened dance floor would whip her into an erotic frenzy, we talked a lot about aphrodisiacs. In fact, with the exception of occasional conjecture over whether Mantle or Maris would break Babe Ruth's single-year home run record, idle conversation in high school boys' locker rooms was devoted almost exclusively to sex, about which we knew virtually nothing. We told one another Munchausen tales of amorous encounters, generally getting things all wrong.

Those were the Dark Ages of sex education, a term somehow associated by our parents with the International Communist Conspiracy. Dwight Eisenhower and Casey Stengel were firmly in control of the nation, and no "nice girl" would have dreamed of venturing forth in the morning without armoring herself in a girdle and several yards of rigidly starched petticoats sufficient to confound even the most inventive and aggressive acne sufferer in our number. Unlike today, when most teenagers possess as much knowledge about the birds and the bees as gynecologists, the first solid data we received on the essential differences between the sexes came to those who let their college deferments lapse and were subjected to Army training films (they always began, "Hi, soldier, new in town?") designed to discourage conjugal union in any form.

If any of us had known how many mundane substances have been credited with aphrodisiac properties over the centuries, there would have been an unprecedented spurt of puerile interest in the culinary arts. Fortunately these philters did not include hamburger grease, deep-frying oil, and lemon Cokes, or the postwar baby boom would have been sustained well into the twenty-first century.

Aside from sniggering references to Iberian insects, about the only aphrodisiac we were all pretty sure of was raw seafood, a fiction kept alive in modern times by the fisheries industry. Today, for example, the Oyster Institute (have you noticed there seems to be an "institute" for every product from avocados to wolfbane?) has printed posters advising, "Eat Oysters: Love Longer." However, we thought seafood worked only on males and was, since all of us lived in an almost constant state of libidinous arousal, useless for our purposes.

At the same time, of course, we also lived in terror of the deadly compound saltpeter, a mysterious chemical we were convinced was secretly incorporated into the fodder doled out in school cafeterias. Except for those few overachievers who made it past Chemistry I, none of us knew that saltpeter is potassium nitrate, a salt then widely used as a preservative and coloring agent in hot dogs and bologna, foods we often consumed to avoid those doped lunches we were sure the home economists were trying to foist on us. Whatever its other demerits, the fact is that saltpeter does nothing to cool a man's ardor, and if you happen to be raising any young louts you would be doing them a kindness to let them in on the secret.

A generation passed, and although I grew up to become obsessed with food and wine, I never did any serious research into aphrodisiacs. Frankly, I never felt the need. Thus, when I undertook to study up on them, I was faced with something of a conundrum: who would I use as a guinea pig? Myself? Be serious. My secretary? First, I don't have one, second I have no desire to seduce strange women and third, even if I did I'd probably botch it and make a fool of myself. That left only one potential victim, my blameless spouse, who already finds me irresistible on an empty stomach. But, what the hell, I thought, it was worth a try. Only she mustn't know or the test wouldn't be valid. After months of scholarly investigation I turned to her one morning and crooned innocently, "Sweetheart, you're going to have a busy day. Why don't I make dinner tonight?"

"Hey, great," she enthused. "What are we having?"

As luck would have it, I had just finished reading an interesting passage from Sir Richard Francis Burton's nineteenth-century translation of Shaykh Nafzawi's work, *The Perfumed Garden for the Soul's Delectation,* a really dirty book if you can get your hands on it. The Shaykh wrote that a person "who boils asparagus, and then fries them in fat, and then pours upon them the yolks of eggs with pounded condiments…will…find in it a stimulant for his amorous desires."

"Oh, I don't know," I answered nonchalantly. "For openers I thought we might try asparagus with hollandaise sauce."

Writers throughout history have tried to define the elusive food of love, from

Ovid, Horace, Petronius and that crowd to the Baron Roy Andries de Groot, who has done about as much as any human to further the literature of comestibles. In between, the subject has been explored by people as diverse as Pliny the Elder, whose scientific curiosity was so intense that it led him to make an unlucky visit to Pompeii in A.D. 79 to check out the volcano; Brillat-Savarin, Benjamin Franklin, Joseph Wood Krutch, Gayelord Hauser, and Dr. David Reuben, not to mention a legion of Near Eastern and Oriental authorities.

Any study of aphrodisiacs must include that most lecherous of literary works, the Old Testament. There one finds an early reference to the startling idiosyncrasies of the mandrake root. Pliny agreed that it was an aphrodisiac, probably because of its rather, uh, unusual shape, but he preferred to rely more on the snouts and feet of hippos to waylay young ladies at his own table.

Aphrodisiac powers have been ascribed to seafood since the dawn of recorded time. According to Brillat-Savarin, Saladin, the Sultan of Egypt who fought Richard the Lion-Hearted to a standstill in the Third Crusade, amused himself when he wasn't tearing up Jerusalem by experimenting with the diet of a couple of dervishes, Islamic monks well known for their abstinence. After feeding them only meat for a period he sent two of his most attractive concubines to visit them. They returned complaining that the holy men had only wanted to while away the afternoon playing Canasta or some such. For the next week or so the sultan fed the dervishes fish three times a day and then ordered his team of women back in for a second series of plays. "This time," Brillat-Savarin recalled (although he wasn't there, of course), "the two happy cenobites succumbed most marvelously."

Now, not everyone has seen fish rather than meat or fowl as a venereal energizer. On the contrary, Saint Thomas Aquinas explained in his *Summa Theologica* that "the Church forbade those who fast to partake of those foods which both afford most pleasure to the palate, and beside are a very great incentive to lust. Such are the flesh of animals that take their rest on the earth, and those that breathe the air, and its products, such as milk from those that walk the earth, and eggs from birds. For, since such animals are more like man in body, they afford greater pleasures as food, and greater nourishment to the human body . . . which . . . becomes a great incentive to lust." Hence the large sale of fish on Fridays throughout Christendom for millennia.

Fruits of all kinds have been described as aphrodisiacs from time to time. In his *Merchant's Tale* Chaucer related how young Lady May, bored with the seldom attentions of her aged and infirm hubby Lord January, hiked out into the orchard to harvest a few pears. A young man was lurking up in the tree and, after she sated her desire for fruit, they concluded a satisfactory dalliance among the branches.

Set with a task similar to mine, Madame du Barry supposedly ordered a meal for Louis XV composed of sweetbreads laced with truffles, venison, pheasant cooked in white wine, capon in Sherry, and various vegetables seasoned with herbs and spices. It is not recorded what happened after dinner, but Brillat-Savarin wrote in *The Physiology of Taste* that truffles "make women more tender and men more apt to love." Perhaps that explains their price.

After consulting many sources I compiled a partial list of "aphrodisiacs" identified through the ages. I emphasize that it's only partial. Still, it's enough to frighten even the most hot-blooded away from the grocery store:

Alligator (tail only), anise, apricots, asparagus, avocados, bamboo shoots (have you ever wondered why there are so many Chinese?), beans, beef (raw), beets (white), birds'-nest soup (see bamboo shoots above), brandy, cabbage, cardamom, carrots, cheese (mainly Parmesan, those wily Italians), chocolate, chutney, cinnamon, clams, cloves, coriander, cocks' combs (no pun intended), crabs (ditto), cubeb pepper, dandelions, dates, ducks' feet, eels, eggs (raw), fennel, fish (most kinds), fowl (skin, wings, and gizzards only), frogs, garlic (I tell you, those Italians are *everywhere*), gelatin, ginger, ginseng root, hearts of palm, honey, jasmine, kidneys, leeks (OK, how come there are so few Welsh then?), limpets, liver, lotus seeds, lobsters, mangoes, mushrooms (especially morels), mutton (but not in my house), nutmeg, olives, onions, oysters (raw), parsley, parsnips, peas, peppermint, peppers, pigs' feet (would I lie to you?), pigs' skins, pimientos, pistachios, radishes, saffron, sharks' fins, shrimp, snake meat, thyme, tomatoes (once called love apples), turtles, truffles, vanilla, veal (shank only), and water chestnuts.

I mean, how can you lose?

Gaily humming a few bars from Cole Porter, I set out to plan the menu. The asparagus would be preceded by a tomato bisque and followed by oysters on the half shell. For the entrée we would devour large portions of osso buco, the braised veal shanks said to have inspired the rulers of Milan to fantastic feats of progeneration. The salad would be chilled slices of cooked fennel and hearts of palm (a double threat). Chocolate mousse topped with whipped cream laced with vanilla would constitute dessert.

For insurance I chilled two bottles of more than adequate Champagne and stacked a couple of hours' worth of Old Blue Eyes on the stereo. (You'd be amazed to know how difficult it is to find a blindfolded violinist on short notice.)

Clad smartly in white ducks, ascot, and the gold-threaded *hapi* coat my brother brought home from Japan after the Korean War, I escorted my prey to the table with visions from *Tom Jones* dancing in my overheated imagination.

"How do you feel, my little cabbage?" I inquired after serving the first two courses and bringing on the third.

"Fine," she replied, delicately applying a napkin to her lips. "By the way, I don't think I've ever seen cubeb pepper on raw oysters before."

The osso buco came and went without comment, although she was a little puzzled by the combination of licorice-flavored fennel and hearts of palm. "Be adventurous," I cried, refilling her wineglass for the third time. "Shut up and eat!"

Following dessert, I whisked her to a couch by the fire, quickly cleared the dishes from the table, and set about brewing a pot of jasmine tea, mindful of the medieval admonition that coffee is "the black enemy of sleep and copulation."

As we stared into the flames she said, "You know, after all that food my clothes feel a little tight. I think I'll go slip into something more comfortable."

"Of course you will," I leered. The hapless wench was completely in my power.

When she returned a few minutes later and found me snoring on the divan, she kissed me gently on my graying forehead, turned off the lights, and tiptoed off to read herself to sleep. She has lived with me long enough to know that overeating acts upon me as a soporific.

After that I took all the books back to the library and went to see a friend of mine, an eminent pharmacologist noted for his work on food and wine.

"Tell me," I implored, "are there really any surefire aphrodisiacs?"

"Yes," he said. "A dry martini and a thousand-dollar bill."

So, as you can see, there's no reason to try to find any hidden meaning in any of these recipes. You can prepare them all with a clear conscience.

# Love Among the Pots and Pans

## MENU

*Shrimp in Cucumber Nests*
*with Dill Dressing*
*Tournedos à la Saint-Valentin*
*Potatoes Dauphine*
*Pineapple in Kirsch Custard*

It's our custom on the Feast of Saint Valentine to blow the budget on an outrageously extravagant and delicious dinner for two. Since it's one of the few holidays Congress hasn't jiggered into a three-day weekend, it often falls during the week. This necessitates a little planning. Neither of us wants to spend a long time in the kitchen at the end of a busy day, and yet we don't want to sacrifice decadence in the interests of simplicity. To satisfy these requirements we try to orchestrate a menu that combines dishes we can prepare ahead with those that require only last-minute attention.

One of the nice things about cooking just for two is that it's possible to splurge every now and then without taking out a second mortgage. While it's true that the price of the cut of beef called for in this main course is more in line with those quoted on the London Gold Exchange than in supermarket ads, two tiny fillets cut from the small end of the loin (tournedos) cost less than, say, tournedos for a family of eight. The same can be said of the tiny shrimp in the first course. Judging from the rates we've seen in the fish markets in recent years, they must be practicing some form of birth control. This recipe for two, however, requires only a minute amount.

In keeping with the theme of this meal, we like to open a half bottle of very dry Champagne with the first course and accompany the tournedos with a nicely aged Pinot Noir.

## Shrimp in Cucumber Nests with Dill Dressing

*1 large cucumber*
*8 cherry tomatoes*
*½ bunch watercress*
*2 ounces cooked and peeled tiny shrimp*

**DRESSING**
*1 egg*
*1 tablespoon fresh lemon juice*
*3 tablespoons olive oil*
*Salt and pepper*
*½ teaspoon dried dill weed*

Peel and seed the cucumber and cut crosswise into 3 sections of equal length. Cut into julienne strips. Place in ice water for several hours to crisp.

Drop tomatoes into rapidly boiling water, remove immediately, refresh in cold water. Peel and cut in half.

Whisk together the egg and lemon juice and then add olive oil, beating until the mixture is as thick as heavy cream. Add salt and pepper to taste and the dried dill.

When ready to serve, make a bed of watercress on each salad plate. Arrange the julienned cucumber in a nest shape on the watercress. Mound the shrimp on top and surround with halved cherry tomatoes. Dress shrimp with some of the dill dressing. Refrigerate any extra dressing to use on a tossed green salad.

## Tournedos à la Saint-Valentin

**FONDUE GARNISH**
*1 tablespoon butter*
*1 tomato, peeled, seeded and diced*
*Pinch salt*
*Pinch superfine sugar*
*2 cooked artichoke bottoms*
*Chicken broth (see p. 220)*

**TOURNEDOS**
*2 fillet steaks, 1–1½ inches thick*
*1 tablespoon butter*
*2 teaspoons oil*
*Salt and pepper*
*¼ cup beef broth (see p. 218)*
*2 tablespoons Madeira*

To make tomato fondue, heat the butter in a small pan. Add the tomato, salt, and sugar and cook just until the tomato is "melting" but has not become a purée. Remove pan from heat.

Warm artichoke bottoms in chicken broth while you cook the steaks.

Dry the steaks with a paper towel. Heat the butter and oil in a small skillet. When the butter begins to foam, add the steaks and sauté them for 3 to 4 minutes on each side. Remove from heat and season quickly with salt and pepper. Keep warm while you make the sauce.

To make the sauce, pour off the fat from skillet and add the beef broth. Boil rapidly, scraping up the browned bits from the bottom of the pan. Add the Madeira and continue boiling until the sauce is thick. Spoon the sauce onto a warm plate. Place the steaks on the sauce and on each steak place an artichoke bottom filled with warm tomato fondue.

## *Potatoes Dauphine*

We like to make and freeze these airy potato puffs ahead of time and reheat them in the oven just before serving. They add style and dash to any menu and yet are quite simple to prepare. Since you may want to make them ahead and freeze them for future evenings or use them for party menus, we are giving you a recipe that serves 6.

| | |
|---|---|
| *1 medium potato, peeled* | *Pinch salt* |
| *1 egg yolk* | *½ cup water* |
| *1 tablespoon butter* | *½ cup flour* |
| *½ teaspoon salt* | *2 large eggs* |
| *3 tablespoons butter* | |

Quarter the potato and place in a saucepan with water to cover. Bring to a boil and cook over medium heat until tender. Drain. Add the egg yolk, 1 tablespoon butter, and salt to the potato and whip until fluffy.

Place the 3 tablespoons butter and pinch of salt in a small saucepan. Add the water and bring to a boil. As soon as the butter has melted, remove the pan from the heat and beat in the flour all at once until smoothly blended. Return the pan to the heat and beat the mixture for one or two minutes or until it leaves the sides of the pan and forms a mass. Remove from heat and beat in the eggs, one at a time, until the dough is well blended and smooth. Combine the *pâte à chou* (egg and flour mixture) with the potato and beat well.

*Heat oil for deep frying to 375 degrees F.* Drop the mixture by teaspoonfuls and cook until puffed and golden brown. Drain briefly on paper towels and serve at once or freeze on a flat tray until firm and then pack in plastic bags. To serve later, *preheat oven to 400 degrees F.* and warm potato puffs 10–15 minutes.

# Pineapple in Kirsch Custard

⅔ cup milk  
3 tablespoons sugar  
2 egg yolks  
1 tablespoon kirsch  

½ teaspoon vanilla  
¼ cup heavy cream, whipped  
½ small fresh pineapple  
Fresh mint leaves (optional)  

Heat the milk in a heavy saucepan until tiny bubbles form on the rim. Add the sugar and stir until dissolved. Whisk the egg yolks and pour the hot milk over them in a slow steady stream, whisking constantly. Return the mixture to the pan and continue whisking over low heat for several minutes until it is quite thick. Remove from the heat and pour the custard into a bowl. Stir in the kirsch and vanilla. Chill. Fold in the whipped cream.

Cut the pineapple out of the shell and core it. Cut the fruit into ½-inch cubes. Cut the shell in half lengthwise (you'll have two quarters of a whole pineapple shell). Arrange the cubed pineapple on the shells and spoon the kirsch custard over them. Garnish with mint leaves if available. Chill until ready to serve.

# PLAN OF ATTACK

**up to one month before**  
1. Make and freeze Potatoes Dauphine.  
**morning before**  
1. Make dessert and put in refrigerator to chill.    2. Cut cucumber into julienne strips, put in ice water, and refrigerate.

## Cook Number One

**ahead of time**  
Prepare artichoke bottoms.  
**30 minutes before**  
1. Make tomato fondue for tournedos.    2. Chill champagne and open red wine.  
**15 minutes before**  
1. Sauté steaks.    2. Warm artichoke bottoms in chicken broth.    3. Make sauce and assemble and serve tournedos.

## Cook Number Two

**30 minutes before**  
1. Peel and cut tomatoes.    2. Make salad dressing.  
**15 minutes before**  
Put frozen Potatoes Dauphine in to reheat.  
**just before**  
Assemble and serve Shrimp in Cucumber Nests.

# *When in Doubt, Punt*

## MENU

---

*Shrimp Pâté*
*Boned Breast of Chicken with Green Peppercorn Sauce*
*Pommes Duchesse*
*Sesame-Spinach Salad*
*Strawberry Cassis Parfait*

---

It's happened to everybody at least once. One or the other of you gets to work in the morning, cheerful and confident that you have the day's events under control. Then you flip the page on the calendar and curse silently as you discover that it's his or her birthday. Or any other day that you have solemnly promised will be etched forever in your memory. (All this evokes a recurring nightmare— the time when, at the end of a rough day, you had just gone to bed and turned off the light and then heard in the darkness from the other pillow words that made your skin crawl: "Happy anniversary, dear.")

Anyway, back to the problem at hand. Cool and graceful under pressure, you fight back the urge to fall down and beat your fists against the floor and, with the desperate guile of a trapped animal, begin plotting your way out of the dilemma. All you have to do is find a present on your lunch hour—which means you don't get lunch—and then come up with an exquisite menu that can be accomplished single-handedly in whatever time is left between an emergency trip to the market on the way home and the dinner hour. This, of course, assumes that in a moment of rashness you instituted the same rule that governs birthday celebrations at our house. That is, no one cooks on his or her natal day. Neither of us can remember who came up with that rule. We both deny it.

One obvious solution is suprêmes, boned chicken breasts that can be sautéed in six to eight minutes. Surrounded by a ring of *pommes duchesse,* they can be masked with a delicate green peppercorn sauce. If you work fast, the whole meal can be prepared in less than an hour, while your partner smiles knowingly over the rim of the glass of Champagne you poured from the chilled bottle you snatched from the cold box at the liquor store. With this entrée, we probably would pour a rich, buttery California Chardonnay, or a great white Burgundy.

The first course can be served on the coffee table in front of the fire, while the honoree admires the slightly too expensive gift you bought. This also keeps him or her out of the kitchen, which enhances your ability to conceal the fact you came home in total disarray.

The lavish spinach salad following the entrée and an opulent strawberry parfait will leave the impression that you planned this dinner for weeks.

# Shrimp Pâté

2 tablespoons sweet butter
¼ pound cooked baby shrimp
1 small clove garlic, minced
4 teaspoons heavy cream

1 teaspoon dry Sherry
¼ teaspoon dried dill weed
Salt and pepper
Dried dill for garnish

Place butter, shrimp, garlic, cream, and Sherry in the container of a blender or food processor. Whirl until smooth. Stir in dill and season to taste with salt and pepper. Spoon into a small ramekin and garnish with an additional sprinkle of dill. This delicate pâté is sumptuous served on crackers or on crisp cucumber slices.

# Boned Breast of Chicken

3 tablespoons clarified sweet butter
  (see p. 225)

1 boned chicken breast, split (or 1 whole
  boned breast apiece, depending on your
  appetites)

To sauté the chicken breasts, use a heavy-bottomed skillet or *sauteuse*. Melt the butter in the pan and sauté the breasts over moderate heat until golden brown, turning once. (High heat would toughen the meat and make it dry.) Remove the breasts to a heated platter and keep warm while you prepare the sauce.

**GREEN PEPPERCORN SAUCE**

2 tablespoons minced onion
¼ cup dry white wine
1 teaspoon whole green peppercorns,
  rinsed and drained
1 teaspoon green peppercorns, rinsed,
  drained, and crushed

½ cup heavy cream
1 teaspoon fresh tarragon leaves or ¼
  teaspoon dried tarragon
Salt and white pepper

Add the onions to the pan in which the chicken breasts were cooked and sauté gently in the remaining butter until limp. Add the white wine and boil to deglaze the pan. Continue boiling gently until reduced by half. Whisk in the whole and mashed peppercorns, cream, and tarragon and continue to reduce the sauce until it has a syrupy cinsistency. Season to taste with salt and white pepper. Spoon the sauce over the cooked chicken breasts.

## Pommes Duchesse

1 large baking potato
Salted water for cooking
1 egg yolk
1 tablespoon butter

1 tablespoon heavy cream
Salt and white pepper
Parmesan cheese
Paprika

Peel the potato and cut it into small chunks for quick cooking. Boil in salted water until tender. Drain and dry the potato by shaking the pieces in the pan over the heat. Put the potato through a ricer or food mill, or beat until smooth. Beat in the egg yolk, butter, and cream. Season to taste with salt and pepper.

Either spoon the potatoes in rings on ovenproof plates or, preferably, scoop into a pastry bag fitted with a fancy large tip and squeeze out decorative borders on heatproof plates. This much can be done ahead of time.

Just before serving, lightly dust the pommes duchesse with Parmesan cheese and paprika and slip the plates under a preheated broiler until tipped with light golden brown.

## Sesame-Spinach Salad

1 tablespoon sesame seeds
3 tablespoons olive oil
1 tablespoon fresh lemon juice
1 teaspoon soy sauce
Dash of Tabasco sauce

Salt and freshly ground pepper
4 water chestnuts, sliced (optional)
2 large mushrooms, thinly sliced
½ pound fresh spinach, washed, stemmed,
    and drained

Toast sesame seeds quickly in a small saucepan or skillet over medium heat, shaking the pan constantly to prevent scorching. Cool. In a small bowl whisk together the olive oil, lemon juice, soy sauce, and Tabasco, and season to taste with salt and pepper. Stir in the water chestnuts and mushrooms. Cover and refrigerate until ready to use.

At serving time, tear spinach into pieces and put into a salad bowl. Add the sesame seeds and dressing and toss well.

## Strawberry Cassis Parfait

1 package frozen unsweetened raspberries
1 tablespoon sugar
2 tablespoons Crème de Cassis
1 cup fresh strawberries, washed, hulled
    and sliced

1 pint vanilla ice cream, slightly softened
2 perfect whole strawberries

Combine the raspberries, sugar, and Crème de Cassis in a blender or food processor and purée until smooth. Transfer to a bowl and gently stir in sliced strawberries. Layer the mixture with ice cream in two parfait or large wine glasses. Place in freezer until ready to serve, each topped with one perfect strawberry.

# PLAN OF ATTACK

*1 hour before*
1. Quickly prepare the Shrimp Pâté.  2. Open cold Champagne and put bottle in ice bucket.  3. Serve pâté and Champagne in living room.  4 Present gift.  5. Excuse yourself and return to kitchen.  6. Pray.

*45 minutes before*
1. Peel, cut up, and start boiling potato.  2. Clean spinach.  3. Toast sesame seeds.  4. Make salad dressing.  5. Return to living room for gulp of Champagne and exactly 1.6 minutes of small talk, including casual request, "Darling, would you mind setting the table? I'm a little tied up right now."

*30 minutes before*
1. Make dessert and put in freezer.  2. Chill dinner wine.

*25 minutes before*
1. Drain potato and prepare Pommes Duchesse.  2. Pipe potato mixture from pastry bag onto ovenproof plates, set aside.  3. Stagger back to living room and, smiling self-assuredly, refill glasses.

*15 minutes before*
1. Start sautéing chicken breasts (you did remember to buy them boned, didn't you. If you didn't, tell your partner you're going out for a pack of cigarettes and catch the first boat for Algiers).  2. Warm a plate to put the chicken on when it's cooked.

*7 minutes before*
1. Set chicken breasts aside on warm plate.  2. Turn up broiler.  3. Make sauce for chicken breasts.

*zero hour*
1. Quickly run Pommes Duchesse under broiler, place chicken breasts on the same plates, and mask with sauce.  2. Open dinner wine.  3. Announce dinner, taking care not to let your voice crack.

*after main course*
1. Dress and serve salad.  2. Clear table and serve dessert.  3. Finish any Champagne or white wine left over—you earned it.

# *The Best-Laid Plans . . .*

## MENU

*Glazed Rock Cornish Game Hens*
*Fettuccine Salad*
*Zucchini in Watercress Dressing*
*Olive-Stuffed Croustade*
*Raspberry Summer Pudding*

A picnic, loosely defined, is any meal eaten out of doors. That covers a lot of territory, and makes about as much sense as saying a great Renaissance painter was any guy who had a charge account at a paint store between the fourteenth and sixteenth centuries. Picnics can be romantic, relaxing, renewing interludes—or they can be frustrating, exasperating and, quite literally, a pain.

We don't want to labor the same cliché throughout this book, but in marriage or nearly any other relationship you can name, opposites seem to attract. Night people end up with partners who believe the day is half shot if they don't rise before dawn, philosophers are fascinated by football fans, ascetics marry sybarites, and dreamers gravitate toward pragmatists. We're no different. One of us (she) is a picnic freak who, from the time the temperature exceeds freezing in the spring until the end of Indian summer, will use any excuse to fill up a hamper, don a white organdy creation, and flutter into the countryside. The other (he) is more cautious, practical to a fault, and hates crowds, traffic jams, and any nasty little surprises such as ants, irate farmers, curious livestock, and summer showers.

How, you wonder, have we managed to avoid the courts of equity all these years? The answer is that the fortuitous research we've done on this subject has led us to evolve a number of rules that satisfy the idiosyncrasies of both of us. They also help assure successful and elegant picnics.

The most important consideration is what folks in the real estate business call site selection. There are 10.66 acres of land for every man, woman, and child in the United States, but most of it is either in private hands or beyond the limits of a day trip. We shudder to recall the time we were traveling separately and were to meet in a large city. One of us (guess who) got there first, went directly to the nearest delicatessen, and bought a basketful of goodies. After meeting at the airport we drove around for hours, unable to find even a vacant park bench, until our stomachs were growling. We returned to our hotel room and consumed the picnic on the floor.

This led us to *Rule No. 1:* DON'T EVER SET OFF FOR A PICNIC UNLESS YOU KNOW WHERE YOU'RE GOING. It's not as limiting as it sounds. The nation not only abounds with urban, suburban, and exurban parks, but owners of rural property are often more hospitable than you would imagine. More than once we've spotted an inviting, tree-shaded glade while driving in the country and managed to get permission at the farmhouse to return for a picnic in the future.

*Rule No. 2:* KNOW WHAT TO EXPECT WHEN YOU GET THERE. Among other things, that means reading the whole weather report, not just the part about whether it's going to rain or not. Once we packed up a luxurious repast and drove many miles to a secluded beach we had visited before. It was clear all right, mainly because the wind was approaching hurricane force, and after blowing sand had infiltrated our pâté, cold artichokes, and wine bottle, we retreated from the coast and glumly ate our gritty lunch in the car at a shopping center parking lot.

*Rule No. 3:* DON'T EVER GO ON A PICNIC ON A LEGAL HOLIDAY UNLESS YOU ARE FORCED TO DO SO AT GUNPOINT. There was the time we planned a big Fourth of July outing with several other couples. Convinced that we could beat the system, we selected a picnic area and volunteered to get there ahead of time to secure the best spot. Augmenting our hamper with a vacuum bottle of coffee and some croissants for breakfast, we arrived before dawn and managed to find the last unoccupied plot, a place about the size of a postage stamp hard by the railroad tracks. Our friends seem able to laugh about it now, though it was touch and go for a while with the ones who had to park three miles away and shlep their ice chests over rough terrain while dodging Frisbees and firecrackers.

*Rule No. 4:* SELECT DISHES THAT CAN BE PREPARED IN ADVANCE, AND SERVE THEM AS GRACEFULLY AS YOU WOULD AT A DINNER PARTY. We believe that frantic, last-minute preparations in the field detract from the leisurely purpose of a picnic. Also, you probably have figured out by now that our favorite picnics are those we share alone in gentle surroundings removed from civilization, but this doesn't mean they have to be exercises in rusticity. Somehow, a fine white Burgundy or California Chardonnay (either would be perfect with this menu) tastes better chilled in an ice bucket and served in crystal than it does poured into a plastic glass. The meal below will be more appealing served on china flanked by silverware than on paper plates with plastic forks and spoons. A painter's drop sheet—a cheap purchase from a hardware store—will protect even the most expensive and delicate tablecloth from moisture or grass stains.

Since strategy is the key to success for all *al fresco* endeavors, we offer here instead of the usual timetable for preparation (all of which can be done a day or two in advance), a checklist of those things each of us considers essential for memorable *déjeuner sur l'herbe.*

# PICNIC PROVISIONS

**For Romantics**
Book of poetry
Scented candles
Linen tablecloth
Damask napkins
Flute (a harp is better, but there is the problem of transportation)
Silver ice bucket
English wicker hamper
Watercolors and easel

**For Realists**
Map
Insect repellent
Plastic drop cloth
Moistened throwaway towelettes
Portable radio
Corkscrew
Garbage bag
Knife and cutting board

## Glazed Rock Cornish Game Hens

One bird apiece is fine for some couples, while others can split one and be perfectly satisfied. Only you can judge the appetites involved. If you choose to divide one hen, it can be accomplished easily with a sturdy pair of poultry shears. When you know you have a busy week coming up it's not a bad idea to roast an extra bird or two to tuck in the refrigerator for a future cold supper. A Rock Cornish game hen weighs about 1 pound.

**FOR EACH BIRD**
*1 clove garlic, pressed*
*1 teaspoon thyme*
*¼ teaspoon salt*
*¼ teaspoon pepper*

**FOR FROM 1 TO 4 BIRDS**
*½ cup butter*
*2 tablespoons lemon juice*
*¼ teaspoon paprika*
*Pinch of thyme*

*Preheat the oven to 450 degrees F.* Rinse the birds and dry the outsides and cavities with paper towels. Season interiors with garlic, thyme, salt, and pepper. Tie the legs together, bend the wings back, and truss the birds with twine. Melt ¼ cup of the butter in a skillet and brown the hens. Place on the bottom of a shallow baking pan. Melt the remaining butter and add the lemon juice, paprika, and thyme. Brush the birds with the mixture and roast for about 40 minutes, brushing often with the butter-lemon mixture. When crisp and brown, remove from the oven. Cool and refrigerate. Wrap in foil for traveling.

# Fettuccine Salad

¼ pound flat egg noodles
1 tablespoon olive oil
4 large raw mushrooms, thinly sliced
1 green onion, thinly sliced
¼ cup minced parsley

¼ cup heavy cream
¼ cup freshly grated Parmesan cheese
1 tablespoon white wine vinegar
Salt and white pepper to taste

Cook the noodles in rapidly boiling salted water until just done. Drain very well in a colander and then on paper towels to remove as much water as possible. Place the noodles in a bowl and toss with the olive oil. Add the remaining ingredients and mix well, tossing gently with two spoons. Refrigerate. Serve at room (or meadow) temperature.

# Zucchini in Watercress Dressing

2 raw zucchini
¼ cup watercress leaves
3 tablespoons olive oil
1¹/₂ teaspoons fresh lemon juice

1 teaspoon white wine vinegar
Pinch tarragon
½ teaspoon Dijon mustard
Salt and pepper

Wash and trim the zucchini. Cut in half lengthwise and then cut across in thin slices. Chop the watercress very fine with a knife or in a food processor. Whisk together the oil, lemon juice, vinegar, tarragon, and mustard in a small bowl. Season to taste with salt and pepper. Stir in the watercress and add the zucchini. Place in a covered bowl and chill until the time comes to pack it in your basket.

# Olive-Stuffed Croustade

1 small French roll, about 3 by 6 inches
¼ cup pitted black olives
1 small clove of garlic, crushed
½ teaspoon lemon juice

Dash Tabasco sauce
½ cup butter, softened
Salt and pepper

Slice the end off the French roll and use your fingers and a long slender knife to remove the core of soft bread from the center without breaking through the crust.

Mince the olives, add the garlic, lemon juice, and Tabasco. Whip the butter until creamy and gradually add the olive mixture, beating well until blended, and season to taste with salt and pepper.

Stand the hollowed roll on end on a piece of waxed paper. Fill with the olive-butter mixture, packing it down as you go. If your hollow and the amount of filling don't quite coincide, cut off any extra roll left at the end. Wrap in foil and refrigerate overnight.

Arm yourself with a serrated knife and a cutting board when you depart for your sylvan retreat and, when you're ready to eat, cut the croustade into ¼-inch slices and serve.

## Raspberry Summer Pudding

This simple but delicious traditional English pudding must be made the night before the excursion. Take it along to the picnic in its own bowl and unmold it onto a plate just before serving.

*2 cups fresh raspberries*
*¼ cup sugar, or more to taste*

*6 slices day-old firm-textured white bread*
*Crème Fraîche (see p. 226) or sour cream*

Place the raspberries and sugar in a skillet, cover, and put over very low heat, shaking the pan occasionally. After 10 to 15 minutes the fruit should be tender and juicy. Cool and taste to see if it needs additional sugar. After correcting the sweetness, strain the fruit, pushing all the pulp through a strainer, to remove the seeds.

For this pudding, fresh bread is too doughy. If yours isn't dry enough, place it in a very slow oven for about 5 minutes. Cut the crusts from the bread and trim a slice to fit the bottom of a 3-cup bowl or dish. Pour a little fruit purée into the bottom of the bowl and place the slice of bread on top. Add more purée and continue layering the fruit and bread until both are used up, making sure each layer is well soaked with purée. Place a small plate with a 1½- to 2-pound weight on it on top of the pudding. Place the bowl on a larger plate to catch any over-flowing juice and refrigerate overnight. Cover tightly with foil before transporting the pudding to the picnic site. Serve it topped with *Crème Fraîche* or sour cream.

# Be Thankful—For Each Other

## MENU

*Pumpkin Soup*
*Roast Cranberry Duck*
*Stuffing Balls*
*Butter-Steamed Green Beans*
*Green Salad*
*Apple-Mince Pie*

Thanksgiving is the first stop on winter's holiday express, and for those who live far from family and Mother's mince pie, the prospect can be melancholy. Memories of past Thanksgivings *en famille* mellow with time, often giving rise to bouts of sugary nostalgia.

Before the blues set in at the idea of celebrating alone together, take stock of the good things about it. Run through a list of what you *won't* have to put up with at an intimate Thanksgiving for two:

Your brother-in-law, Harlow, won't tell you about the killing he just made on the stock you dumped at a loss two months ago.

You won't have to listen to the details of your godmother's latest surgical adventure.

Your old next-door neighbor, the one who still hasn't returned the hedge clippers he borrowed from your father fifteen years ago, won't be around to be persuaded he should run home for his slides of Disney World.

You won't have to applaud your eight-year-old nephew's virtuoso performance of "Lady of Spain" on the accordion.

You won't have to take gum out of any child's hair.

You won't have to nod sympathetically when Aunt Agatha reveals breathlessly that your cousin Mona, the one with the smoldering eyes who went to Paris to study Post-Impressionism, wound up instead running off with an Algerian *garagiste* on the back of a Vespa.

And, although it may sound like heresy, you won't have to eat turkey.

For all of these things, you both can be truly thankful.

Here, instead, is a sumptuous banquet for two built around a glistening roast duck in cranberry glaze, surrounded by many of the traditional dishes of the season set forth in slightly new ways.

In the event you've ever been intimidated by the old white-wine-with-fowl rule (which never was a rule, by the way), throw it away in the case of duck, one of the richest of poultries and best accompanied by a red wine. This is supposed to be something of an occasion, after all, so we suggest a mature red Bordeaux or a California Cabernet Sauvignon at least five years old. With the soup, a *copita* of chilled, light *fino* Sherry will do wonders for the appetite.

## Pumpkin Soup

If you can find a well-formed but slightly undernourished small pumpkin, scoop it out and use it as a tureen for two. Pumpkin soup is excellent served either hot or cold, so suit its temperature to your climate. We like to throw convention a curve by beginning our Thanksgiving dinner with pumpkin instead of putting it in a pie at the end.

*1 tablespoon butter*
*2 tablespoons finely chopped onion*
*1 tablespoon flour*
*1 cup chicken broth (see p. 220)*
*1 cup solid-pack canned pumpkin*
*½ teaspoon brown sugar*

*Pinch of mace*
*Salt and white pepper to taste*
*½ cup half-and-half or light cream*
*2 tablespoons Sherry*
*Minced parsley for garnish*

Place the butter in a saucepan and melt over medium heat. Add the onion and sauté until limp but not brown. Stir in the flour and cook until bubbly. Remove the pan from the heat and whisk in the chicken broth. Add the pumpkin, brown sugar, mace, salt, and white pepper to taste. Cook, stirring, until the mixture simmers. Add the half-and-half or light cream and continue heating, stirring, without letting the soup come to a boil. Cool and chill at this point if the soup is to be served cold. To serve hot, refrigerate the soup now and reheat later. Just before serving, hot or cold, stir in the Sherry and garnish with minced parsley.

## Roast Cranberry Duck

*1 duck (4 to 5 pounds)*
*1 lemon, cut in half*
**GLAZE**
*1 can whole cranberry sauce (8 ounces)*

*2 tablespoons honey*
*¼ cup Port*
*1 teaspoon lemon juice*

*Preheat oven to 350 degrees F.* Remove the giblets and neck. Rinse and dry the duck with paper towels and sprinkle the cavity with salt. Fasten the neck skin to the back with a skewer and tie the ends of the legs together with twine.

Place the duck on a rack in a roasting pan and scratch the skin all over with the tines of a fork to allow the fat to drain during roasting. Rub the outside of the duck with the cut lemon. Roast in the oven for about 2½ to 3 hours or until the skin is crisp and browned and the thigh of the bird is tender when pricked with a fork. After 1½ hours, pour the fat off and add 1 pint of water to the bottom of the pan. The duck should be turned from one side to the other and then onto its back during roasting to assure even crisping of the skin.

Mix together the cranberry sauce, honey, Port, and lemon juice and coat the duck with the glaze using a pastry brush. Increase the oven temperature to 425 degrees F. and continue cooking for another 10 to 15 minutes. Allow the duck to rest 10 minutes before carving. Serve the remaining glaze on the side as a sauce.

## Stuffing Balls

Domestic ducks lead such a soft life that they tend to be plump and placid little creatures. As a result, any stuffing put into them soaks up an enormous quantity of rendered fat and becomes, well, to put it bluntly, greasy. But what's Thanksgiving without dressing? These stuffing balls neatly solve the problem and make a nice garnish for the duck platter to boot.

*1 cup fresh bread crumbs (whole-wheat bread makes a nice change and gives a good strong flavor to complement the duck)*
*4 tablespoons melted butter*
*2 tablespoons chopped pistachios* or *walnuts*

*1 teaspoon poultry seasoning*
*1 tablespoon minced parsley*
*1 small egg, beaten*
*Salt and pepper*

Mix together the bread crumbs, 2 tablespoons of the melted butter, nuts, poultry seasoning, parsley, and beaten egg. Season to taste with salt and pepper. Roll the mixture into balls about the size of walnuts. Put the remaining butter in a skillet and sauté the balls over medium heat until browned (they may also be drizzled with the melted butter and baked in a baking dish at 350 degrees F. for about 20 minutes or until browned).

# Butter-Steamed Green Beans

½ pound green beans
2 tablespoons butter
3 tablespoons water
½ teaspoon dill
Salt and pepper

**GARNISH**
2 strips orange peel

Remove the strings and stem ends from the beans and break the beans in half. Melt the butter in a skillet over high heat. Add the beans and water. Cover and cook, shaking the pan occasionally, for seven minutes. Remove from heat and toss the beans with the dill and salt and pepper to taste.

To arrange the platter, place the duck in the center with the stuffing balls at either end, tucking parsley or watercress between the balls. Divide the beans into two bundles and place them on either side of the duck. Put a strip of orange peel across each stack of beans.

To contrast with the richness of the duck, serve a crisp green salad with a simple oil-and-vinegar dressing after the main course and before dessert.

# Apple-Mince Pie

Those who cook for two know that the urge to make a pie or quiche often results in half of it languishing in the refrigerator until the time comes to make that awful decision and give the remains a decent burial. We bless the day we bought a seven-inch tart pan which gives us enough dessert for one dinner with just a bit left over for a midnight snack or lunch the next day.

7-inch tart pan lined with unbaked pastry
1 cup prepared mincemeat
1 tart apple, sliced
2 tablespoons sugar

1 teaspoon lemon juice
¼ cup sugar
¼ cup flour
2 tablespoons butter

*Preheat oven to 450 degrees F.* Spoon the mincemeat into the pastry shell, spreading it evenly. Mix the apple slices with the 2 tablespoons sugar and the lemon juice and arrange them on top of the mincemeat. Mix together the ¼ cup sugar and the flour and cut in the butter, using a pastry knife, until the mixture is the consistency of coarse meal. Sprinkle the mixture over the apples, covering well. Bake for 10 minutes, then reduce the heat to 325 degrees F. and bake for 40 minutes longer.

# PLAN OF ATTACK

Ordinarily we regard the consumption before 7 P.M. of any meal that passes for dinner as barbaric, but the holidays are different. To begin with, morning newspapers throughout the nation achieve their apogee of pre-Christmas advertising on Thanksgiving Day, and there are five or six pounds of newsprint to wade through over a late and leisurely breakfast. Then, those fascinating televised parades staged by department stores from Toronto to Philadelphia provide the opportunity to sit by the fire and watch thousands of other people freezing to death in the icy rain along streets such as Broadway in New York. Finally there is the unharried preparation of dinner all afternoon in a kitchen redolent of roasting duck. We usually polish off one bottle of Champagne in the process, and are quite ready to eat about 5 P.M.

## Cook Number One

**2 hours before**
1. Wash and truss duck.   2. Put duck in preheated oven.

**1¹/₂ hours before**
1. Clean green beans, set aside.   2. Set table (it's never too early to get it done).

**¹/₂ hour before**
1. Glaze duck.   2. Open red wine and let it breathe.

**15 minutes before**
Remove duck from oven to let juices set.

**just before**
1. Cook green beans.   2. Place duck on serving platter, put in warm oven.

**after soup**
1. Decorate duck platter with stuffing balls and green beans.   2. Take platter to table and carve.

## Cook Number Two

**2 hours before**
Make soup and refrigerate.

**1¹/₂ hours before**
Form stuffing balls, set aside.

**1 hour, 15 minutes before**
Make apple-mince pie and put it in to bake.

**1 hour before**
Assemble salad, refrigerate.

**20 minutes before**
1. Take pie out of oven and put it on a rack.   2. Sauté or bake stuffing balls.

**just before**
Reheat and serve soup.

**after soup**
1. Clear away soup plates.   2. Dress salad, put it on plates and put them in the refrigerator to be served between the entrée and the dessert.

# With Apologies to Clement Clarke Moore

## MENU

Onion Soup with Calvados
Sweetbreads in Toast Cups
French Peas
Endive and Walnut Salad
Christmas Torte

# THE NIGHT BEFORE CHRISTMAS

On the night before Christmas
  at the stove in the manse,
A creature was stirring,
  for the sauce was from France;
A carafe was stashed by the
  chimney with care
With St. Nicholas' ration
  of *vin ordinaire.*
Two cooks were nestled
  quite close to the fire,
While the fragrance of sweetbreads
  kindled desire.
One chef in an apron,
  the other a cap,
Had just settled down
  with some gifts to unwrap,

When out in the pantry
  there rose such a clatter
They sprang to their feet
  to see what was the matter.
Away to the kitchen
  they flew like a flash,
Threw open the oven,
  tripped over the trash.
The moon on a bottle of
  lovely Bordeaux
Gave the luster of midday
  to objects below;
When what to their wondering eyes
  should appear,
But a miniature tray
  and some glasses of cheer,

With a little imbiber, so lively
  and quick,
They knew in a moment it must
  be St. Nick!
More rapid than stir-fry
  he showed them his game,
Unpacked his goodies and
  called them by name:
"Now, truffles! Now, morels! And
  butter that's sweet!
Now, Cognac! Now, garlic! And
  Brie for a treat!"
To the top of the shelf
  at the end of the hall
He put away, put away,
  put away all.
As vegetables within food
  processors fly,
He made it all look
  just as simple as pie.
His eyes, how they twinkled! His
  dimples, how merry!
His cheeks were like apples, his
  nose a raspberry.
His droll little mouth had been
  fashioned from dough

And the beard on his chin
  was quite apropos.
He had a broad face and a little
  round belly
That shook when he laughed
  like a fine calf's-foot jelly.
He was chubby and plump—
  a right jolly old sort—
Who took from his backpack
  a rich chocolate torte.
And laying a finger aside
  of his nose,
He proposed a toast that was
  quite grandiose.
"All year you've been cooking
  with two at the helm,
The problems of which quite
  overwhelm.
But for better or worse,
  you're cooking together—
Try some of this torte,
  it's as light as a feather."
And they heard him exclaim ere he
  drove out of sight,
"Happy Christmas to all...may
  your sauce be just right!"

Something about the holiday season makes people's minds snap. The foregoing is proof of that.

Traffic, crowds, new bicycles that arrive with one screw missing, self-stick ribbon that won't stick, the sure and certain realization that in a couple of months you'll have to *pay* for all this—by the time Christmas Eve arrives, we all long for a moment of peace and quiet. One year we actually pulled it off and had a cozy and relaxed private Christmas Eve party for just the two of us. With this menu, Champagne should be (and was) served throughout.

## *Onion Soup with Calvados*

The familiar French onion soup with its unctuous crown of crouton and cheese is delightful, but we think too substantial to begin this meal. Instead, we like this lighter broth in which you can taste the pure flavor of slowly cooked onions heightened by the addition of a bit of Calvados.

*2 tablespoons butter*
*1 large onion, chopped*
*2 cups chicken broth (see p. 220)*
*¼ teaspoon thyme*

*1 bay leaf*
*Salt and pepper*
*1¹/₂ ounces Calvados (or applejack)*

Heat the butter in a heavy skillet. Add the chopped onion and sauté slowly until it has become a light caramel color, about 7 to 10 minutes. Add the chicken broth, thyme, bay leaf, and salt and pepper to taste. Cover and continue cooking for 20 minutes. Just before serving, stir in the Calvados or applejack.

# Sweetbreads in Toast Cups

Once you've made these glamorous little devils you'll find dozens of uses for them. Fill them with scrambled eggs, use them for vegetables or any creamy entrée. They can hold sauces and dips, and they beautify every plate or platter on which they appear. Tiny ones, made in miniature muffin tins and filled with mushroom duxelles in cream, (p. 133) are great appetizers. We like to make a dozen or so at a crack and freeze them to be reheated for future use.

**TOAST CUPS**
*4 slices firm-textured, homemade-type*
  *bread*
*6 tablespoons butter, melted*

*Preheat oven to 375 degrees F.*
   Trim the crusts from the bread. Using a rolling pin and rolling in both directions, flatten each slice until it is very thin. Dip each slice in the melted butter and fit it into a muffin tin or custard cup. Bake 15–20 minutes, or until golden brown. Place on a plate covered with a paper towel and keep warm. (To reheat from the frozen state, preheat oven to 400 degrees F. and warm them for about 5 minutes.)

**SWEETBREADS**
*½ pound veal sweetbreads*
*Juice of ½ lemon*
*3 tablespoons flour*
*3 tablespoons butter*
*1 tablespoon oil*
*½ cup medium mushrooms, sliced thin*

*½ cup heavy cream*
*½ cup white Port*
*½ cup Madeira*
*Salt and pepper*
*Parsley for garnish*

To prepare the sweetbreads for cooking, place them in a pan with the juice of ½ lemon. Cover with cold water and slowly bring to a boil. Simmer for 5 minutes. Immediately plunge the sweetbreads into a bowl of ice water. Carefully peel away the outside membrane and remove all fat and tubing. Place the sweetbreads between two pieces of waxed paper and then between two plates. Press under a heavy weight (a table leg is just dandy, or several volumes of the Encyclopedia Britannica) for several hours.

When ready to cook, cut the sweetbreads into bite-sized pieces, lightly flour them, and then sauté slowly in the butter and oil for 20 minutes, turning them once after 10 minutes. Remove them from the pan and keep them warm. Raise the temperature under the pan and add the mushrooms, sautéing them until they are slightly browned. Add the cream, white Port, and Madeira to the pan and, stirring, bring to a boil. Reduce the sauce until it is thick and smooth. Remove from the heat, season to taste with salt and pepper, and return the sweetbreads to the pan, stirring them into the sauce.

Spoon the sweetbreads into two toast cups for each serving. Garnish with parsley.

# French Peas

We're both fresh-vegetable addicts, but unfortunately in the matter of peas, the fresh ones we usually find in our market are great hulking marbles that are tough and starchy. As a result we prefer to use the tiny frozen ones (especially in the winter, when the fresh ones generally aren't available in the first place). If, however, you grow your own or have a sensitive greengrocer who deals in infant peas out of season, by all means use them.

| | |
|---|---|
| 1 package frozen small peas (10 ounces) | 1 sprig fresh mint (if available) |
| 2 tablespoons butter | 1 sprig fresh parsley |
| 2 tablespoons boiling water | ¼ teaspoon salt |
| 1 teaspoon sugar | A couple of grinds of fresh black pepper |
| ¼ teaspoon chervil | ⅔ cup shredded lettuce |

Remove the peas from the freezer and allow to thaw for about an hour before cooking time.

Melt the butter in a heavy pan. Add the water, sugar, chervil, mint, parsley, salt, and pepper. Add the peas and toss to combine with seasonings. Gently stir in the lettuce, then cover the pan and cook over medium heat for about 5 minutes or just until the peas are tender. Remove the mint and parsley sprigs before serving.

# Endive and Walnut Salad

Walnut oil, if available, gives a distinctive touch to this salad. If it is not, olive oil is a good alternative.

*2 heads Belgian endive, cleaned and
    quartered lengthwise*
*¼ cup coarsely chopped walnuts*

*2 tablespoons walnut oil or olive oil*
*1 tablespoon fresh lemon juice*
*Salt and pepper*

Divide the endive spears evenly between two salad plates. Sprinkle with walnuts. Whisk together oil and lemon juice. Season with salt and pepper to taste. Drizzle dressing evenly over the two plates.

## Christmas Torte

*3 tablespoons strong coffee*
*2 tablespoons Cognac*
*4 ounces semi-sweet chocolate*
*2 tablespoons superfine sugar*
*¾ cup heavy cream*
*1 tablespoon confectioners' sugar*

*¼ teaspoon vanilla*
*3 pieces of sponge cake, each 5 by 3 ½
    inches and 1 inch thick*
*3 teaspoons Cognac*
*Confectioners' sugar*
*Holly leaves*

Put the coffee and 2 tablespoons Cognac in the top of a double boiler. Add the chocolate and melt, stirring, over gently boiling water. When the mixture is smooth, add the superfine sugar and continue stirring until smooth and glossy. Remove from heat and allow to cool.

Whip the cream until very thick and add the confectioners' sugar and vanilla. Thoroughly fold the chocolate mixture into the whipped cream.

Arrange one piece of sponge cake on a serving plate. Drizzle it with a teaspoon of Cognac. Spread about ¼ of the chocolate cream on top of the cake, and repeat the process to make three layers, ending with chocolate cream on top, and then use the last ¼ of the chocolate cream to ice the sides of the torte.

Refrigerate for 12 to 24 hours. Sprinkle with powdered sugar and decorate with holly leaves before serving in slices.

# PLAN OF ATTACK

It's obvious from the length of time the torte needs to be refrigerated (to allow the flavors of the chocolate and Cognac to marry and permeate the sponge cake) that it must be made in the morning or, if Christmas Eve falls on a workday, the night before.

## Cook Number One

***ahead of time***
1. Make toast cups to reheat when ready to use. 2. Simmer, peel, and press sweetbreads to prepare for final cooking.

***30 minutes before***
1. Begin cooking sweetbreads. 2. Chill champagne.

***10 minutes before***
1. Make sauce for sweetbreads. 2. Reheat toast cups if necessary, put sweetbreads in cups to serve.

## Cook Number Two

***ahead of time***
1. Clean and quarter Belgian endive and refrigerate. 2. Make and refrigerate salad dressing. 3. Make dessert.

***1 hour, 15 minutes before***
Take peas out to thaw.

***1 hour before***
Begin making soup.

***15 minutes before***
1. Cook peas. 2. Stir Calvados into soup and keep warm.

***just before***
1. Dress salad. 2. Serve peas.

---

# *Christmas Morning*

---

*Sherry Eggnog*
*Papaya Crescents or Fresh Pineapple Spears*
*Orange-Nut Waffles with Orange Syrup*
*Homemade Sausage Patties*

---

You've done it. You've baked several kilos of cookies. The tree is trimmed. The presents are wrapped and the cards are in the mail. For weeks you've shopped and cooked, made lists and sped through Christmas preparations with all the skill and stamina of a broken field runner. But now the pandemonium is behind you and it's time to relax with a serene Christmas breakfast for two before the pace of the holiday whirl picks up again.

We suggest starting the day slowly, edging into it with a gentle celebratory drink, something festive and frosty but not overwhelmingly alcoholic. A Sherry eggnog fills the bill perfectly. While sipping this you can prepare the rest of the menu. If papaya is available to you, peel and cut it into crescent-shaped slices for a festive beginning to the day. If not, fresh pineapple spears can stand in.

For this special morning all thoughts of calories must be set aside while you plunge into the main attraction, orange-nut waffles with orange syrup. When it comes to dieting in December, we follow the philosophy of Scarlett O'Hara: we'll think about it tomorrow.

The pistachio-studded sausage is best made a couple of days ahead to give the flavors a chance to snuggle up and get acquainted. Making your own sausage meat is no more difficult than preparing a meat loaf, and the result is infinitely better than the packaged products which often contain bread or cereal extenders. Although this same mixture can be stuffed into sausage casing, we find it easier during busy times merely to form it into patties that can be sautéed quickly.

Use this basic recipe as a starting point for your own seasoning improvisations. Instead of pistachios, you could include chopped roasted chestnuts or truffles. Alter the spices to suit your taste: a pinch of mace hints at the flavor of English "bangers," and red pepper flakes put snap into the mixture. Onion or garlic is never amiss, and chopped spinach, parsley, or sorrel adds both flavor and handsome green flecks.

Be sure the pork mixture has at least 25 percent fat to assure a tender, juicy patty. Wrapping the sausage meat in gossamer-thin white caul fat instantly makes it into *crépinettes,* the succulent little sausage parcels one sees in French *charcuterie* shops.

Altogether, it's not a breakfast for the fainthearted, but then Christmas comes just once a year—thank heavens.

## Sherry Eggnog

*1 egg*
*2 teaspoons sugar*
*1 cup cold rich milk or half-and-half*

*3 tablespoons medium Sherry*
*¼ teaspoon vanilla*
*Nutmeg, grated*

Place egg, sugar, milk, Sherry, and vanilla in a blender and whirl until frothy. Pour into wine glasses and sprinkle with nutmeg.

## Orange-Nut Waffles with Orange Syrup

*2 eggs, separated*
*½ cup milk*
*½ cup fresh orange juice, strained*
*1 tablespoon finely grated orange peel*
*1½ cups cake flour*

*2½ teaspoons baking powder*
*3 tablespoons sugar*
*½ teaspoon salt*
*½ cup walnuts, finely chopped*
*6 tablespoons melted butter*

Beat egg yolks until thick. Beat in milk, orange juice, and grated orange peel. Sift the cake flour, baking powder, sugar, and salt together and gradually stir the dry ingredients into the liquid until thoroughly mixed. Stir in the walnuts and melted butter.

Beat egg whites until stiff but not dry. Fold them into the waffle mixture. Bake the waffles in a preheated waffle iron until steam stops rising from the edges.

### ORANGE SYRUP

*1 cup sugar*
*⅔ cup fresh orange juice*
*Peel of 1 orange, grated coarsely*

*2 tablespoons dark rum*
*1 tablespoon Curaçao*

Combine sugar and orange juice in a saucepan and cook, stirring, over low heat just until the mixture boils. Take the pan off the heat, add the orange rind, rum, and Curaçao and let the syrup steep until cool. Just before serving, strain and reheat the syrup.

## Homemade Sausage Patties

*1 pound fresh pork (at least 25 percent fat, or use additional fat if meat is too lean)*
*1 teaspoon powdered sage*
*Pinch powdered bay leaf*

*Pinch ground allspice*
*Pinch ground red pepper*
*¾ teaspoon salt*
*¾ teaspoon freshly ground pepper*
*1 ounce pistachio nuts, chopped*

Cut the pork into cubes and grind, using the fine disk of a grinder, or chop in a food processor. Add sage, bay leaf, allspice, red pepper, salt, pepper and pistachio nuts and mix thoroughly. Sauté a small portion of the mixture in a skillet and sample to check seasoning; adjust to taste. (If using as a crépinette, wrap in caul membrane.) Refrigerate the sausage overnight or longer to allow flavors to develop.

Form into patties and cook until well browned on the outside and cooked all the way through.

# PLAN OF ATTACK

---

## Cook Number One

*ahead of time*
Make sausage and refrigerate.
*½ hour before*
1. Make and serve Sherry Eggnog.
2. Prepare papaya crescents or pineapple spears.
*just before*
Fry sausage patties.

## Cook Number Two

*ahead of time*
Make syrup.
*½ hour before*
Make waffle batter and bake waffles (it takes about 10 minutes to cook 2 of them).

# *Christmas Dinner*

## MENU

*Chicken and Clam Broth*
*Roast Beef and Yorkshire Pudding for Two*
*Horseradish Cream Sauce*
*Sautéed Broccoli and Tomatoes*
*Chocolate Christmas Pudding*

For years we have shared a Christmas fantasy. It goes something like this.

There's a little hotel we know in London, in Knightsbridge to be precise, convenient to Harrods and a number of other expensive pitfalls. It's one of those places favored by people from the country whose visits to the capital generally coincide with holidays or the necessity of acquiring a tractor or some new brogues. The lounge, which looks more like the living room of an English manor house, is peopled with ruddy men in tweeds and women who still favor flowered hats.

The accents are decidedly British, as is the comfortable oak-paneled dining room. Although we chanced upon this relic of a more gracious time one damp and chilly spring long ago, the talk was of Christmas. Our venerable waiter, who also confided that we were among the few "foreigners" he had ever served, regaled us with tales of the hotel's Rabelaisian Yuletide dinners. In the dining room, festooned with garlands of evergreen and holly and made warm with hundreds of candles, the guests spent hours consuming an Edwardian meal built around great slabs of roast beef accompanied by Yorkshire pudding.

As you may have guessed, we have always dreamed of spending Christmas in London. As you also may have guessed, we've never quite been able to accomplish it. That hasn't prevented us from yearning for a classic English Christmas dinner, however. The problem was that we simply couldn't face the prospect of some enormous leftover chunk of beef shadowing us into the New Year, so we never attempted it by ourselves until we discovered a method of roasting a single beef rib (about 2½ pounds) without turning it into overcooked shoe leather.

This menu begins with an understated chicken and clam broth and includes Yorkshire pudding for two, a colorful mélange of broccoli and cherry tomatoes, and an ethereal steamed pudding that arrived in England by way of Austria.

At the hotel where our fantasy began, Champagne was served before dinner, a well-aged *Deuxième Cru* Bordeaux with it, and vintage Port after dessert.

Who are we to argue?

# Chicken and Clam Broth

This deceptively simple but glamorous soup is a nice, light beginning for a hearty Christmas dinner.

$1^1/_3$ cups rich chicken broth (see p. 220)
⅓ cup clam juice
2 teaspoons Sherry
Salt and pepper

**GARNISH**
Small spinach leaves
Carrot curls
Grated lemon peel

Heat the broth and clam juice together and add the Sherry. Adjust the seasoning with salt and pepper if necessary (depending on how much was already in the broth and clam juice). Ladle into warmed soup bowls, each garnished with a leaf of spinach, a slender carrot curl, and a sprinkling of grated lemon peel.


# Roast Beef and Yorkshire Pudding for Two

1 rib of a standing rib roast (about $2^1/_2$ pounds)

**YORKSHIRE PUDDING**
1 egg
¼ teaspoon salt
½ cup flour
½ cup milk
2 tablespoons roast beef drippings

*Preheat oven to 400 degrees F.* The meat must be thoroughly frozen to cook properly this way, so be sure to buy it a couple of days ahead to wrap and freeze. About an hour and 45 minutes to 2 hours before dinner, unwrap the frozen meat and place it in a roasting pan, fat side up and balanced on the bone. Roast for 1 hour and 30 minutes for rare, 1 hour and 40 minutes for medium, depending on the thickness of the meat (a meat thermometer should read 140 degrees F. for rare, 160 for medium, and 170 for well done). Allow the roast to stand, tented with foil to keep it warm, for 10 to 15 minutes before carving.

To make the Yorkshire Pudding, put the egg, salt, flour, and milk in a blender or food processor and blend until smooth. Divide the drippings equally among four ovenproof custard cups. Pour ¼ of the batter into each cup and place in the oven with the roast for the last 20 minutes the rib cooks. When you remove the roast to set, lower the temperature to 350 degrees F. and bake puddings for another 10 to 15 minutes.

# Horseradish Cream Sauce

2 tablespoons prepared horseradish
1 teaspoon tarragon-flavored white
   vinegar
½ teaspoon sugar

½ teaspoon dry mustard
¼ cup heavy cream, lightly whipped
Salt and pepper

Mix together the horseradish, vinegar, sugar, and dry mustard in a bowl. Fold in the whipped cream and season to taste with salt and pepper.


# Sautéed Broccoli and Tomatoes

½ pound fresh broccoli
6 cherry tomatoes
2 tablespoons butter, melted

1 teaspoon lemon juice
Pinch basil
Salt and pepper

Wash broccoli, discard tough outer leaves, and cut stalks lengthwise into quarters. Using a small knife, peel the branches almost to the flower end. Blanch the broccoli in rapidly boiling salted water 4–6 minutes. Refresh in cold water. Drain on paper towels and chop coarsely. This can be done ahead and the broccoli refrigerated.

Just before serving, cut the tomatoes in half. Combine the butter with the lemon juice and basil. Place the broccoli and tomatoes in a skillet over medium heat, pour over the butter mixture and toss gently until vegetables are heated through. Season to taste with salt and pepper.


# Chocolate Christmas Pudding

2 slices firm home-style bread
¼ cup heavy cream
2 tablespoons butter
1 egg
1 egg yolk
6 tablespoons confectioners' sugar

2 tablespoons ground almonds
1 ounce semi-sweet chocolate, melted
¼ teaspoon almond extract
**GARNISH**
Confectioners' sugar
Unsweetened whipped cream

Cut the crusts from the bread and break the bread into small pieces. Place in a bowl and pour the cream over the bread. Beat until the cream is absorbed.

With an electric mixer, cream the butter 5 minutes until fluffy. Add the bread mixture and beat again until light. Combine the egg and egg yolk and beat lightly with a fork. Alternately add the eggs and the sugar to the bread mixture, beating well after each addition. Add the almonds, melted chocolate, and almond extract and beat until well blended.

Butter a 2-cup mold and turn the pudding mixture into it. Cover with buttered waxed paper and foil, then tie the coverings over the top of the mold with string. Place on a rack in a steamer (a round cake cooling rack set into a large pot works well) and add boiling water just to the bottom of the rack. Cover the pot and place over medium heat on top of the stove and steam for two hours, checking occasionally to see if more boiling water needs to be added. Remove from the steamer, take off the foil and waxed paper, and allow the pudding to set for 5 minutes. Unmold onto a serving dish, dust with confectioners' sugar, and garnish with whipped cream (and, for traditionalists, a sprig of holly).

# PLAN OF ATTACK

## Cook Number One

*ahead of time*
Wrap and freeze beef.
*2 hours before*
Prepare beef for roasting and put into oven at appropriate time for desired doneness.
*1 hour before*
1. Blanch, refresh, and chop broccoli.
2. Make Yorkshire Pudding batter.
*35 minutes before*
1. Put Yorkshire Pudding in to bake.   2. Open wine.
*15 minutes before*
1. Remove roast and tent with foil to set juices before carving.   2. Reduce heat to complete baking of Yorkshire Pudding.
*just before*
Heat broccoli and tomatoes in butter sauce.

## Cook Number Two

*2 hours, 15 minutes before*
Make Chocolate Christmas Pudding and begin steaming.
*1 hour before*
1. Wash and chill endive and watercress.   2. Make salad dressing.
*just before*
1. Prepare soup.   2. Unmold dessert.

# The Last Celebration of the Year

## MENU

*Avocado à la Madrilène*
*Lobster Newburg Crêpes*
*Château Salad*
*Cheeses*
*Marron Coffee Parfait*

Hating New Year's Eve is one of America's favorite national conceits. The same people who swear they never watch television except for old Bogart movies and the MacNeil-Lehrer Report are equally adamant against celebrating the passing of the old year. "You'll never catch me out on the road," they say smugly. "I plan to stay home and read a good book."

Why is it, then, that on December thirty-first these same individuals can be found wearing lampshades on their heads and doing the limbo while deftly tipping their drinks down the décolletage or shirtfronts of their partners?

Naturally, we have a theory.

There seems to be some sort of atavistic short circuit in the mental wiring of people in all cultures that use calendars—Julian, Gregorian, Hebrew, Mayan, Chinese or whatever—to observe each successful passage of the planet around the sun. This could be an act of gratitude that they've made it through another year, or perhaps rejoicing in the sweet promise of one yet to come. Things can only get better, right?

In Western civilization, though, the New Year's Eve bash has become a rite, an obligation. Why else would an otherwise rational person spend the waning hours of December standing around in a roomful of bibulous acquaintances wearing ridiculous hats, all the while knowing that some sober traffic cop with no sense of humor is lying in ambush somewhere on the road home with his Breathalyzer?

Before we are accused of being antisocial, let us admit that we like parties as much as anyone, but events shouldn't provide the motive for celebration—people should. Besides, one of us is a football fan, and she hates to watch the Cotton Bowl on New Year's Day through bloodshot eyes.

Yet we would be less than candid if we didn't confess to all the folly we have decried above. There was the New Year's Eve in Boston when we braved an ice storm to drive to a party that turned out to be about as much fun as a tax audit.

Or the time in San Francisco when we were talked into joining a convivial group of strangers in a restaurant. The level of conversation was so stimulating we had to fight to stay awake until midnight (we were roused abruptly when the time came to divide the bill which, appropriately enough, contained the same number of figures as the New Year).

One December, we finally decided to take our own advice and planned a late evening supper for two at home. Instead of making resolutions we knew we'd never keep in the New Year, we reminisced about the good things that had happened in the old, with the result that we stayed up long past the witching hour, talking quietly until the wine supply was exhausted.

As a matter of curiosity we recited the menu a few days later to a friend in the restaurant business and asked him how much it would have cost to duplicate it in his august tavern. "Oh, about a hundred bucks, I guess," he replied, "if you'd be satisfied with a rather indifferent Champagne."

That was several years ago. We think you can see why we vowed on the spot to make New Year's Eve at home a tradition.

We haven't ever changed the menu much, with the exception of trying some of the high-value substitutes for Champagne. In addition to the obvious California contenders, the French themselves make very creditable sparkling wines in the regions of Anjou (Saumur) and the Loire Valley (Vouvray), and the Panedés district near Barcelona in Spain produces some remarkable (and price-worthy) examples of the *méthode champenoise*, particularly those of Segura Viudas, Codorniu, and Freixenet.

## Avocado à la Madrilène

1 avocado
Lemon juice
1 small tomato, peeled, seeded, and diced
½–1 cup chilled consommé madrilène
   (depending on the size of the avocado's
   cavity)

2 tablespoons sour cream
Chopped chives or minced parsley

Cut the avocado in half without peeling it. Twist gently to separate the halves and remove the seed. Sprinkle the exposed surfaces with lemon juice to keep them from darkening when exposed to the air.

Spoon the diced tomato into the avocado. Break up the chilled consommé with a fork and then spoon it over the tomato. (If you have leftover consommé, save it for another night and serve it with a bit of whipped or sour cream flavored with curry.)

Chill the filled avocados until ready to serve. Serve on a lettuce leaf, or on watercress. Top with sour cream and chives or parsley.

# Lobster Newburg Crêpes

These are so sinfully rich that two per person should suffice for all except those challenging a Guinness world record. Any unfilled crêpes can be frozen, layered with foil, for future use.

**CRÊPES**

¼ cup cold water
¼ cup cold milk
1 egg
⅛ teaspoon salt

½ cup flour
1 tablespoon melted butter
Cooking oil

Whirl all the ingredients except the cooking oil in a blender or food processor until smooth. Refrigerate batter for 2 hours.

To make crêpes, oil a 6-inch crêpe pan and preheat over medium heat. Ladle a scant ¼ cup of the batter into the pan and tilt it until all of the surface is covered. Cook on one side until the edges begin to brown, turn with a spatula, and cook on the other side for half a minute. Cool on cake racks.

**FILLING**

1 cup lobster meat or 1 lobster tail (½ pound)
2 tablespoons butter
¼ teaspoon paprika
¾ cup heavy cream

3 egg yolks
¼ cup dry Sherry or Madeira (Sercial or Verdelho)
Salt and white pepper to taste
¼ cup grated Parmesan cheese

*Preheat oven to 350 degrees F.* If using a lobster tail, cook in simmering salted water for 8 minutes. Cool, then remove the meat from the shell and chop. If using lobster meat, chop or shred into manageable pieces.

Melt the butter in the top of a double boiler. Add the paprika and cream and place over (not in) simmering water. Beat the egg yolks and then beat a little of the hot cream mixture into the yolks before adding them in a slow stream to the cream mixture on the double boiler, beating constantly with a whisk. Add the Sherry or Madeira and continue cooking slowly, stirring, until the sauce thickens. Season to taste with salt and white pepper and stir in lobster meat.

Butter a small shallow baking dish. Using a slotted spoon, place ¼ of the lobster and a little sauce across the middle of each of 4 crêpes. Roll up crêpes and put them into the baking dish, seam side down. Spoon the remaining sauce over the rolled crêpes (the crêpes can be refrigerated at this point until ready for final cooking).

To cook, sprinkle crêpes with grated cheese and bake 12–15 minutes, or until sauce bubbles.

# Château Salad

½ head Bibb lettuce
½ head romaine lettuce
3 tablespoons olive oil
1 tablespoon garlic wine vinegar
2 teaspoons fresh or ¾ teaspoon dried chervil, crumbled

2 teaspoons fresh or ¾ teaspoon dried sweet basil, crumbled
1 teaspoon fresh or ¼ teaspoon dried marjoram, crumbled
Salt and freshly ground pepper

Tear lettuce into large bowl. Combine remaining ingredients in a jar with tight-fitting lid and shake well. Just before serving, pour over salad and toss.

A cheese course continues the relaxed tempo of this meal and also gives you an excuse for an interesting shopping trip. Cheese shops have sprouted up all over the country, and now even supermarkets offer good, if less varied and esoteric, selections. Two or three cheeses of different types, either old favorites or new discoveries, will give you both a chance to pause, contemplate, and consider the diversity of the seductive treasures that man has created since he first went into partnership with the cow.

# Marron Coffee Parfait

1 pint coffee ice cream
2 ounces Kahlúa

1 cup chopped marrons glacés in syrup
Sweetened whipped cream (optional)

Place a scoop of ice cream in each of two parfait glasses or large wine glasses. Add ½ ounce of Kahlúa to each and then a layer of chopped chestnuts. Repeat the layers with another scoop of ice cream, the rest of the Kahlúa, and the rest of the chestnuts. Place the glasses in the freezer.

Remove from the freezer a few minutes before serving and top with whipped cream if you like. (You can keep whipped cream for garnishing on hand by freezing small mounds of it on a cookie sheet until firm and then storing them in tightly closed plastic bags in the freezer. Thaw at room temperature 5–10 minutes before using.)

# PLAN OF ATTACK

As we mentioned before, this menu has earned a permanent place in our hearts because, despite the fact it's reasonably elegant, it's simple to prepare and can be made almost entirely ahead of time. In honor of the occasion we've suggested some ideas below for making everything look as good as it tastes. We usually serve this supper at about 11 P.M. so we can finish the last of the bubbly with the final minutes of the old year. Of course, then you have to pull the cork on a fresh bottle to welcome the new one, but that's all right too. This schedule is predicated on the assumption that New Year's Eve doesn't fall on a workday. If it does, there's still plenty of time to get everything prepared in a leisurely fashion, provided neither of you tarried too long at the saloon across the street from the office.

## Cook Number One

*morning*
1. Prepare crêpe batter and refrigerate. 2. Wash and dry salad ingredients, place in a plastic bag, and refrigerate.

*two hours later*
1. Cook crêpes, refrigerate the best four and freeze the rest. 2. Put Champagne in to chill (okay, we know that it's always better to chill wines in ice immediately before serving, but who's going to be around to catch you?).

*late afternoon*
1. Halve avocados and sprinkle with lemon juice. 2. Set the table.

*10:30 P.M.*
Remove cheese from refrigerator to let come to room temperature.

*10:45 P.M.*
1. Preheat oven for crêpes. 2. Open Champagne and pour two glasses (you may already have done this).

*11 P.M.*
Place crêpes in oven to bake during first course.

*11:15 P.M.*
1. Clear first-course dishes. 2. Toss salad to serve with crêpes or afterward.

*11:30 P.M.*
Serve cheese.

## Cook Number Two

*morning*
1. Make parfaits and place in freezer. 2. Cook lobster, if necessary, and cool.

*two hours later*
1. Make Newburg sauce. 2. Fill crêpes and arrange in baking dish (an oval copper gratin pan would be lovely), cover with plastic wrap, and refrigerate.

*late afternoon*
1. Peel, seed, and chop the tomato and put it into the cavities of the avocados your partner has prepared. 2. Spoon on the consommé, place the avocados on two plates lined with pretty (nonpoisonous) leaves from the garden, and refrigerate.

*10:30 P.M.*
Make salad dressing.

*11 P.M.*
Serve the filled avocados.

*11:15 P.M.*
1. Serve the crêpes. 2. Refill Champagne glasses (see, isn't this fun?).

*11:30 P.M.*
Clear main-course dishes.

*11:45 P.M.*
Serve parfaits.

# FOUR

# THE PLEASURE OF COMPANY

Those who love to cook usually also enjoy entertaining. To them, there's nothing quite so soul-satisfying as those faint little cries of delight uttered by guests as they dig into another culinary triumph. Even those for whom cooking is a necessity and not a diversion can't ignore the subject of home entertaining entirely unless they have unlimited credit and a warm personal relationship with a local maître d'.

It's part of the social minuet that when you have been entertained you are expected to return the favor within a decade or two. Add in the family, business associates, and old roommates who arrive from out of state with three children, a dog, and several evenings' worth of memories to be sorted through, and you find there's just no escape.

We have found, though, that with two cooks in the kitchen to handle the back-stage chores, everyone has a better time. These are the moments when cooking in tandem really pays off.

The menus we have included in this chapter take into account some of the most common (and some downright unlikely) occasions when you're called on to dust off the welcome mat. From an omelet brunch to a mussel lunch—with side trips into an elegant duck extravaganza, a quick dinner for which the guests do the cooking, a casual cassoulet party, a tailgate picnic, an unconventional holiday celebration, and a whole weekend of house-party menus—this chapter is designed to expand your repertoire of entertaining ideas.

## *Brave New Brunch for Six*

## MENU

*Sangrita*
*Strawberry-Filled Cantaloupe*
*Susan's Oven Omelet*
*Chicken Livers in Marsala*
*Orange Marmalade Bread*
*Café Dimanche or Espresso*

Aside from breakfast served in bed on a wicker tray resplendent with a single red rose and a crisp copy of the New York *Times,* morning meals are not things to be mentioned in polite society. However, as the sun reaches its apex on sleepy week-end mornings, civilized souls occasionally gather to mingle and munch. Some call it brunch—although that term has fallen out of favor lately, perhaps because too many of us have attended brunches at which the main course was some anonymous substance suspended in a cream sauce and served up on English muffins after our sense of taste had been anesthetized by round after round of cute drinks. But whatever you call it, lazy Sundays provide just the right atmosphere for entertaining. Busy people can relax in the slow-paced hours between a social Saturday and a frenzied Monday.

Since brunch should be an easygoing affair, you can make up your own rules to suit the occasion. If your friends are late risers and don't feel they can set out in the world until they've filled in the last blank in the Sunday crossword, make the time late enough to accommodate their eccentricities.

The food can be as simple or complex as you care to make it. It need not be even vaguely related to anything you've ever seen on a breakfast table. This is one occasion when people are usually happy to throw off their prejudices in the spirit of adventure. However, it's comforting for those of a conservative bent to come across something familiar, something that spells "breakfast," something like the special super-duper oven omelet that is one of Jinx's sister's morning spectaculars.

Before getting to the meat of the matter, offer your Sunday loafers a gala libation, a sunny tequila concoction from Mexico, Sangrita. After the main event, round things out nicely with Café Dimanche or espresso. Anyone who is devoted to gadgets longs to have one of those massive brass or copper espresso machines that wheeze and burble on the bars of Italian cafés. Unfortunately, they cost about as much as a modest condominium, so most of us must make do. It's quite impossible to prepare good espresso without a machine, but Café Dimanche can be accomplished in even the most modestly equipped kitchen. Simply warm heatproof glasses or mugs and place in each *1¹/₂ ounces Kahlúa or Bahía and 1 ounce white Crème de Menthe,* and fill with *strong, hot black coffee.* Stir and top with *whipped cream.*

To create the proper effortless ambience for a brunch, to strike the right note of easy relaxation, the two of you can't be seen scurrying around the kitchen in a damp frenzy. This unhappy state of affairs can be avoided if the scullery chores are done ahead of time, leaving you, too, a lazy Sunday.

## *Sangrita*

4 cups tomato juice
4 cups orange juice
1¹/₂ cups lime juice

½ teaspoon Tabasco sauce or more to taste
Tequila

Stir together the juices and Tabasco. Pour a jigger of tequila into each chilled, stemmed goblet and fill with Sangrita mix. Float an orange slice on the surface. Makes 6 drinks.

## Strawberry-Filled Cantaloupe

3 cups strawberries  
Sugar  

Kirsch or Crème de Cassis  
3 small cantaloupes

Hull and rinse the strawberries and flavor them with sugar and kirsch or Crème de Cassis. Allow them to marinate for at least half an hour. Cut the cantaloupe in half, scoop out the seeds, and fill center of each half with the strawberries. Chill until ready to serve.

## Susan's Oven Omelet

Butter  
12 eggs  
Salt  
Pepper  
Tarragon  
10 ounces packaged sausage, cooked and crumbled  
½ pound mushrooms, sliced and sautéed  
½ cup cashews, chopped  
2 small to medium potatoes, peeled, boiled, and diced  

2 green onions, sliced, or equal amount chopped chives  
½ cup each, two of your favorite cheeses, grated  
1 cup grated Cheddar cheese  
¼ cup minced parsley  
1 cup chopped cooked zucchini or asparagus  
½ cup butter  
¼ cup sliced ripe olives  
1 cup sour cream

Simply use this ingredient list as a guide—vary it to suit your own taste. *Preheat oven to 450 degrees F.* Heat 2 tablespoons butter in an omelet pan. Whip together 2 eggs, salt, pepper, and tarragon with 1 tablespoon water. When the butter has foamed, pour egg mixture into pan. As the eggs set up, keep them moving around the bottom of the pan. Continue cooking until the egg mixture is almost cooked but the top is still slightly creamy. Slide omelet into buttered casserole dish about the same size as the omelet pan. Cover with one of the prepared fillings or any mixture, setting aside ½ cup Cheddar cheese, the olives, and the sour cream for the top.

Prepare five more omelets following the above instructions and covering each with a different filling. On top of the last omelet sprinkle the remaining Cheddar cheese and sliced olives, and spoon dollops of sour cream around the outside edge. Place in a preheated oven 6–8 minutes.

# Chicken Livers in Marsala

2½ pounds chicken livers, cut in half
Marsala to cover
6 tablespoons butter
4 green onions, minced with some of the
    green tops
Flour seasoned with salt, pepper, and
    paprika

2 tablespoons fresh lemon juice
⅔ cup Marsala
Pinch dried sage
Salt and pepper
Minced fresh parsley

Place the chicken livers in a bowl and pour on enough Marsala to cover. Marinate 1 hour. When ready to cook, melt the butter in a skillet and add the green onions. Sauté until limp. Pat the livers dry with paper towels and dip them lightly in seasoned flour. Add to the onions and sauté about 3 minutes over medium heat, or until the livers are firm. Add the lemon juice, Marsala, sage, and salt and pepper to taste. Cook gently until the Marsala is slightly reduced. Sprinkle with fresh parsley and serve.

Any leftover chicken livers can be whirled in the blender or food processor with some butter and a hard-cooked egg for a terrific spread to go with crackers and cocktails the following evening.

# Orange Marmalade Bread

3 cups flour
1 teaspoon baking powder
1 teaspoon baking soda
1 teaspoon salt
1½ cups sugar
2 eggs
1¼ cups milk

¼ cup butter, melted
⅔ cup marmalade
½ cup finely chopped pecans
2 tablespoons orange juice
¼ tablespoon Grand Marnier or other
    orange liqueur
½ cup sugar

Preheat oven to 350 degrees F. Sift together the flour, baking powder, soda, salt, and 1 cup sugar into a large bowl. In another bowl beat the eggs and stir in the milk and melted butter. Place the marmalade in a small saucepan and simmer over low heat until melted. Pour the egg mixture all at once into the flour mixture and stir just until combined. Stir in the simmering marmalade and chopped pecans. Pour the batter into a greased 8×5×2-inch loaf pan. Bake for 55 to 60 minutes, or until a toothpick inserted in the bread comes out clean. Place the pan on a cake rack.

Heat the orange juice, liqueur, and the remaining ½ cup sugar in a small saucepan until the sugar dissolves. Using a long wooden pick, poke about ten holes in the loaf of bread. Pour the orange mixture over the warm loaves and allow them to stand for 15 minutes. The bread will absorb the liquid. Remove from the pan and cool completely on the rack. Wrap in foil and refrigerate for at least one day before slicing. This bread freezes very well.

# PLAN OF ATTACK

---

## Cook Number One

*ahead of time*
Make Orange Marmalade Bread.
*1 hour before*
1. Make Sangrita and serve a round.
2. Cut chicken livers in half and marinate.
*½ hour before*
Prepare remaining ingredients for chicken livers.
*15 minutes before*
1. Slice bread. 2. Cook chicken livers. 3. Refill Sangrita glasses and serve breakfast.

## Cook Number Two

*ahead of time*
Prepare fillings for omelet: cook and crumble sausage, wash, slice, and sauté mushrooms, chop cashews, boil and dice potatoes, chop chives, grate cheeses, chop parsley, cook vegetables.
*1 hour before*
1. Wash and hull strawberries; marinate. 2. Set the table.
*½ hour before*
Halve and seed cantaloupe. Fill with strawberries and refrigerate.
*15 minutes before*
Make and layer omelets with fillings in a buttered casserole.
*just before*
Bake oven omelet and serve.

# Mussel Beach Lunch

## MENU

*Mussels in Mustard Cream*
*Cheese Gougère*
*Mushroom-Zucchini Salad with Green Dressing*
*Apricot Crêpes Flambé*

SIX SERVINGS

These days one of the biggest problems for would-be hosts is finding a time when everyone can get together. A year's worth of Saturday nights doesn't begin to allow for most people's social obligations, and to entertain during the week means resigning yourself to guests who keep one eye on the main course and the other on their watches. Since a relaxed atmosphere is essential to a successful party, we like to entertain on Sunday afternoons, a time conducive to good conversation, interesting food, and reasonable departures.

A favorite menu on these occasions is one that features mussels, a shellfish that is still reasonably inexpensive, perhaps because it is not yet as popular in this country as it is in Europe. Like many Americans we had to be drawn, gently protesting, into the circle of mussel aficionados. But it took only one meeting for us to be seduced by these handsome shellfish with their shiny blue-black shells and brilliant orange meat. Their buttery texture and delicately rich flavor respond beautifully to the simplest treatment, yet they also make suitable partners for a number of other ingredients, resulting in dishes of great complexity and elegance.

For many years mussels were not readily available in American markets, but now commercial harvesting of Eastern mussels has changed all that. And for those who live near the sea there are still plenty available directly from nature. But there are a few simple rules you should know before planning a mussel hunt.

During the warm months a toxic plankton can affect mussels and other bivalves. State public health agencies warn of this problem by posting beaches, but it's a good idea always to check with the local health department. On both coasts, you should avoid harvesting mussels from areas with possible water pollution. Again, the health department is your best guide.

Because mussels attach themselves with great tenacity to their homes among rocks and wharves, a tool for coaxing them off their perches is essential. You can use a crowbar, tire iron, claw hammer, or even a strong, broad screwdriver. Whether shopping at nature's store or in the regular marketplace, select mussels of uniform size which will cook in the same length of time. Choose only those with tightly closed and unbroken shells.

Mussels prepared in this smooth, mustard-flavored cream sauce are enhanced by a crisp salad of raw mushrooms and zucchini with a brilliant green dressing touched by garlic and parsley. A gougère, the great Burgundian cheese pastry, rich with the flavor of Gruyère, is a splendid companion as is a glass or two of chilled Muscadet from the Loire Valley, a California Chardonnay, or a Pinot Blanc.

The finale for this menu is far more spectacular than its simple preparation would indicate. Flaming apricot crêpes that can be made ahead, reheated in the oven, and torched with great ceremony just before serving are a marvelous dessert for entertaining.

## Mussels in Mustard Cream

3 quarts fresh mussels
1 onion, chopped
1 branch celery, cut in pieces
2 sprigs parsley
1¹/₂ cups white wine
1¹/₂ cups water

3 tablespoons butter
3 tablespoons flour
¹/₂ cup heavy cream
1 tablespoon Dijon mustard
Salt and pepper
Minced fresh parsley

Select mussels carefully, discarding any with open or broken shells. To clean, rinse mussels well under running water and scrub with a stiff brush or pot cleaner. Clip off the exposed "beard" (the hairlike fibers common to mussels) with scissors.

Place cleaned mussels in a large saucepan with the onion, celery, and parsley. Add the wine and water. Cover the pan and steam until the mussels open. Discard any that haven't opened. Remove the top shells, but leave the mussels in the bottom shells and arrange in large shallow soup plates. Strain the liquid and reserve.

Heat the butter in a saucepan and stir in the flour. Cook just until slightly colored. Add 1 cup mussel broth and stir until smooth. Add the cream and mustard, and season to taste with salt and pepper. Adjust thickness of the sauce to your preference by stirring in additional broth if necessary (save and freeze remaining broth to use as the base for your next fish stew or chowder).

Spoon some of the sauce over each mussel in its shell. Sprinkle with finely minced parsley and serve immediately.

# Cheese Gougère

1 cup water
½ cup butter
1 cup flour, sifted
Salt

4–5 eggs
¾ cup diced Gruyère cheese
1 egg yolk beaten with 1 tablespoon water

*Preheat oven to 400 degrees F.* Place the water and butter in a saucepan. Bring to a boil. When boiling rapidly, remove from the heat and add flour all at once and a dash of salt. Beat vigorously until the dough is smooth and pulls away from the sides of the pan. Cool mixture for about 5 minutes. Add eggs, beating after each addition, until mixture is glossy and smooth (this also can be done in a food processor). Stir in the diced cheese.

Dampen a baking sheet with cold water (this will help the pastry rise). On the sheet, place large spoonfuls of dough touching one another in a circle. Brush the tops with beaten egg yolk. Place in a preheated oven and bake for 30 minutes or until puffed and brown. Serve hot or cold.

# Mushroom-Zucchini Salad with Green Dressing

Lettuce leaves
3 large zucchini, thinly sliced
6–8 large white mushrooms, sliced
4 radishes

**GREEN DRESSING**
¾ cup olive oil
3 tablespoons fresh lemon juice
1 cup fresh parsley
2 cloves garlic, crushed
Salt and pepper

Make a bed of lettuce leaves on six salad plates. Place the mushrooms in a circle in the middle of the plate and surround with a ring of sliced raw zucchini, making a pinwheel effect. Grate the radishes and reserve for garnish.

To make the dressing, place all of the ingredients in the jar of a blender and blend until smooth. Season to taste with salt and pepper. Spoon some of the dressing over each salad and sprinkle with grated radishes. The dressing will keep refrigerated for 3 to 4 days.

# Apricot Crêpes Flambé

**CRÊPES**
3 eggs
1 cup instant-blending flour
3 tablespoons sugar
1 cup milk
2 tablespoons melted butter

**FILLING**
¾ cup sweet butter
6 tablespoons apricot jam
1 tablespoon sugar
1 tablespoon dark rum

**SAUCE**
3 tablespoons sugar

3 tablespoons orange liqueur
3 tablespoons dark rum

To make the crêpes, whirl all the crêpe ingredients in a blender or food processor for about 1 minute or until smooth. Or beat the eggs in a bowl, add the remaining ingredients, and beat until smooth.

To cook, brush a crêpe pan with a bit of oil. When it sizzles, pour in just enough batter to cover the bottom of the pan. Tip the pan to spread the batter. When the crêpe is firm on the underside, after about 1 minute, turn it and cook on the other for a few seconds. Cool on a cake rack. Repeat with the remaining batter.

Beat the butter, jam, sugar, and rum together. Divide the filling among the crêpes and spread on the lower third of each. Roll filled crêpes into cylinders and arrange them in individual gratin dishes or one large flat baking dish. At this point the crêpes can be covered and refrigerated until you're ready for dessert.

About 10 minutes before serving time, sprinkle the top of the crêpes with sugar and place in a *preheated 375 degree F. oven* until the sugar has become slightly caramelized. Warm the orange liqueur and rum together in a small pan. Bring the crêpes to the table, pour the spirits over them, and ignite. Spoon the sauce over the crêpes until the flames die down.

# PLAN OF ATTACK

## Cook Number One

*ahead of time*
1. Clean and de-beard mussels.  2. Prepare and bake Cheese Gougère if serving cold.
*15 minutes before*
Cook mussels, remove top shells, and keep warm.
*10 minutes before*
Make mustard cream sauce.
*just before*
Mask mussels individually with sauce and sprinkle with parsley.

## Cook Number Two

*ahead of time*
1. Make crêpe filling.  2. Fill, roll, and refrigerate crêpes.
*40 minutes before*
1. Prepare and bake Cheese Gougère if serving hot.  2. Make and chill salad.  3. Chill wine.
*just before*
1. Remove salad from refrigerator and serve.  2. Uncork wine.  3. Remove Cheese Gougère (unless done ahead) from oven to table and reduce oven heat to 375 degrees F. for crêpes.
*after main course*
1. Sprinkle crêpes with sugar.  2. Reheat crêpes in oven.  3. Heat rum and orange liqueur together.  4. Flame crêpes.

## British Tailgate Picnic

# MENU

Gin and Bitters
or
Scotch Toddy
Baby Sprouts with Curry Cream
Scotch Eggs
Veal-and-Ham Pie
Carrot Salad Vinaigrette
Mustard Maison
Fruit and Cheese
Lemon Cookies
Beer

SIX TO EIGHT SERVINGS

Something has happened to the once simple art of tailgate picnicking. Old grads who in their youth were perfectly satisfied with pallid hot dogs and thin beer now sit around quaffing Champagne and nibbling caviar at damask-covered folding tables tricked out with fresh flowers and silver candelabra. Clearly the bird and bottle that once seemed the ultimate outdoor menu won't win any points in the heady gastronomic atmosphere in stadium parking lots today.

Tailgate chefs who want to set the proper tone can take their lead from the English who have a flair for this sort of thing. English food, while sometimes snubbed by the cognoscenti, is just right for tailgate picnicking and more fun than fancy Continental concoctions.

Start with a choice of three favorite British drinks—gin and bitters, beer, or a scotch toddy to take the chill off. Brussels sprouts dunked in a curry-flavored cream sauce and that pub favorite, Scotch Eggs, will appease hunger pangs while the rest of the meal is arranged.

The main attraction is an elegant veal-and-ham pie served with sweet-tart homemade mustard. A golden carrot salad in vinaigrette sets it all off. Dessert is simply fruit, a selection of lovely English cheeses, and lemon cookies. For the cheese, consult a good merchant and try some of the mature English farmhouse Cheddars now increasingly available in this country. Also look for Cheshire, the oldest of the British cheeses, which is crumbly, nutty, and salty; Gloucester, a robust straw-colored cheese; Caerphilly from Wales or Somerset; Wensleydale with its delicate sour buttermilk flavor; Sage Derby; or the granddaddy of all the English cheeses, Stilton. By the time this final course appears, some trenchermen may wonder whether it's really worth it to fight their way into the stadium. After all, a football game is only a football game, but this picnic is a feast.

## Gin and Bitters

For each serving, pour 2 ounces of gin into a mug or old-fashioned glass. Add bitters to taste. Stir gently, and if you're a purist you'll never let ice near it, though a rub of lemon around the edge of the glass is considered good form. It's possible to make an exception for ice-loving guests, but frown when you do it.

## Scotch Toddy

*1 cup water*
*½ cup sugar*
*2 cups scotch whisky*
*8 cloves*
*½ teaspoon ground cinnamon*

*1 quart hot water*
*Nutmeg to taste*
*8 thin slices lemon*
*Juice of 2 lemons*

Boil sugar and water together until clear. Combine with remaining ingredients except nutmeg and lemon slices. Fill thermos. Serve hot in mugs. Float lemon slice on each and dust with nutmeg. Makes 6–8 drinks.

## Baby Sprouts with Curry Cream

*1½ pounds brussels sprouts*
*Caraway seeds (optional)*

**CURRY CREAM**

1 package cream cheese (8 ounces), softened
½ pint sour cream
¼ cup mayonnaise (see p. 221)
1 tablespoon curry powder (or more to taste)

¼ teaspoon powdered ginger
1 clove garlic, minced
2 tablespoons minced onion
Lemon juice
Salt and white pepper

Find the tiniest, tenderest sprouts you can, then wash thoroughly and trim. Cook, uncovered, in a large pot of rapidly boiling salted water until tender but still crisp, about 7 to 10 minutes. Drain and chill. Sprinkle with caraway seeds if you wish.

To make the Curry Cream, blend together the cream cheese, sour cream, and mayonnaise until smooth. Stir in the seasonings and serve in a dish surrounded by the brussels sprouts for dipping.

# Scotch Eggs

Follow the directions for Trattoria Eggs (see p. 00), using regular sausage rather than Italian and omitting cheese from the bread-crumb coating.

# Veal-and-Ham Pie

The use of lard is traditional in this rather sturdy English crust. Vegetable shortening can be substituted, but the result will be slightly different both in flavor and texture.

**PASTRY**

5 cups flour
½ teaspoon salt
½ cup plus 2 tablespoons lard

6 tablespoons milk
2 tablespoons water

**FILLING**

2 pounds boneless veal, cut into ¼-inch cubes
1 pound ham, cut into ¼-inch cubes
¼ cup minced parsley
4 tablespoons brandy
6 tablespoons chicken or beef broth (see p. 220 or 218)
2 tablespoons fresh lemon juice
1 teaspoon thyme

2 teaspoons salt
¼ teaspoon pepper
4 hard-cooked eggs, peeled
1 egg yolk combined with 1 tablespoon heavy cream
1 envelope unflavored gelatin
2 cups chicken broth (see p. 220)

To make the pastry, which traditionally is thick and heavy, combine the flour and salt in a bowl. Warm the lard, milk, and water in a pan over moderate heat until the lard has melted. Beat the liquid into the flour, a few tablespoons at a time, until the dough can be gathered into a ball. On a floured board, knead the dough until it is smooth and elastic, about 2 to 3 minutes. Place the dough in a bowl, cover with a cloth, and allow to rest for 30 minutes.

In a large bowl, combine the veal, ham, parsley, brandy, 6 tablespoons chicken or beef broth, lemon juice, thyme, salt and pepper. Stir together until the ingredients are thoroughly mixed.

*Preheat the oven to 350 degrees F.* and grease the inside of a 10×5×4-inch loaf pan. Reserve about a third of the pastry and roll out the remaining dough into a rectangle about 20 inches by 10 inches. Press the pastry into the loaf pan and trim off any extra.

Fill the pastry shell not quite to the halfway point with the veal-and-ham mixture. Arrange the hard-cooked eggs in single file down the middle of the filling and cover the eggs with the remaining meat mixture, leaving a 1-inch space at the top.

Roll the remaining pastry into a rectangle large enough to cover the loaf pan and about a quarter inch thick. Drape it over the pan and trim off any excess. With your fingers, crimp the edges to make a fluted crust and secure the pastry to the rim of the pan.

Cut a 1-inch round hole in the middle of the top crust. If you're feeling artistic, you can roll out any scraps of dough and cut them into leaf designs to surround the hole in the top. The extra pieces will stick if you moisten them with the egg-cream mixture before attaching them. Then paint the entire top with the egg-cream mixture.

Bake for 2 hours, or until the top is a handsome golden brown. Cool for 15 minutes.

In a saucepan, combine the gelatin and chicken broth and allow the gelatin to soften for 2 to 3 minutes. Simmer over low heat, stirring constantly, until the gelatin is completely dissolved. Using a funnel, pour the broth mixture into the hole in the top of the pie. Cool the pie to room temperature and refrigerate for 6 to 8 hours or until the aspic is firm.

If you want to unmold the pie, simply run a knife around the edges and dip the bottom in hot water. Place an inverted plate on top and, holding the plate firmly in place, turn the whole thing over. A few solid shakes should release it. Turn over the pie onto another plate and serve in half-inch slices.

## Carrot Salad Vinaigrette

10 large carrots (about 1 3/4 pounds)
4 green onions, chopped with some of the
   green tops
2 tablespoons minced parsley
2 tablespoons grated lemon rind

½ cup olive oil
3 tablespoons lemon juice
¼ teaspoon dry mustard
Salt and pepper

Peel the carrots and cut in julienne strips about ¼ inch thick or coarsely grate. Cook, covered, in about 1 inch of boiling water until barely tender (about 5 minutes). Drain and plunge into cold water. Drain again and turn into a serving bowl. Add the onions, parsley, and lemon rind and mix thoroughly. In a small bowl combine the olive oil, lemon juice, mustard, and salt and pepper to taste. Whisk together to blend. Pour over carrots and toss until carrots are filmed with the dressing.

## Mustard Maison

*1 can Colman's dry mustard (2 ounces)*　　*3 eggs*
*1 cup malt vinegar*　　*1 cup sugar*

Blend the dry mustard and vinegar in a blender. Add the eggs and sugar and blend at high speed until frothy. Put in the top of a double boiler over simmering water and stir until the mixture thickens, about 10 minutes. This is a thin mustard with an authoritative sweet-hot bite. When cool, pour into jars and refrigerate. Mustard Maison also makes a lovely gift.

## Lemon Cookies

*2 cups flour*　　*½ cup butter*
*1 teaspoon baking powder*　　*1 cup sugar*
*⅛ teaspoon salt*　　*1 egg*
*½ teaspoon grated lemon zest*　　*1 tablespoon lemon juice*

Sift together the flour, baking powder, and salt. Cream together the lemon zest and butter and add sugar gradually. Beat until fluffy. Add egg and lemon juice and beat well. Beat in flour mixture. Shape into rolls and wrap in waxed paper and chill. (If you're going to freeze rolls, wrap them in foil or put waxed-paper rolls in plastic bags and seal tightly.) When ready to bake, slice into ¼-inch rounds and place them on greased baking sheets. *Preheat oven to 375 degrees F.* and bake 8–10 minutes.

Because all of the preparations for this picnic can be done ahead at your leisure, you can work out whatever plan of attack suits you.

# THE GRAND GESTURE

## *Formal Dinner for Six*

## MENU

*Shrimp Rémoulade*
*Canard à l'Orange*
*Zucchini and Spinach Timbales*
*Green Salad*
*Cheeses*
*Cold Sherry Soufflé*

Even if you are the barefoot-and-blue-jean type, there are occasions that call for serious sit-down entertaining. It's always a good idea to have a few reliable menus on call that are impressive enough to knock the socks off the most dedicated food snob. At our house this is one.

The main course is duck, a fowl which when properly prepared is a glorious treat. It's likely that the bird you buy will be frozen and, happily, duck is one meat that takes this process well. Thaw it in the bag in the refrigerator overnight or submerge it, bag and all, in cold water for several hours. Now remove the neck, giblets, and any surplus fat in the duck cavity and rinse and dry the bird thoroughly. By the way, rendered duck fat is marvelous for cooking hash browns or other fried-potato dishes. Before cooking, scratch the duck lengthwise with a sharp fork to release the fat that will baste the meat. For roast duckling, allow 45 minutes per pound in an oven preheated to 350 degrees F.

The easiest way to serve duck is to quarter it. Judge the number of servings by the size of the duck, the complexity and richness of the dish in which it stars, and the supporting cast of side dishes. For this menu we figure that 2 ducks—8 quarters—will feed six people; increase it to 3 ducks if you're having a group of sumo wrestlers to dine.

Many busy cooks think preparing duck is just too time-consuming, but by following the techniques developed for restaurant kitchens, as we have in the following recipe, it's possible to cook duck ahead and even have it at the ready for impromptu dinners.

This menu begins with a piquant Shrimp Rémoulade, then progresses to our version of Canard à l'Orange decorated with handsome fruit baskets and served with individual Zucchini and Spinach Timbales. If you're really out to impress with this meal, follow this course with a simple green salad of one or two types of lettuce with an oil and vinegar dressing and then a selection of cheeses to accompany the last of the wine. Dessert is a fanciful cold Sherry soufflé decorated with candied violets.

There are two schools of thought when it comes to serving wine with duck. Because it tends to be full-flavored, some hold that only an authoritative red is appropriate. Others believe that because the flesh tends to be quite rich, the solvent qualities of some dry whites make for a more pleasant combination. Our own preference with this menu would be to serve a well-aged California Cabernet Sauvignon or one of the more exalted growths of the Médoc with the entrée, and a Sauternes with the dessert.

## Shrimp Rémoulade

*2 pounds large shrimp*
**RÉMOULADE SAUCE**
*6–8 small green onions chopped with 2 inches of green tops, or about ⅔ cup chopped green onions*
*1 stalk celery*
*1 clove garlic*
*¼ cup parsley*

*4 tablespoons Creole mustard*
*1 tablespoon paprika*
*2 tablespoons white wine vinegar*
*6 tablespoon olive oil*
*Salt and pepper*
**GARNISH**
*Watercress*
*Lemon wedges*

Cook the shrimp in rapidly boiling salted water for 2 to 3 minutes. Drain and rinse under cold water, then peel and devein.

To make the sauce, mince together the onions, celery, garlic, and parsley until very fine. This can be accomplished easily in a food processor using a steel blade and on and off bursts of power, but do not make a mush. Add the mustard, paprika, and vinegar and stir. Whisk in the olive oil and season to taste with salt and pepper. Combine the shrimp with enough rémoulade to coat well and refrigerate for about 2 hours to allow the flavors in the sauce to permeate the shellfish. Serve on a bed of watercress and garnish with lemon wedges.

## Canard à l'Orange

*2 ducks (4 to 5 pounds)*
*2 navel oranges*
*1 can (8 ounces) mandarin oranges*
*Watercress sprigs*
*½ cup sugar*
*½ cup water*
*4 tablespoons red wine vinegar*

*1 teaspoon meat glaze (see p. 219) or Bovril*
*½ cup concentrated chicken broth (see p. 220)*
*½ teaspoon arrowroot*
*1 ounce Grand Marnier*

*Preheat the oven to 350 degrees F.* Place the ducks breast up on a rack in a roasting pan and scratch skin all over with a fork. Roast for a total of 2½ to 3 hours, pouring off the accumulated fat after 1½ hours. Add a pint of water to the bottom of the pan at this time and turn the duckling breast down. Roast for another half hour and then return to the original position to complete cooking.

The moment the duck has finished roasting, remove from the pan and place it on a baking sheet and chill rapidly, moving it directly from the oven to the refrigerator or even to the freezer for a brief period until the duck is thoroughly chilled. When it is cool, cut the duck in quarters and slip each into a plastic bag and close. Refrigerate. Pour all the fat from the roasting pan and then scrape the remaining juices and bits of meat into a small bowl. Reserve. This much can be done ahead of time.

To make the garnish, cut two navel oranges into basket shapes, scooping them out and leaving a piece of the rind in place on each as a handle. Fill the baskets with the mandarin oranges, or with peeled tangerines, and garnish with watercress sprigs.

When ready to serve, *preheat the oven to 425 degrees F.* and reheat the cooled ducks for 15 to 20 minutes.

While the duck is being reheated, mix the sugar and water together in a heavy skillet and bring to a boil, cooking over a medium heat until the syrup is a medium-brown caramel color. Without removing the pan from the heat, add the red wine vinegar all at once, but stand back as it will sizzle and steam. Continue to boil and stir, and when the mixture begins to thicken again add the scrapings from the roasting pan, the meat glaze, and the chicken broth. Continue to boil and stir until it thickens again and then stir in the arrowroot mixed with the Grand Marnier. Continue stirring the sauce until it is reduced to a syrupy consistency. Arrange duck on a serving platter, pour the sauce over the quarters, and garnish the platter with the orange baskets.

# Zucchini and Spinach Timbales

**VEGETABLE MIXTURE**
1 pound zucchini
½ pound fresh spinach
1 tablespoon butter
1 tablespoon oil
1½ cups minced onions

**CUSTARD MIXTURE**
¾ cup grated cheese, Swiss and
   Parmesan mixed

¾ cup heavy cream
6 eggs, well beaten
Salt and pepper

**TOPPING**
3 tablespoons butter
½ cup dried bread crumbs
¼ cup minced fresh parsley
Salt and pepper

Cut rounds of waxed paper to fit the bottoms of six individual ½-cup ramekins or dariole molds. Butter the sides and bottoms of the molds, fit in the paper, and butter it as well.

Trim the ends of the zucchini and wash well. Grate coarsely and place in a colander. Sprinkle with salt and toss. Allow the squash to drain for a few minutes and then squeeze dry, one handful at a time.

Rinse the spinach carefully and remove stems. Place in a large pot with only the water that clings to the leaves. Set over low heat and cook just until the spinach has wilted. Place the cooked spinach in a sieve and press out liquid. Chop very fine.

Place the butter and oil in a skillet and sauté the onions slowly until tender and clear. Add the zucchini and spinach and raise the heat to medium and stir 5 minutes.

Place the vegetables in a bowl and add grated cheese and cream. Stir to blend. Fold beaten eggs into the mixture. Add salt and pepper if necessary. Pour the timbale mixture into molds. These can now be covered and refrigerated for later baking.

When ready to bake, *preheat oven to 375 degrees F.* Stir the mixture to reblend and place the molds in a shallow pan. Pour enough boiling water into the pan to reach one third of the way up their sides. Bake 15–20 minutes, or until the tops are set and the mixture shrinks away from the sides of the molds. A knife inserted in the middles should come out clean. Allow the molds to set for about 5 minutes.

For the topping, heat the butter in a skillet. Stir in the bread crumbs and toss until toasted. Remove the pan from the heat, stir in parsley and salt and pepper to taste. Unmold the timbales. Sprinkle with the crumb mixture.

# *Cold Sherry Soufflé*

2 packages ladyfingers
1 envelope (1 tablespoon) unflavored
  gelatin
½ cup cold water
1 cup sweet Sherry
6 eggs, separated

¾ cup sugar
1 tablespoon lemon juice
1 cup heavy cream
**GARNISH**
Whipped cream
Candied violets

Place a waxed-paper collar around a 7-inch soufflé dish and line the sides of the dish with ladyfingers.

Soften the gelatin in ½ cup of cold water for 5 minutes. Place over boiling water and stir until dissolved. Remove from the heat, add the Sherry, and cool. Chill for 30 minutes or until the mixture begins to thicken.

Beat the egg whites until foamy and gradually add ½ cup of the sugar, beating constantly. Add the lemon juice and continue beating until the mixture is stiff but not dry. In a separate bowl beat the egg yolks until frothy, gradually add the remaining ¼ cup of sugar, and beat until the mixture is thick and lemon-colored. Add the slightly thickened wine gelatin slowly to the egg yolks and continue beating until light and thick. Fold the beaten egg whites into mixture. Whip the cream and fold it in. Pour into the collared soufflé dish and chill for three hours until firm.

Serve decorated with piped whipped cream and candied violets.

# PLAN OF ATTACK

## Cook Number One

*ahead of time*
1. Prepare shrimp and sauce; blend and chill. 2. Prepare individual ramekins or dariole molds for timbales.

*1 hour before*
Make timbales; cover and refrigerate.

*20–25 minutes before*
Put timbales in to bake.

*15 minutes before*
Make crumb topping for timbales.

*just before*
1. Unmold timbales and dress with crumb topping. 2. Serve shrimp.

## Cook Number Two

*ahead of time*
1. Precook duck and chill. 2. Make Cold Sherry Soufflé and decorate; chill. 3. Make orange baskets.

*1 hour before*
1. Uncork wine. 2. Remove cheeses from refrigerator. 3. Wash and chill salad greens. 4. Make salad dressing.

*15 minutes before*
1. Reheat duck. 2. Make sauce.

*after main course*
Toss salad with dressing and serve.

---

# USE YOUR BEAN

## *Informal Dinner for Six*

# MENU

*Scallop Soup*
*California Cassoulet*
*Lemon-Dressed Salad*
*Orange Tart*

This is the sort of meal we like to serve to a group of good friends for no occasion at all except the fun of getting together. It's an unpretentious menu, but the food is good and there's plenty of it. Beans mean the meal's in the budget range (if scallops are selling for the equivalent of Krugerrands, substitute another soup), but it's clear that thought and attention—ingredients far more important than truffles and caviar—have gone into the preparation.

In some kitchens beans have a way of hanging around forever, always self-effacing and modestly residing on the dusty back shelf of the pantry. Eventually they become one of the kitchen fixtures—never noticed, never cooked. And yet, beans have long fulfilled a vital role in the kitchens of other lands. In China, as far back as the first century A.D., merchants made fortunes peddling bean relishes, and delicacies such as Italian bean soups, Greek bean stews, and Brazilian *feijoada* are all built around the bean. Of course the French cassoulet, from which we take our inspiration for this lighter version, is a monument to the artistry of Gallic kitchens.

Dried beans must be soaked to replace the water lost in drying. There are two ways to do this. Those organized cooks who are always on top of matters will, of course, remember to put their beans to soak overnight. Those of us whose checkbooks never balance and who can't remember where we parked the car undoubtedly will resort to the quick-soaking method. In bean cooking there is, thankfully, always something for everyone.

The cooking time for dried beans can't be pinpointed. It can vary depending on variety of bean, where they were grown, their age, and the hardness of the water in which they are cooked. Generally speaking, though, most beans will take 1½ to 2½ hours to cook, with lentils requiring less time and garbanzos more.

To be sure you have beans ready to go when you are, it's a smart idea to pre-cook some and either store them in the refrigerator, where they'll keep for up to a week, or freeze them to be incorporated into a dish at a later date. And don't forget that if you have cooked beans on hand, they also can become a wonderful spur-of-the-moment salad with a dressing of oil and vinegar, herbs, and a few chopped green onions. Or make an impromptu dip by putting cooked white beans in a blender or food processor with some olive oil, lemon juice, and a peeled clove of garlic. Whirl until smooth and season with salt and pepper. Chill.

This menu begins with a very light, scallop-flavored broth. Cassoulet is a hearty dish by any measure, so a light first course is essential. The cassoulet is followed by a green salad dressed with a sprightly lemon dressing. A fresh orange tart is the perfect ending for this meal of many flavors. With the cassoulet we like to serve a strong young red wine such as a Côtes-du-Rhône or a Petite Sirah.

## *Scallop Soup*

2½ *cups chicken broth (see p. 220)*
1 *cup beef broth (see p. 218)*
¼ *cup clam broth*
¼ *cup white Port*

*Salt and pepper*
¼ *pound scallops, cut into julienne strips*
1 *tablespoon thinly sliced green onion or chopped chives*

Put the broths and Port in a saucepan and bring to a boil. Season to taste with salt and pepper. Divide scallops among bowls and ladle broth over the top. Garnish with green onions or chives.

# California Cassoulet

1 quart chicken broth (see p. 220)  
1 quart water  
1 pound dried Great Northern beans  
½ pound bacon, diced  
4 sweet Italian sausages  
½ pound ham, cubed  
1 onion, chopped  
1 clove garlic, mashed and finely chopped  
½ teaspoon thyme  
Bouquet garni of 3 sprigs parsley, 1 leek,  
   3 celery tops, 1 bay leaf  

1 pound pork, cubed  
1 pound lamb, cubed  
2 Rock Cornish game hens  
4 tomatoes, peeled, seeded, and chopped  
Salt and pepper  
1 cup dry white wine  
¾ cup dry bread crumbs  
3 tablespoons minced parsley  

Bring the chicken broth and water to a boil, add the beans, boil 2 minutes, then cover and remove from the heat. Allow to stand, covered, 1 hour.

Sauté the diced bacon in a skillet until crisp, remove and drain on paper towels. Prick the sausages and sauté in the same pan. Drain, reserving the fat.

Add the bacon, whole sausages, and cubed ham to the beans. Bring to a boil and skim. Reduce the heat and add the chopped onion, garlic, thyme, and bouquet garni. Simmer, uncovered, for about 45 minutes. Remove and discard the bouquet garni and remove and reserve the sausage. Drain the beans, saving the broth, and set aside.

Brown the pork and lamb in the bacon and sausage fat, drain on paper towels, and set aside. *Preheat the oven to 450 degrees F.* Place the game hens on a rack in a roasting pan and put in the oven. Immediately reduce the oven temperature to 350 degrees F. and cook the birds about 30 minutes or until tender and cooked through. Cool and cut in quarters.

**TO ASSEMBLE THE CASSOULET** *Preheat the oven to 350 degrees F.* In an ovenproof casserole, spread a 1-inch layer of beans. Cover with half of the sausage cut into ½-inch pieces, half of the other meats, and 2 chopped seeded tomatoes. Salt and pepper lightly. Repeat and end with a layer of beans. Pour in the bean broth mixed with 1 cup dry white wine until the ingredients are just covered. Sprinkle the top with half of the dry bread crumbs mixed with half of the minced parsley. Bring to a boil on top of the stove, then bake, uncovered, 1½ hours. After an hour, push the crust down, sprinkle with remaining bread-crumb mixture, and allow another crust to form.

# Lemon-Dressed Salad

**DRESSING**

1 whole egg
1 tablespoon grated Parmesan cheese
2 tablespoons Dijon mustard
3 tablespoons fresh lemon juice

1 teaspoon Worcestershire sauce
Pinch thyme
½ cup oil
Salt and pepper

Combine all the ingredients in a bowl and whisk until thoroughly mixed. Refrigerate for an hour, if possible, before tossing with your choice of crisp salad greens.


# Orange Tart

**PASTRY CRUST**

1 cup flour
2 tablespoons sugar
1 egg, separated
⅛ teaspoon salt
6 tablespoons cold butter (or frozen butter, if you are using a food processor)
1 tablespoon cold water
1 teaspoon finely grated orange peel
¼ teaspoon almond extract

**FILLING**

1½ tablespoons cornstarch
1 cup milk
2 tablespoons sugar
2 egg yolks, lightly beaten
¼ teaspoon vanilla
10–12 ladyfingers
3 large oranges

**GLAZE**

½ cup apricot preserves
1½ tablespoons orange liqueur

**FOR PASTRY** If using a food processor fitted with the steel blade, place flour, sugar, egg yolk, and salt in work bowl. Process, turning on and off rapidly for about 5 seconds. Add butter and process again until mixture is crumbly. Mix in water, orange peel, and almond extract and continue processing until just before mixture forms a ball. Press together into a ball and chill.

For non-space-age pastry, combine flour, sugar, and salt and stir thoroughly. Cut in butter until mixture resembles a coarse meal. Stir in egg yolk, water, orange peel, and almond extract, mixing until it forms a ball. Wrap and chill.

*Preheat oven to 425 degrees F.* Roll out pastry and place in 9-inch tart pan with removable bottom. Prick pastry all over with a fork. Or, line shell with foil or waxed paper and weight it down with raw rice or beans. Bake 5 minutes. Remove beans and lining. Bake another 5–6 minutes, or until golden brown. Brush with lightly beaten egg white. Let dry before adding filling.

**FOR FILLING** Dissolve cornstarch in 2 tablespoons of the milk. Heat remaining milk in saucepan and stir in dissolved cornstarch. Cook, stirring constantly, until thickened. Mix in sugar. Whisk a little hot milk into egg yolks. Return egg mixture to pan and continue cooking over low heat until very thick, about 8 to 10 minutes. Cool before stirring in vanilla.

Spread custard in pastry shell. Place a layer of split ladyfingers on top (this will soak up juices from oranges and prevent tart from becoming soggy). Peel oranges, cutting away all bitter white pith. Cut crosswise into very thin slices. Arrange oranges on top of ladyfingers.

**FOR GLAZE** Heat preserves and liqueur until blended. Press through sieve and brush on top of oranges in tart. Chill before serving.

# PLAN OF ATTACK

## *Cook Number One*

*ahead of time*
1. Cut scallops into julienne strips and refrigerate.   2. Make pastry crust.   3. Slice green onions and refrigerate.
*1 hour before*
1. Make tart filling.   2. Assemble tart and chill.   3. Make salad dressing and chill.   4. Crisp salad greens.
*just before*
Make soup.

## *Cook Number Two*

*ahead of time*
1. Boil beans 2 minutes, cover, and allow to stand 1 hour.   2. Roast Rock Cornish game hens.   3. Make bread crumbs.
*3 hours before*
1. Sauté bacon and sausages.   2. Simmer beans with flavorings for 45 minutes.   3. Brown pork and lamb.
*2 hours before*
Assemble cassoulet.
*1 1/2 hours before*
Bake cassoulet.
*1/2 hour before*
1. Add another layer of bread crumbs to cassoulet.   2. Uncork wine.
*just before*
1. Toss salad.

# The Great American Melting Pot

## MENU

Deep-Fried Cheese
The Great American Melting Pot
Green Peppercorn Herb Sauce
Sesame Yogurt Sauce
Horseradish Sauce
Soy Dipping Sauce
Cold Hot Tomato Sauce
Carrot Cake

### SIX SERVINGS

There are times when the urge to entertain washes over us at the most inopportune moments. An old friend arrives in town at the very moment we're racing to meet a deadline. Someone has a birthday and we're repainting the house. You know how it goes. Sometimes parties just can't wait. When this happens we often serve what we call "The Great American Melting Pot," a dish for which our only responsibilities are purchasing and arranging the food and making a few simple sauces. The guests do the cooking.

This is a most cooperative and flexible dish and can be cooked in a fondue pot, electric wok, Mongolian Hot Pot, or casserole set over a portable burner. Since the whole thing is a moveable feast, it can be served in the kitchen, dining room, or in front of a roaring fire. We often take along the ingredients on ski weekends. It's a good way to get invited back.

The Deep-Fried Cheese is fine for nibbling with apéritifs or cocktails and the dessert is a luscious down-home carrot cake. The eclectic nature of this menu demands a beverage that will complement a variety of flavors. Although some might be tempted—and correctly so—to wash all this down with steins of chilled lager, we also like a dry Sauvignon Blanc, such as a Sancerre or a California Fumé Blanc.

# Deep-Fried Cheese

*2 eggs*
*1 cup fine dry bread crumbs*
*¾ pound or about 3 cups Swiss or*
  *Gruyère cheese, cut into 1-inch cubes*
*Oil for deep frying*

In a small bowl beat the eggs with 2 tablespoons of the bread crumbs. Place the remaining crumbs in a small bowl.

Dip the cheese cubes into the egg mixture, then into the bread crumbs to coat well. Pour a 2-inch depth of oil in a small skillet and heat to 380 degrees F.

Fry cheese cubes, a few at a time, for 1 minute or until crisp and golden. Remove with a slotted spoon and drain well on paper towels. Serve immediately with cocktail picks for spearing.

# The Great American Melting Pot

*6 cups boiling chicken broth (see p. 220)*
*Choose from the following list one or two meat or fish selections and several vegetables:*
*¾ pound asparagus, trimmed and cut in 2-inch lengths*
*¾ pound broccoli flowerets*
*¾ pound cauliflower flowerets*
*¾ pound flank steak, cut across the grain in paper-thin slices*
*2 chicken breasts, skinned, boned, and cut in strips*

*1 pound medium shrimp, shelled, deveined, and split lengthwise*
*¾ pound scallops, rinsed (if large, cut in half)*
*1½ cups whole small oysters*
*2 onions, thinly sliced*
*½ pound stemmed spinach leaves*
*18 large mushrooms, thickly sliced*
*½ pound Chinese pea pods*

*1 cup cooked rice or ½ pound cooked broken vermicelli*

Blanch asparagus, broccoli, and cauliflower in rapidly boiling salted water for 5 minutes. Drain and rinse in cold water. Drain again.

Arrange the meats and vegetables you have chosen on a large platter. Set up your cooking equipment and add the hot broth to the pot over the portable fire as your guests gather to eat. Using fondue forks or long picks, each guest will select from the tray a bit of meat, fish, or vegetable and hold it in the broth until cooked to his or her liking. The cooked morsel is then dipped in one of the sauces.

After the meat and vegetables have been eaten, add rice or noodles to the richly flavored broth which guests can calmly sip from cups or bowls.

# Green Peppercorn Herb Sauce

1 cup sour cream
¼ cup plain yogurt
2 tablespoons white wine
1 tablespoon chopped chives

1 tablespoon green peppercorns, rinsed
  and crushed
1¹/₂ teaspoons Dijon mustard
Salt to taste

Mix together all ingredients and chill.

# Sesame Yogurt Sauce

½ cup tahini (sesame seed paste)
½ cup plain yogurt
¼ cup fresh lemon juice

1 tablespoon Dijon mustard
⅔ cup feta cheese
¼ cup water (approximately)

Mix together all ingredients, adding enough water to make the mixture creamy.

# Horseradish Sauce

¼ cup grated fresh horseradish
1 teaspoon sugar
Pinch salt

1 cup mayonnaise
½ cup heavy cream, softly whipped

Mix together the horseradish, sugar, salt, and mayonnaise and then gently fold in the lightly whipped cream. Chill.

# Soy Dipping Sauce

¼ cup lemon juice
¼ cup soy sauce
¼ cup dry Sherry

Pinch sugar
½ teaspoon grated fresh ginger
2 green onions, minced

Combine all ingredients and let stand for an hour before serving.

# Cold Hot Tomato Sauce

4 tomatoes, peeled, seeded, and chopped
1 onion, minced
2 cloves garlic, minced
2 tablespoons red wine vinegar
1 teaspoon coriander

1 teaspoon oregano
2 tablespoons chopped green chilies or
  more to taste
Salt to taste

Place all ingredients except about 2 tablespoons of the chopped tomatoes in the container of a blender or food processor. Purée and stir in remaining tomatoes. Chill.

# Carrot Cake

2 cups flour
2 cups sugar
1 teaspoon salt
2 teaspoons baking soda
2 teaspoons cinnamon

1½ cups cooking oil
4 eggs, beaten
3 cups shredded carrots
1 cup chopped walnuts

*Preheat oven to 350 degrees F.* Sift dry ingredients together. Add oil, eggs, carrots, and nuts. Pour batter into a well-greased 9½×5½×3-inch loaf pan and bake for about 65 minutes or until center is done. Cool, then divide cake into 3 layers for frosting.

**FROSTING**
1 package (8 ounces) softened cream
    cheese
¼ cup butter, softened
3½ cups confectioners' sugar

2 teaspoons vanilla
**GARNISH**
Walnut halves
Oranges

Blend together cream cheese and butter and beat until fluffy. Beat in sugar and vanilla. Spread between layers and on top of carrot cake. Garnish with walnut halves and orange slices.

# PLAN OF ATTACK

## Cook Number One

**ahead of time**
Cut cheese into cubes.
**1 hour before**
Make sauces.
**15 minutes before the cocktail hour**
Dip cheese cubes in egg-and-bread-crumb mixture. Place on cake racks until ready to cook.
**just before the cocktail hour**
Deep-fry cheese cubes and serve with drinks.

## Cook Number Two

**ahead of time**
Make carrot cake (this freezes well so we try to keep one on hand for just this sort of emergency).
**1 hour before**
1. Blanch vegetables. 2. Arrange platter of meat, fish, and vegetables. 3. Chill beer or wine.
**just before**
Heat broth for Melting Pot.

# Season's Eatings

## MENU

*Mushroom-Hazelnut Tarts*
*Grape-Stuffed Rock Cornish Game Hens with Orange Butter*
*Sweet-Potato Bouchons*
*Broccoli Medallions with Peas*
*Apple-Cranberry Charlotte*

**SIX SERVINGS**

Holiday gatherings at our house inevitably go hand in hand with the collapse of some essential piece of kitchen equipment. One year when our table groaned under the makings of dinner for twenty, the garbage disposal ground to a halt while attempting to chew up the peelings of about a bushel of potatoes. Another memorable season saw us carting dishes to the neighbors' house after the dishwasher sighed its last and took with it the majority of the kitchen plumbing.

Yet even with the certain knowledge that for us Thanksgiving and Christmas mean burst pipes and balky appliances, we always wind up hosting at least one party between the end of November and the beginning of the new year. The menu we present here works well for either Christmas or Thanksgiving and can be considered an all-purpose holiday spread.

We begin our slightly unconventional bill of fare with fresh mushrooms cooked in tarragon-flavored cream, which is reduced to a satiny sauce and studded with toasted hazelnuts. This is served either in tart shells of your own making or in commercially prepared puff pastry patty shells.

Rock Cornish game hens are perfect for individual portions, but since we sometimes find the meat a little dry, we insert orange-and-ginger-flavored butter between the skin and meat of the breasts to keep them moist. Crisp sweet-potato bouchons and a vivid green broccoli stem and fresh pea combination are the accompaniments. For dessert we suggest a charlotte of apples and cranberries to take advantage of two of the best products of the season.

A good wine selection with this menu would be a fruity white like a Johannisberg Riesling or, if you prefer a slightly sweeter, softer wine, a Chenin Blanc.

# Mushroom-Hazelnut Tarts

¾ cup chopped hazelnuts
36 mushrooms
1½ cups heavy cream
1 teaspoon tarragon
Salt and pepper
6 small brioche tins or tart molds lined
   with pastry (see p. 231), or 6 pre-baked
   puff pastry shells

**GARNISH**
Cherry tomatoes
Parsley

Preheat oven to 350 degrees F. Place hazelnuts on baking sheet and toast in the oven for 15 to 20 minutes. Clean and slice mushrooms. Place in a skillet with the cream and tarragon. Cook over medium-high heat until the cream is reduced to form a thick, syrupy sauce. Stir in the nuts and season to taste with salt and pepper. Remove the pastry shells from molds and spoon in the mushroom mixture. Garnish with thin slices of cherry tomato and sprigs of parsley.

# Grape-Stuffed Rock Cornish Game Hens
## with Orange Butter

6 Rock Cornish game hens
6 tablespoons butter
3 tablespoons finely grated orange rind
1 tablespoon minced fresh ginger
1 tablespoon minced shallots
**DRESSING**
6 slices day-old firm white bread
1 onion, chopped

6 tablespoons butter
¼ cup minced parsley
1 teaspoon thyme
1½ cups seedless red or black grapes
Salt and pepper
**BASTING SAUCE**
¼ cup melted butter
2 tablespoons soy sauce

Rinse and dry the game hens. Loosen the breast skin of the birds by slipping your fingers between the skin and flesh, being careful not to pierce the skin. Mix together the butter, orange rind, ginger, and shallots. Insert equal amounts of the mixture between the skin and breast of each bird, pushing into all areas and patting the skin to smooth into a uniform layer.

Remove the crusts and crumble or cut the bread into tiny cubes. Sauté the onion in butter until golden. Add the bread, parsley, and thyme and toss until well mixed. Stir in the grapes and season to taste with salt and pepper.

Preheat the oven to 425 degrees F. Stuff the cavities of the birds with the bread mixture and truss. Mix together the melted butter and soy sauce and paint the hens with the mixture. Arrange on their sides in a rack in a roasting pan. Roast in the lower third of the oven for 10 minutes. Turn to the other side and roast another 10 minutes. *Reduce heat to 375 degrees F.,* turn breast up and continue roasting for another 40 minutes, or until hens are done.

## Sweet-Potato Bouchons

| | |
|---|---|
| 2 white potatoes | Nutmeg |
| 2 sweet potatoes | Flour |
| 6 tablespoons butter | 2 eggs, beaten |
| 3 egg yolks | Bread crumbs |
| Salt and pepper | Oil for deep frying |

Peel potatoes and boil until tender in salted water. Drain and mash together with the butter, egg yolks, salt and pepper to taste, and a dash of nutmeg (you may have to adjust the number of yolks according to the size of your potatoes). Spread the mixture 1 inch thick in a buttered shallow dish. Cover with plastic wrap and chill. Just before serving, form the potato mixture into cylindrical shapes about 2 inches long and 1 inch in diameter. Dust them with flour and then dip in beaten egg and roll in bread crumbs. Deep-fry in hot oil (375 degrees F.) for 2 to 3 minutes, or until golden. Drain and serve at once.

## Broccoli Medallions with Peas

Most people just lop off broccoli stems and consign them to the garbage. That's a big mistake. The stems have wonderful crunchy texture and lovely flavor. Save the broccoli flowerets for another night.

| | |
|---|---|
| 3 cups broccoli stems | ¼ cup water |
| 3 tablespoons butter | Salt and pepper |
| 4 green onions, sliced, including some of the green tops | ½ teaspoon lemon juice |
| | 2 teaspoons minced parsley |
| ½ cup tiny fresh or frozen peas | Salt and pepper |

Cut broccoli stems into ¼-inch slices. Heat butter in a skillet and add the broccoli, onions, peas, water, and salt and pepper. Cover and cook about 5 minutes or until vegetables are just tender. Stir in the lemon juice and chopped parsley. Season to taste with salt and pepper.

# Apple-Cranberry Charlotte

¾ cup butter, melted
8–12 slices firm white home-style bread
3 cups whole raw cranberries, washed and
    chopped
¾ cup water
1 cup sugar
3 tablespoons flour
½ teaspoon salt
2 tablespoons butter

¾ cup chopped walnuts
¼ cup butter
3 large tart apples, peeled, cored, and
    sliced
3 tablespoons dark rum
1 tablespoon lemon juice
**GARNISH**
Whipped cream or vanilla ice cream

Melt ¾ cup butter. Trim crusts and cut bread into shapes to fit in the bottom and sides of an 8-cup charlotte mold or soufflé dish. Dip both sides of bread in melted butter and arrange in dish.

Place cranberries and water in a saucepan and simmer 5 minutes. Stir together the sugar, flour, and salt and gradually stir into the cranberry mixture. Cook over low heat, stirring constantly, until thickened. Stir in 2 tablespoons butter and walnuts. Cool.

Heat ¼ cup butter in a skillet. Add apple slices, rum, and lemon juice and sauté until juices are absorbed and apples are beginning to brown. Cool.

*Preheat oven to 350 degrees F.* Place a layer of apples in the bread-lined soufflé dish. Place the cranberry mixture on top of the apples and cover with remaining apples. Cover with foil and bake for 1 hour.

Serve at room temperature or reheat. Turn out of dish, if you wish, and top with whipped cream or vanilla ice cream.

# PLAN OF ATTACK

## Cook Number One

**ahead of time**
Make sweet-potato mixture; spread in baking dish and chill.
**2 hours before**
Shape bouchons, dip in flour, eggs, and crumbs. Refrigerate.

## Cook Number Two

**ahead of time**
Make tart shells for Mushroom-Hazelnut Tarts.
**2 hours before**
Stuff and truss Rock Cornish game hens.

## Cook Number One

*1¹/₂–2 hours before*
1. Make Apple-Cranberry Charlotte; bake and cool.
*¹/₂ hour before*
Chill wine.
*after first course*
Deep-fry Sweet-Potato Bouchons.

## Cook Number Two

*1 hour before*
Put hens in to roast at 425 degrees F.
*50 minutes before*
1. Turn hens to the other side. 2. Clean and cut broccoli stems, cut up green onions and mince parsley for vegetable dish.
*40 minutes before*
Reduce heat to 375 degrees F. for hens and continue cooking.
*¹/₂ hour before*
Cut mushrooms for tart filling.
*15 minutes before*
Make mushroom tart filling.
*just before*
Fill tarts and serve.
*after first course*
Make Broccoli Medallions with Peas.

# BLITHE SPIRITS

## *The Cocktail Party*

The cocktail party of our fantasies has a cast of fascinating, witty people gathered in a penthouse high above some great city's glittering skyline. Everyone is sipping very dry martinis and in one corner Cole Porter noodles a few tunes on a white baby grand. When he tires, Noel Coward moves in to take a turn.

The cocktail parties of our experience, on the other hand, are peopled largely by guests who pass the time knocking back scotch on the rocks and guessing our astrological signs or sipping Perrier and comparing the tread on their running shoes.

It seems clear that the cocktail party has fallen on hard times. It's not that the idea isn't sound. Gathering together a group of convivial people to lift a glass is a gracious gesture. But the occasion has been tarnished by its predictability, its aura of forced gaiety, and a flood of clam dip.

It may not be too late to resuscitate this hallowed pastime. We've found that people often perk up when they find that you haven't used the occasion to tidy up your social obligations for the past year (when, that is, there are fewer than three hundred people in a studio apartment) and that there's plenty to eat as well as sip.

While it's true that white wine has become the fashionable drink, it's still important to have a well-stocked bar on these occasions and someone with at least a nodding acquaintance with the more common mixed drinks. One cannot be expected to please the bizarre or exotic tastes of every guest, however. There was, for example, a pressman for the San Francisco *Examiner* who ritually entered a legendary bar called Jerry & Johnny's at six o'clock every morning and announced in thunderous tones, "I shall have a Pousse-Café." The bartender then poured him a water tumbler full of Muscatel.

Although the white wine and mineral water stampede has simplified life for the home bartender, the making of mixed drinks still is a skill worth perfecting. and in some quarters the martini is the standard by which all bartenders are judged, although agreement on the precise formula is hard to come by. Alexis Lichine says the formula is simply four parts gin to one part dry French Vermouth. Food and wine authority Roy Andries de Groot boasts of having had great success with something made of four ounces of Russian vodka, four or five drops of dry Vermouth, a drop of lemon oil, and just a dash of ice-cold Holland gin, garnished with a Tuscan red pepper. British author Alec Waugh says the best martini he ever drank was served to him at a tea shop in Tangier. Sir Winston Churchill, by his own account, made martinis by pouring gin into a pitcher and glancing briefly at a bottle of Vermouth across the room.

Jeff has quite definite ideas about the creation of this drink. His ideal martini is made as follows: three parts London-style gin and one part dry Vermouth stirred together in a Mason jar ("The tendency toward drier and drier martinis probably has contributed as much as anything to their dwindling popularity," he grouches). The exact amounts will depend on the company, but nine ounces of gin and three ounces of Vermouth will make four martinis. Close the jar with a tight-fitting lid and put it in the freezer about two hours before pouring time, along with as many long-stemmed cocktail glasses as you will have drinkers. When the magic moment comes, pour the liquid, which by now will have the specific gravity of glycerin, into the chilled glasses. Twist a lemon peel over the surface of each drink to extract the oil and rub the zest around the rim of each glass. If you must, drop the peels in for decoration. If you have any green olives, pickled onions, or tiny preserved tomatoes on hand, put them in a salad.

(NOTE: All hysterical mail on this subject should be addressed to Jeff. Jinx fancies an olive now and then and will defend to the death her right to do so.)

Of course, the martini is only one of the mixed drinks that might be requested if you allow the subject to come up. You can make things easier on yourself by limiting your provisions to wine and a selection of apéritifs such as Sherry, Vermouth, Byrrh, and Dubonnet.

Planning is essential for one of these bashes. A successful party means having plenty of everything: liquor, wine, food, glasses, napkins, ashtrays, and ice. Try to place the food as far from the bar as possible to avoid traffic jams, and put out lots of little nibbles like nuts, pumpkinseeds, cheeses, olives, and other goodies to augment the more substantial offerings. And don't make more hot appetizers than your oven or ovens can accommodate.

Food can make the ritual of the cocktail party not only bearable, but even memorable. Here is a selection of some of our favorite party fare. Choose a few that you like and make lots.

# MENU

---

*Cornucopia with Crab-Filled Puffs*
*Mushroom Duxelles in Toast Cups*
*Tiny Cheeseburgers on Sourdough Biscuits*
*Curry Turnovers*
*Chinese Barbecued Pork*
*Sausage Rolls*
*Crudités with Two Dips*

---

## Cornucopia with Crab-Filled Puffs

This is particularly appropriate for holiday get-togethers. We often use it as the centerpiece for a Christmas or New Year's party table.

**CORNUCOPIA**
*1 package (17¹/₂ ounces) prepared puff pastry*

*1 egg, beaten*
*Coarse salt*

One of the convenience foods that we find very useful is the prepared puff pastry made by the Pepperidge Farm people. We usually keep a box in the freezer. The pastry makes it convenient to add handsome top crusts to pot pies or soups and to make bottom crusts for tarts and quiches. For the cornucopia, thaw the puff pastry at room temperature for about half an hour. Meanwhile cut two 18-inch squares of heavy-duty aluminum foil. Fold each in half diagonally and then roll into a cone. Put one cone inside the other so the front edges are even. Twist and bend the opposite end up to resemble a cornucopia. Place a folded strip of foil around the open edge to form a collar. Fasten with a paper clip.

Place the thawed puff pastry on a lightly floured surface. Roll each sheet into a rectangle roughly 12 by 18 inches. Cut into 1½-inch strips. Starting at the tip of the foil cornucopia form, wind the strips one at a time around the form. Use a bit of beaten egg where necessary to secure the strips, but place the side of the strip without egg next to the foil. Be sure to overlap the pastry strips at least ¼ inch, as the pastry will shrink as it bakes. Place on a baking sheet, sprinkle with coarse salt, and bake in a preheated 425-degree F. oven for 25 minutes or until golden brown. Remove from the oven and cool on a rack. When cool, carefully remove the foil form. Don't worry if all the foil can't be removed, since the cornucopia won't be eaten and the foil won't show.

### PUFFS

| | |
|---|---|
| 1 cup water | 1 teaspoon dry mustard |
| ½ cup butter | 4 eggs |
| 1 cup sifted flour | ⅛ teaspoon Tabasco sauce |
| 1 teaspoon salt | 1 cup grated Swiss or Gruyère cheese |

*Preheat oven to 400 degrees F.* Bring the water and butter to a rolling boil in a large saucepan. Mix together the flour, salt, and mustard and add all at once to the boiling water. Stir with a wooden spoon until the mixture forms a thick, smooth ball and leaves the sides of the pan. Cool slightly.

Add the eggs, one at a time, beating well after each addition until the paste is shiny-smooth. Stir in the Tabasco and cheese. Use a pastry bag to make small mounds of the dough (about 1 teaspoonful) on greased cookie sheets.

Bake 25 minutes or until puffed and golden. Cool completely before filling. These may be frozen in a single layer on cookie sheets and then placed in plastic bags for future use.

### FILLING

| | |
|---|---|
| 8 ounces cream cheese, softened | 1½ cups flaked crab meat |
| ¼ cup heavy cream | 1½ teaspoons dill |
| 2 tablespoons Cognac | 1 tablespoon minced chives |
| 3 teaspoons lemon juice | Salt |

Beat together the cream cheese, cream, Cognac, and lemon juice until fluffy. Fold in crab, dill, and chives. Season to taste with salt. Fill the puffs by cutting in half horizontally and putting in a small amount of filling. Replace tops. This filling also could be used in hollowed-out cherry tomatoes for a colorful one-bite delight.

# Mushroom Duxelles in Toast Cups

### MAKES 24

**MUSHROOM FILLING**
½ pound mushrooms, minced
¼ cup finely minced green onions and
   tops
¼ cup butter
¼ teaspoon salt
¼ teaspoon pepper

¼ teaspoon oregano
½ teaspoon lemon juice
2 tablespoons flour
1 cup heavy cream
2 tablespoons minced parsley
1 tablespoon minced chives
3–4 drops Tabasco sauce

Place mushrooms in a clean dishtowel. Wrap the towel around them and wring out moisture.

Sauté the onions in butter for 3 minutes, add the mushrooms, seasonings, and lemon juice and cook, stirring often, until the moisture is almost evaporated. Sprinkle on the flour and cook, stirring, for another 3 minutes. Gradually whisk in the cream and cook, stirring, until sauce is thickened. Add the parsley, chives, and Tabasco. Adjust seasoning and cool. (Frozen in small containers, this filling will keep as long as a month.) Yield: 1½ cups.

**TOAST CUPS**
12 thin slices home-style white bread (Pepperidge Farm, for example)
½ cup butter, melted

*Preheat oven to 375 degrees F.* Remove the crusts and roll each slice of bread between pieces of waxed paper to flatten. Using a round cookie or biscuit cutter slightly larger than the cups of the smallest available muffin tin, cut two rounds from each slice of bread. Dip each round in the butter and press evenly into muffin tins. Place in oven and bake 20–30 minutes, or until the bread is toasted and a deep golden brown. Remove from oven and let stand about five minutes before unmolding the toast cups. Cool to room temperature and then fill with 1 tablespoon fresh or thawed duxelles mixture. Refrigerate. Just before serving, bring to room temperature and bake in a 375-degree F. oven for several minutes or until heated through. These cups can be made in standard-size muffin tins (see p. 000) and filled with scrambled eggs, creamed sweetbreads, or whatever your heart desires.

# Tiny Cheeseburgers on Sourdough Biscuits

Dipping the biscuits in the warm bacon fat before baking is the secret to their crisp, savory nature. If you can't bring yourself to use bacon grease, butter will do, but the result may not be plucked from the platter quite as quickly as these.

## SOURDOUGH BISCUITS

½ cup sourdough starter (see below)  ¾ teaspoon salt
1 cup milk  1 teaspoon baking powder
2½ cups unsifted flour  ½ teaspoon soda
1 tablespoon sugar  Bacon fat

Mix together the starter, milk, and 1 cup of the flour in large bowl to make the sponge. Allow to stand for several hours or overnight.

Sift together the remaining flour, the sugar, salt, baking powder, and soda and stir into the sponge. Knead the mixture in the bowl until the ingredients are well blended. Turn the dough onto a well-floured board and pat out to a thickness of ½ inch. Cut out biscuits with a small cutter and dip each biscuit in warm bacon grease.

Place close together in a baking pan and allow to rise in a warm place for about half an hour. *Preheat oven to 375 degrees F.* and bake for 30 to 35 minutes.


## CHEESEBURGER MIXTURE

1 pound ground beef  1 small onion, minced
1 cup grated Tillamook or other sharp  1 teaspoon Worcestershire sauce
   Cheddar cheese  ½ cup ketchup
1 teaspoon salt

*Preheat oven to 425 degrees F.* Mix together all of the ingredients. Cut sourdough biscuits in half and spread each half with some of the mixture. Bake open-face cheeseburgers about 15 minutes or until hamburger is cooked to your liking.


## SOURDOUGH STARTER

Commercial sourdough starter is available in many markets and gourmet shops across the country and it's great fun to work with. If you want to make your own, however, boil about four peeled potatoes in 1 quart of water until they're soft but not mushy. Drain and save the potato water. Thoroughly mix two cups of lukewarm potato water with about two cups of unsifted flour, a tablespoon of sugar, and a teaspoon of salt. Put the batter in a crock or a jar and leave it loosely covered in a warm place for three or four days. By then it should be bubbling merrily from the fermentation of wild yeast. If it doesn't work, throw the whole mess out and start over, adding a teaspoonful of active dry yeast and a few drops of vinegar at the beginning to make up for the obvious lack of cooperative wild spores in the air. Be sure the liquid is not over 130 degrees F. when mixed with the flour, or some of the yeast will die.

Once your starter is going, it can be kept refrigerated indefinitely as long as you replenish the amount you use each time with equal amounts of flour and water. The ½ cup of starter used in this recipe should be replaced by ¼ cup flour and ¼ cup water, which will begin to ferment and freshen the established starter.

# Chinese Barbecued Pork

This is available already prepared in most Chinese markets, but making your own is a snap.

2 pounds boneless pork butt or tenderloin
2 cloves garlic, pressed
2 teaspoons sugar
1 teaspoon salt
2 tablespoons dry Sherry

¼ cup soy sauce
2 tablespoons honey
½ teaspoon Chinese 5-spice seasoning or allspice
½ teaspoon red food coloring (optional)

If using pork butt, cut into strips 2 inches wide, 2 inches thick, and 5 inches long. These are approximate dimensions—all the strips won't be the same size. Mix together the remaining ingredients and marinate the pork for 2 hours, turning frequently. Drain, reserving marinade. *Preheat oven to 425 degrees F.* Place pork strips on a rack over a shallow roasting pan containing some water. Roast 10 minutes. Lower heat to 325 degrees F. and roast for 1 hour. Baste strips occasionally with marinade during cooking. Cool.

Slice very thin and serve with a dipping sauce of ½ cup soy sauce blended with 1 teaspoon prepared hot mustard. Don't forget the napkins!

# Curry Turnovers

2 tablespoons oil
1 onion, chopped
1 clove garlic, minced
1½ teaspoons minced fresh ginger
2–3 teaspoons curry powder
¼ teaspoon ground turmeric

½ pound ground veal
1 teaspoon salt
1 package (10 ounces) frozen patty shells, thawed, or 2 sheets (17¼ ounces) frozen prepared puff pastry, thawed

Heat oil in skillet. Add onion, garlic, ginger, curry, and turmeric. Sauté over medium heat until onions are transparent. Add veal and salt. Cook, stirring to break up veal, for about 15 minutes or until meat is done. Cool.

If using prepared patty shell dough, overlap and press edges together before rolling to piecrust thickness. Prepared puff pastry sheets should be rolled to the same thickness. Cut into 3-inch circles and place a generous teaspoon of cooled filling in center of each. Fold over, moisten edges with water and press with a fork to seal.

*Preheat oven to 400 degrees F.* Place turnovers on a cookie sheet, prick tops with a fork, and bake about 20 minutes or until puffed and golden. Curry turnovers can be made ahead and frozen. Defrost before baking. Makes about 2½ dozen.

# Sausage Rolls

In this very simple recipe, it is important to use a thin French-style baguette, not the larger loaf of French bread.

*Baguettes of French bread*
*Kielbasa or other fully cooked smoked sau-*
  *sage, the links totaling the length of the*
  *bread*

*Preheat oven to 375 degrees F.* Cut the baguettes in half crosswise. Using the handle of a wooden spoon, bore a tunnel through each half to the ends. Stuff the sausage into the bread as far as it will go and trim the ends of the bread.

Wrap the half loaves individually in heavy foil and bake them for 15 minutes. Unwrap and slice. Serve with mustard.

(NOTE   These loaves freeze well after they're wrapped in foil. To serve from the freezer, bake 25–30 minutes.)

# Crudités with Two Dips

A display of crisp fresh vegetables can be the centerpiece of your party table. Try to find some unusual varieties such as jicama, Chinese long beans, baby artichokes (cook these and chill), sugar snap peas, or Belgian carrots as well as zucchini, asparagus, broccoli, cauliflower, cherry tomatoes, fresh mushrooms, and other reliables. Arrange them beautifully in a basket and add some prosciutto-wrapped breadsticks and two excellent dips.

**GREEN HERB DIP**

*½ cup watercress leaves, pressed down in cup*
*½ cup parsley sprigs, pressed down in cup*
*1 shallot, sliced*
*1½ teaspoons fresh or ½ teaspoon dried tarragon*
*1½ teaspoons fresh or ½ teaspoon dried thyme*
*½ teaspoon salt*
*¾ teaspoon dry mustard*
*2 tablespoons white wine vinegar*
*1 egg*
*1 cup oil*

Place all of the ingredients except the oil in the container of a blender. Whirl until liquefied. With the motor still running, remove the top and slowly add the oil, pouring it in a thin stream, until the mixture has thickened. Then add remaining oil at a faster pace until it is all incorporated.

**BAGNA CAUDA**

*1½ cups heavy cream*
*2 tablespoons butter*
*1 tablespoon olive oil*
*3 large cloves garlic, minced (or more to taste)*
*8 anchovy fillets, drained and minced*
*Black pepper*

Reduce the cream by one third over high heat. Heat the butter and oil in a saucepan and sauté the garlic until golden. Add the anchovy fillets to the pan and then the cream, in a slow stream. Add freshly ground black pepper to taste and serve hot.

# HOUSE PARTY WEEKEND FOR SIX

The only reason we can think of for having a weekend house party is to provide a suitable location for Hercule Poirot or Miss Marple to ply their trade. Anyone who has done hosting duty on one of these occasions is not surprised that they are such a popular setting for fictional poisonings, bludgeonings, and other assorted mayhem. The wonder is that it doesn't happen more often in real life.

And yet it all seemed easy enough two weeks ago when you invited friends to your country place, or the beach house, cabin, or boat for the weekend.

"It'll be very casual," you said, the words springing from your lips with careless abandon.

But as the date grows near, you know that entertaining even the most undemanding guests places a certain burden on those who must organize and prepare the meals. This is one of the many times when two cooks is none too many.

There are a few guidelines that can help ease your way through a successful house party weekend. These menu plans work just as well if you happen to have parents or friends spending a three-day furlough with you in your city apartment or suburban ranch house. (Despite rumors to the contrary, we know that not everyone scurries off to the Hamptons every Friday afternoon, and that includes us.)

The first thing you should do is consult the recipes well in advance and note down all the ingredients you'll need, even the most obvious. Without your list you may find yourself up a creek minus the salt and pepper. Measure as many ingredients ahead of time as possible. Put them into plastic bags or small jars, label according to when each will be used (Saturday lunch, Sunday brunch, etc.) and bag or box together with other items for that menu.

You'll also be well ahead of the game if you prepare as much food as possible in advance. Friday's main course, a glistening cold chicken dish from South America called *Escabeche*, should be made the day before to allow the flavors to reach their full potential. With this you can serve marinated tomatoes and onions, again prepared ahead and carried from home. The one hot dish, a heavenly corn purée called *Humitas*, can be made easily once you've reached your destination. If you pass a vegetable stand on the way and can pick up some corn fresh from the field, so much the better. If not, you may find it more convenient to cut the corn from the cobs at home and transport the kernels in a plastic bag. Beer or a jug of sturdy white wine would be a fine companion for this simple meal.

Dipping the dessert strawberries in fondant is so pleasant an occupation that you may feel free to foist this step on one of your guests.

Breakfast, with the exception of a lavish Sunday brunch, is a matter best left to each individual. Since people tend to rise at odd hours when stripped of their alarm clocks, on Saturday you need provide only a pot of coffee, some fruit or juice, and a selection of crusty rolls, flaky croissants, or something in the sticky Danish department.

Double-duty dishes are dear to the hearts of weekend cooks, and one you might consider is Honey Nut Cake: serve it spread with cream cheese and preserves for breakfast and bring it back for a reprise as Saturday night's dessert.

Lunch on Saturday provides an opportunity to use local seafood if you happen to be stopping by the shore. If not, whatever is fresh in the market will suffice. The soup, which needs no cooking, can be made in the cool unhurried minutes of the morning and left to chill until noon. The accompanying bread, oozing with melted cheese and drenched in herb-flavored butter, can be assembled at home and buttered just before it is heated. Open a chilled bottle of Gewürztraminer for the occasion. Dessert is fresh fruit and brownies.

Seasoned ground lamb and eggplant chunks alternate on skewers for Saturday night dinner. It's a dish that's easy to put together, and if done on an outdoor grill, guests can cook their own. Pita bread makes a convenient pastry pocket to hold the lamb. The *tabbouleh* can be made anytime during the day. Either a fresh-flavored Beaujolais or California Gamay would be a good wine choice.

Sunday morning brunch probably is the last meal you'll serve on a getaway weekend. An out-of-the-ordinary eye-opener starts brunch on the proper note. You can follow this with a pretty melon presentation and then a lavish French toast dish designed to use up most of the bread, milk, cream, and eggs you have left. In fact, if you've planned things well, there should be next to nothing to pack for the return trip.

So you see, it isn't any harder to plan for a house party than it was to organize, say, the flight of the space shuttle.

# *Friday Dinner*

*Escabeche*
*Humitas*
*Marinated Tomatoes and Onions*
*Strawberries in Fondant Chemises*

## *Escabeche*

2 chickens (each 3 pounds), cut into serving pieces
½ cup olive oil
2 cups dry white wine
2 cups cider vinegar
2 cups hot water
6 carrots, sliced diagonally ⅛ inch thick
4 medium onions, cut into eighths

4 celery stalks, sliced
2 small leeks (including some of the green
   tops), sliced
Bouquet garni (4 parsley sprigs, 1 bay
   leaf, 2–3 whole cloves, and ½ teaspoon
   thyme)
GARNISH
2 lemons, thinly sliced

Pat chicken dry with paper towels. Heat oil in heavy 6–8 quart Dutch oven or stockpot. Add chicken in batches and brown well on all sides. Pour off fat and return chicken to pot. Add remaining ingredients except lemons and bring to a boil over high heat. Reduce heat to medium low, cover and simmer gently until chicken is tender, about 30 to 35 minutes. Remove from heat and let chicken cool to room temperature in stock.

    Discard bouquet garni. Remove skin and bones from chicken and cut meat into finger-size pieces. Remove vegetables. Cool broth; discard fat and strain broth through cheesecloth. Pour small amount of broth into large, deep serving bowl (glass is very pretty for this). Arrange chicken in spoke pattern in the bottom. Top with carrot slices in overlapping pattern. Distribute onion wedges, leeks, and celery around outer edge. Pour remaining broth evenly over vegetables. Refrigerate until set. Just before serving, twist lemon slices and place around outer edge.

# Humitas

(Because of the rather liquid consistency of the Humitas, you may want to serve it in small bowls.) See p. 252.

6 cups fresh corn kernels (about 12 to 16 ears) or 6 cups frozen corn, thawed
½ cup milk
3 eggs
2 teaspoons paprika
Salt and freshly ground pepper
⅓ cup butter

6 green onions, chopped
⅓ cup chopped green pepper
⅔ cup freshly grated Parmesan cheese
GARNISH
Red pepper rings
Parsley

Combine corn and milk in food processor or blender in batches and mix 30 seconds, or purée through food mill set over a bowl. Add eggs, paprika, salt and pepper to taste and mix until smooth.

Melt butter in a large skillet over medium heat. Add onion and green pepper and sauté until soft but not brown. Add corn mixture and blend well. Reduce heat and simmer uncovered, stirring frequently, until thickened, about 5 to 10 minutes. Stir in cheese. Pour into large serving bowl or soup tureen, garnish with pepper rings and parsley.

# Marinated Tomatoes and Onions

This dish can be prepared early in the day, transported to your getaway site, and chilled again before serving.

½ cup red wine vinegar
⅓ cup olive oil
3 tablespoons chopped fresh basil or 1 tablespoon dried
1 tablespoon chopped fresh tarragon or 1 teaspoon dried

1 tablespoon chopped fresh oregano or 1 teaspoon dried
6 large tomatoes, peeled and thinly sliced
2 medium red onions, thinly sliced
1 tablespoon sugar
Salt and freshly ground pepper

Combine first 5 ingredients in a small bowl and whisk until well blended. Layer half of tomatoes in a large serving bowl and cover with half of the onions. Sprinkle with half of the sugar, and salt and pepper to taste. Drizzle with some of the marinade. Repeat with remaining ingredients. Cover and chill before serving.

# Strawberries in Fondant Chemises

If the weather is cool, berries can be dipped in advance and taken to your week-end retreat in empty egg cartons.

*2 pints large strawberries, preferably with stems*
*3 ounces cream cheese, softened*
*3 cups powdered sugar*

*2 egg yolks*
*2 tablespoons kirsch*
*Heavy cream (optional)*

Wash strawberries and dry on paper towels. Beat cream cheese until light and fluffy. Add sugar, egg yolks, and kirsch and continue beating until fondant has reached dipping consistency. Add cream if mixture seems too thick. Dip each berry halfway in fondant and place on baking sheet or waxed paper in cool area until firm.

# PLAN OF ATTACK FOR FRIDAY DINNER

## Cook Number One

*ahead of time*
Make Escabeche.
***15 minutes before***
1. Scrape kernels from ears of corn or thaw frozen corn. 2. Prepare Humitas and cook 5–10 minutes or until thick. 3. Stir in cheese and serve.

## Cook Number Two

*ahead of time*
Make marinated tomatoes and onions.
***½ hour before***
1. Make fondant and set your guests to dipping. 2. Chill wine or beer.

# *Saturday Lunch*

## MENU

*Shellfish Gazpacho*
*Spiedini*
*Fresh Fruit*
*Best-Ever Brownies*

SIX SERVINGS

## *Shellfish Gazpacho*

¼ cup French or Italian bread crumbs
4 tomatoes, peeled, seeded, and chopped
2 cucumbers, peeled and coarsely chopped
1 onion, chopped
1 green pepper, seeded and chopped
2 teaspoons minced fresh garlic
4 cups water
¼ cup wine vinegar
¼ cup olive oil
1 tablespoon tomato paste
1¹/2 pounds cleaned, cooked shellfish
   (shrimp, lobster, crab, scallops, or a
   combination), chopped or shredded
Salt and pepper

**GARNISHES**
1 cup croutons
½ cup minced onions
½ cup peeled, chopped cucumber
½ cup minced green pepper
½ cup minced fresh parsley
¼ cup chopped fresh chives

Combine first six ingredients in a large bowl and blend well. Add water and vinegar and stir thoroughly. Purée about 2 cups at a time in blender, food processor or food mill. Return to bowl and slowly whisk in oil and tomato paste. Cover and chill at least 2 hours. Just before serving, salt and pepper to taste and add shellfish. Pass garnishes in separate bowls.

# Spiedini

This is another excellent getaway dish. The butter and the loaf can be prepared ahead, ready for assembling just before broiling.

*1 cup (2 sticks) unsalted butter*
*2–3 garlic cloves, minced*
*½ cup chopped fresh basil or 4 tablespoons dried*
*2 tablespoons capers, rinsed, drained, and minced*

*Salt*
*1 baguette (12 inches long)*
*12–16 ounces Mozzarella cheese*

Cream butter in a small bowl. Blend in garlic, basil, capers, and salt. Cover and chill if not using immediately. Trim off top and side crusts of bread, leaving bottom crust intact. Slice bread almost through at about ¾-inch intervals. Cut cheese into as many slices as there are cuts in bread. Place a slice of cheese in each cut. Secure loaf with skewer if necessary. Wrap and refrigerate.

Just before serving, preheat broiler. Place loaf on piece of heavy foil and bring up edges to form a cradle, but don't cover the top of the bread. Transfer to baking sheet. Spread top and sides with butter and run under broiler until brown and bubbly.

## Best-Ever Brownies
### ABOUT 2 DOZEN

*½ cup butter at room temperature*
*1 cup sugar*
*2 eggs*
*1 teaspoon vanilla*
*¾ cup flour*
*⅓ cup unsweetened cocoa*

*½ teaspoon baking powder*
*¼ teaspoon salt*
*½ cup chopped nuts*
*Miniature marshmallows*
*Frosting*

*Preheat oven to 350 degrees F.* Generously grease a 6½×10½-inch baking pan. Cream butter and sugar in a large bowl. Beat in eggs and vanilla. Sift together flour, cocoa, baking powder and salt. Add to creamed mixture, blending thoroughly. Stir in nuts. Pour into prepared pan. Bake about 25 minutes or until brownies test done; *do not overbake.* Remove from the oven and immediately cover entire top with marshmallows. Return to oven and bake an additional 2–3 minutes. Cool completely in pan. Spread with frosting and let stand until set before cutting into squares.

**FROSTING**

*¼ cup butter at room temperature*
*¼ cup unsweetened cocoa*
*1 teaspoon vanilla*

*Pinch salt*
*2 cups confectioners' sugar*
*2 tablespoons milk*

Cream butter. Blend in cocoa, vanilla, and salt. Add sugar alternately with milk and beat until light and fluffy.

# PLAN OF ATTACK
# FOR SATURDAY LUNCH

## Cook Number One

*ahead of time*
1. Prepare vegetables for garnishes and chill.   2. Make bread crumbs for Gazpacho.   3. Make base for Gazpacho, pack in a covered jar, and refrigerate.
*½·hour before*
Chill wine.
*just before*
Finish preparing Gazpacho and serve.

## Cook Number Two

*ahead of time*
1. Make brownies and pack them up.
2. Cream butter with seasonings for Spiedini and pack in a covered jar.
3. Slice and stuff bread with cheese for Spiedini.
*just before*
1. Butter Spiedini loaf and run it under the broiler.   2. Wash and arrange fresh fruit.

# Saturday Dinner

# MENU

*Ground Lamb and Eggplant Kebabs*
*Pita Bread*
*Yogurt Relish*
*Tabbouleh*
*Honey Nut Cake*

SIX SERVINGS

# Ground Lamb and Eggplant Kebabs

Seasoned ground lamb, known as everything from *köfta* to *kuftah* in the Middle East, can be barbecued on an outdoor grill or cooked under the broiler. Either way, it's a fine aromatic filling for pita bread as well as an easy main dish to prepare after an active day—or any day.

| | |
|---|---|
| 1 1/2 pounds ground lamb | 1/4 teaspoon cayenne pepper |
| 1/2 cup minced onions | 6 slender Japanese eggplants, each about |
| 1/2 cup minced fresh parsley | 6 inches long, or 1 medium regular |
| 3 tablespoons flour | eggplant (1–1 1/2 pounds), cut |
| 3 tablespoons red wine or water | lengthwise into 6 wedges |
| 1 1/2 teaspoons salt | Olive oil |
| 1/2 teaspoon freshly ground pepper | Garlic salt |
| 1/2 teaspoon allspice | Freshly ground pepper |
| 1/4 teaspoon cinnamon | |

Prepare charcoal and generously grease grill. If broiling indoors, preheat the broiler briefly just before cooking. Grease 6 skewers. Combine first 10 ingredients and mix well. Shape into 18 meatballs. Cut each unpeeled eggplant (or eggplant wedge) into 4 equal pieces. Alternate with meatballs on skewers, pressing firmly together. Brush cut surfaces of eggplant with olive oil and sprinkle with garlic salt and pepper. Place about 4 to 6 inches above glowing coals or broil about 4 inches from the heat source about 15 to 20 minutes, turning often, or until eggplant is tender and lamb is done. Serve with pita bread.

# Yogurt Relish

The tangy zing of yogurt is perfect with lamb. Guests can spoon a bit of this sauce into their pita pockets along with the lamb and eggplant kebabs.

| | |
|---|---|
| 1 cup plain yogurt | 1/2 cup chopped onion |
| 2 cloves garlic, minced | 1 teaspoon Dijon mustard |

Combine all ingredients and mix well. Cover and chill before serving.

# Tabbouleh

A zesty salad of bulgur wheat tossed with herbs and an oil and lemon dressing is splendid with lamb cooked in any fashion, but seems especially well suited to its supporting role in this menu.

1³/₄ cups bulgur wheat
7 cups boiling water
¾ cup minced fresh parsley
⅓ cup minced fresh mint
½ cup minced green onion
1 cup peeled, seeded, and chopped
   tomatoes

⅓ cup fresh lemon juice
⅓ cup olive oil
Salt and freshly ground pepper to taste
Romaine leaves

Measure bulgur into large bowl or saucepan and add boiling water. Cover and let stand 2 to 3 hours, or until wheat has expanded and is light and fluffy. Drain off excess water. Transfer bulgur to sieve and shake until very dry. Return to bowl. Add remaining ingredients, except romaine, and mix thoroughly. Cover and chill well.

To serve, mound tabbouleh in center of a large platter and surround with greens. Romaine leaves can be used to scoop up the tabbouleh.

## Honey Nut Cake

¼ cup butter at room temperature
1 cup sugar
3 eggs
2 cups flour
2 teaspoons baking powder
1 teaspoon cinnamon
¼ teaspoon salt

¼ teaspoon cloves
¼ cup milk
2 cups ground walnuts
**GLAZE**
1 cup sugar
1 cup water
2 tablespoons honey

*Preheat oven to 350 degrees F.* Generously grease a 10-inch tube pan. Cream butter and sugar in a large bowl until light and fluffy. Add eggs one at a time, beating well after each addition. Sift together flour, baking powder, cinnamon, salt, and cloves. Using electric mixer on low speed, gradually add dry ingredients alternately with milk and beat until just blended. Stir in nuts. Spoon batter into prepared pan and bake 35 to 40 minutes, or until cake tests done.

Meanwhile, combine sugar and water and bring to a boil over medium-high heat, stirring until sugar is dissolved. Stir in honey and simmer until syrupy.

Remove cake from oven. Prick surface with a long toothpick and spoon glaze over evenly. Cool completely in the pan. Invert onto platter, then turn right side up for serving. Slice with a serrated knife.

# PLAN OF ATTACK
# FOR SATURDAY DINNER

## Cook Number One

*ahead of time*
Make tabbouleh.
*1 hour before*
Season lamb for kebabs and shape into balls.
*½ hour before*
1. Make yogurt relish.  2. Open wine.

## Cook Number Two

*ahead of time*
Make Honey Nut Cake.
*45 minutes before*
1. Start barbecue.  2. Cut eggplant, brush with oil and seasonings, and string with lamb balls on skewers.
*20 minutes before*
Put kebabs on the barbecue or under broiler.

---

# *Sunday Brunch*

---

# MENU

---

*Gerry Sturges's Washington Indiscretion*
*Melon Balls with Lime*
*French Toast with Apple Custard Sauce*
*Canadian Bacon*
*Coffee*

---

# Gerry Sturges's Washington Indiscretion

We were introduced to this lovely drink by a friend who works in the nation's capital and attributes a good bit of the funny business that goes on there to this innocent-appearing libation.

**FOR EACH DRINK**
*1 1/2 ounces fresh orange juice*
*1 1/4 ounces tequila*
*1/4 ounce coffee liqueur*
*Crushed ice*

**GARNISH**
*Orange slice*
*Fresh mint sprig*

Combine orange juice, tequila, and liqueur in a tall glass filled with crushed ice and stir well. Garnish with orange slice and sprig of fresh mint.

# Melon Balls with Lime

*1 large ripe honeydew melon*
*1 ripe cantaloupe*
*6 wedges fresh lime*

Cut honeydew into 6 equal pieces and discard seeds. Halve cantaloupe and discard seeds. Using a melon baller, carefully scoop out honeydew and cantaloupe balls. Arrange in honeydew shells. Cover and chill, if preferred. To serve, slit each lime wedge and secure to one end of melon shell. Extra melon balls can be passed separately.

# French Toast with Apple Custard Sauce

*Oil*
*4 eggs*
*1 cup heavy cream*
*1/4 teaspoon salt*
*6 large thick slices day-old egg bread or*
  *challah (crusts removed), cut*
  *diagonally into 12 triangles*

*Confectioners' sugar*
*Apple Custard Sauce (below)*

Heat 1/2 inch of oil in an electric skillet to 325 degrees F. *Preheat oven to 400 degrees F.* Beat eggs, cream, and salt in medium bowl. Dip into it each slice of bread, allowing it to soak up as much liquid as possible. Fry in hot oil until browned, turning only once. Transfer to baking sheet and bake until puffed, about 3 to 5 minutes. Drain on paper towels. Arrange on heated platter, sprinkle with powdered sugar and serve immediately with Apple Custard Sauce on the side.

**APPLE CUSTARD SAUCE**

1 cup milk
2 eggs
2 tablespoons sugar
1 teaspoon vanilla

Pinch salt
½ cup applesauce
1 teaspoon minced lemon zest

Heat milk in top of double boiler over gently simmering water until small bubbles form around the edge. Combine eggs, sugar, vanilla, and salt in mixing bowl and beat well. Slowly whisk milk into egg mixture, beating constantly until well blended. Return to double boiler and continue cooking over low heat until sauce thickens. Stir in applesauce and zest and heat through.

# PLAN OF ATTACK FOR SUNDAY BRUNCH

## Cook Number One

*ahead of time*
Squeeze fresh orange juice.
*½ hour before*
1. Make melon balls and arrange in honeydew shells; refrigerate. 2. Set up coffee.
*just before*
Set up bar and mix drinks.

## Cook Number Two

*ahead of time*
1. Make Apple Custard Sauce and cover with plastic wrap. 2. Trim bread for French toast.
*½ hour before*
Mix together eggs, cream, and salt for French toast; refrigerate.
*15 minutes before*
Begin cooking Canadian Bacon.
*just before*
1. Cook French toast. 2. Reheat sauce. 3. Make coffee.

# FIVE

## TWO FOR THE ROAD

One of the things that make travel broadening, both for the mind and the hips, is the opportunity it affords to sample the cuisines of other cultures. A magical quality of cooking is its ability to transport us to a different time and place without worrying about passports, travel agents, shots, gimlet-eyed customs functionaries, and the vulcanized swill that generally passes for airline food. Often we're able to recall past destinations with just a whiff of an herb, the taste of some alien spice. What's even more remarkable is that some dishes whisk us off to places we've only visited in our imaginations. In that sense, food is one way of leading a rich fantasy life.

Cuisine reflects not only countries but cultures. Geography may dictate the ingredients, but the character of a people determines how they are used. Simply put, dour folk tend to eat dull food. Show us an ascetic and we'll show you someone with a quarrelsome digestion and no sense of humor. On the other hand those who are given to song, dance, and erratic driving usually are equally flamboyant in their cooking and tend to throw at least one extra garlic clove in the pot.

The dozen menus in this section literally girdle the earth, from Europe down to Africa, across the Atlantic to the Americas, into the Pacific and beyond to Asia. Two of them, from Louisiana and New Mexico, deal with a couple of the more uninhibited regional cuisines of our own country, which is often unjustly maligned as a culinary wasteland. The basis for that, of course, lies in the image of American cooking that we have chosen to export. When, for example, did you see jambalaya and crawfish étouffée or corn pudding and shoofly pie for sale under the Golden Arches in Paris or London?

# FRANCE

## MENU

*Sweet Pea and Zucchini Soup*
*Poulet Sauté à la Bordelaise*
*Tarragon Tossed Salad*
*Strawberry-Hazelnut Crêpes*

This chicken dish is similar to one we first tasted at the Terminus Hotel in Bordeaux after a harrowing train journey involving lost tickets, disappearing porters, and what seemed to be enough luggage to transport a modest circus. After hours of wandering about with suitcases thudding against our legs, our tempers grew short and hisses of recrimination filled the air.

"Did you have to bring every lens for your camera?" she demanded, panting hard.

"That's rich," he shot back. "I was not the one who brought six pair of shoes including lavender sandals."

"I suppose you expected me to run through France in my bare feet," she replied through thin lips.

Fortunately, these escalating hostilities were brought to a halt by our arrival at the hotel desk. After depositing the offending baggage in the room, we repaired to the restaurant where a kind waiter sensed our plight, opened a bottle of wine for us, and suggested the Poulet Sauté à la Bordelaise. It was delicious and a rapprochement was achieved. If you ever need a disarmament dinner we can't recommend a better one than this.

Trust the wily French to combine romance with economy. For as other prices continue to escalate, the reliable and prolific chicken remains as it has always been: cheap, plentiful, and infinitely versatile. Low-cost chicken can be even more of a bargain if you buy your birds whole and cut them up yourselves. When chicken is on sale we take home three or four, keep one intact for roasting, and cut up the others to freeze in portions for two. Spare parts are tossed into a pot with some water, a carrot, an onion, some peppercorns, celery, and a bay leaf and in a couple of hours we have a good rich chicken broth suitable for soups, sauces, or nursing the pip (see p. xxx).

To dissect a chicken, first sharpen a boning knife and then place the chicken on its side on a cutting board with the wings on your left. Remove the paper packet of innards (isn't it amazing how science has been able to breed fowl with the giblets and neck tidily contained in a Cryovac package?). Place the liver in a small plastic bag to start a collection in your freezer for a future meal. Add the other bits and pieces to the broth. Now wiggle the wing around until you sense where the shoulder joint is. Put the knife in and cut around the wing and remove it.

Turn the chicken around so the leg is on the left and lift it up until the skin is stretched tight. Cut through the skin and around the leg and thigh to remove them in one piece. To separate the leg and thigh, run your finger along the outside curve of the leg and you'll feel a little notch where the joint is. Cut through there. Turn the bird over and repeat with the other wing and leg and thigh.

All that's left now is the breast and back. To separate them, hold the back in one hand and cut directly down behind the breast to remove it in one motion.

For this menu we use only the legs and thighs of the chicken, so freeze the breast for a later date when you can bone it out to make suprêmes and sauce to suit your fancy (consult the index for ideas).

With this lusty chicken dish, a handsome Bordeaux would be the obvious choice to salute its origins, but it also would snuggle up comfortably with the less rarefied delights of a Gamay or a Beaujolais.

# Sweet Pea and Zucchini Soup

The vivid green color of this fresh-tasting low calorie soup makes it a beautiful overture to any meal.

*1 medium zucchini*
*½ cup fresh or frozen petite peas*
*¼ cup chopped onions*
*1½ cups rich chicken broth (see p. 220)*

*1½ teaspoons fresh or ½ teaspoon dried chervil*
*1 tablespoon butter (optional)*
*Salt and pepper*

Wash and cut the zucchini into ½-inch slices. Place the zucchini, peas, onions, chicken broth, and chervil in a saucepan and simmer for 10 minutes or until zucchini is tender. Place the mixture in the container of a blender and whirl until smooth. Return to the pan and heat. Whisk in the butter and season to taste with salt and pepper.

# Poulet Sauté à la Bordelaise

*5 tablespoons butter*
*1 tablespoon olive oil*
*2 chicken legs and thighs, cut in 4 pieces*
*Salt and pepper*
*1 artichoke (or substitute ½ package frozen artichoke hearts prepared according to package instructions)*
*1 medium potato*
*1 onion, peeled and thinly sliced*
*Milk*
*Flour*
*Oil for deep frying*
*Fresh parsley*

**SAUCE**
*1 small clove garlic, minced*
*½ cup chicken broth (see p. 220)*
*½ cup dry white wine*
*1 teaspoon Meat Glace (see p. 219) or commercial meat concentrate such as Bovril*
*1 tablespoon tomato paste*
*Salt and pepper*

Heat 2 tablespoons of the butter and the olive oil in a heavy skillet. Add chicken parts, turning to brown on all sides. Sprinkle with salt and pepper. Cover and cook chicken about 45 minutes or until tender. While chicken cooks, cut away and discard tops and outside leaves of the artichoke and simmer it for about 35 minutes. Discard choke from center and cut artichoke in quarters. Reserve.

Peel potato and slice very thin. Dry on paper towels. Separate sliced onion into rings and dip rings first in milk and then in flour. Wash and thoroughly dry parsley.

When the chicken is ready, move into high gear and divide up these jobs:

## Cook Number One

1. Sauté artichoke quarters in 1 table-spoon butter.   2. Sauté potatoes in 2 tablespoons butter.

## Cook Number Two

1. Fry onion rings in 2 inches of hot oil at about 375 degrees F.   2. Fry a few sprigs of parsley in hot oil for about 3 seconds.

The choreography is smoother if the jobs are divided between sautéeing and deep frying since the artichokes and potatoes can be done in one pan while the onions and parsley are cooked in another.

When all is ready, one partner should arrange the dish attractively on a heated platter with the golden chicken in the center ringed with the garnishes of potato, onion, artichoke hearts, and deep-fried parsley.

Meanwhile the other kitchen hand can make the sauce by adding the garlic to the butter remaining in the pan in which the chicken was cooked and sautéeing it briefly. Add the chicken broth, wine, and meat glaze and cook, stirring to release the good brown bits sticking to the pan, until sauce is reduced and thickened. Strain sauce, stir in tomato paste, and season to taste with salt and pepper. Heat and spoon over chicken.

## Tarragon Tossed Salad

2 cups salad greens
**DRESSING**
1 tablespoon white wine vinegar
¼ teaspoon dry mustard

3 tablespoons olive oil
Salt and pepper
1 tablespoon chopped fresh tarragon or 1
    teaspoon dried

Wash and dry lettuce leaves. In a salad bowl whisk together vinegar, mustard, olive oil, and salt and pepper to taste. Stir in tarragon. Add salad greens and toss until each leaf is thoroughly coated.

## Strawberry-Hazelnut Crêpes

**CRÊPES**
1 egg
⅓ cup instant-blending flour
1 tablespoon sugar
6 tablespoons milk
2 teaspoons melted butter
**SAUCE**
1 tablespoon sugar
1 tablespoon brandy
1 tablespoon strawberry liqueur

**FILLING**
¼ cup sweet butter
1 teaspoon sugar
½ cup strawberries plus 2 whole
    strawberries
Dash lemon juice
**GARNISH**
Sliced strawberries
Minced hazelnuts

To make the crêpes, whirl all the crêpe ingredients in a blender or food processor for about a minute or until smooth. Or beat the eggs in a bowl, add the remaining ingredients, and beat until smooth.

To cook, brush a crêpe pan with a bit of oil. When it sizzles, pour in just enough batter to cover the bottom of the pan. Tip the pan to spread the batter. When the crêpe is firm on the underside, about 1 minute, turn it and cook on the other side for a few seconds. Cool on a cake rack. Repeat with the remaining batter.

Cream together the butter and sugar in a bowl. In another bowl mash the strawberries with the lemon juice. Incorporate the mashed strawberries into the butter mixture, a little at a time, until they are well blended. Spread each crêpe with some of the strawberry butter, fold into quarters, and arrange in a small baking dish. At this point the crêpes can be covered and refrigerated until you're ready for dessert.

About 10 minutes before serving time, sprinkle the top of the crêpes with sugar and place in a *preheated 375-degree oven* until sugar has become slightly caramelized. Warm the brandy and strawberry liqueur together in a small pan. Bring the crêpes to the table, pour the spirits over them, and ignite. Spoon the sauce over the crêpes until the flames die down. Garnish with sliced strawberries and minced hazelnuts.

# PLAN OF ATTACK

## Cook Number One

*ahead of time*
1. Make soup and refrigerate. 2. Make salad dressing.

*1 hour before*
Cook chicken.

*½ hour before*
Prepare potatoes, onions, and parsley for cooking.

*just before*
1. Sauté artichokes and potatoes. 2. Heat soup.

*10 minutes before dessert*
Sprinkle crêpes with sugar and place in oven.

## Cook Number Two

*ahead of time*
1. Make crêpes. 2. Fill crêpes and refrigerate.

*1 hour before*
Prepare and cook artichoke.

*½ hour before*
Wash and crisp salad greens. 2. Open wine.

*just before*
1. Deep-fry onions and parsley. 2. Arrange chicken platter.

# DENMARK

## MENU

*Danish Pickled Oysters*
*Viking Meat Patties*
*Dilled Potatoes*
*Scandinavian Red Cabbage*
*Garnet Fruit Pudding*

We have always thought that Shakespeare was playing a little joke when he cast Hamlet as a Dane. They are among the least melancholy people in the world and certainly are the jolliest of the Scandinavians, probably because they are the only ones who live in a country where they don't have to hibernate in the winter.

From Tivoli Gardens to the statue of the Little Mermaid down by the harbor the city of Copenhagen has a fairy-tale quality, yet the food there is sturdy and simple, reflecting the bounty of nature and the changes of season.

While pastries and those wildly inventive open-faced sandwiches may represent Danish cuisine to the rest of the world, the Danes know their food is distinctive in other ways as well. Everything that's served at a Danish table tastes of itself and the freshness of the sea or land from which it came. Seasonings are low-key and subtle. Even dill, the most popular herb in Scandinavia, only points up the freshness of the other ingredients with its own clean, sweet flavor.

This menu begins with an unusual but easy to make first course of pickled oysters. The club soda in the recipe for the veal and pork patties isn't a typo, by the way. It helps lighten the mixture before it's fried. And don't try to automate the making of the meat mixture: it takes a wooden spoon and elbow grease. If you attempt to use the food processor, you'll end up with carbonated baby food. The vegetables and dessert are like the Danes themselves—uncomplicated.

Although the beverages of choice in Denmark tend to be aquavit and beer, we've never been completely comfortable with drinking what amounts to boiler-makers at table. With this dinner, on this side of the Atlantic, we would probably open a California Sauvignon Blanc.

If all the essential ingredients of the meal—food, drink, good company—come together right, the result is what the Danes call *Hygge*, which probably translates better to the German *Gemütlichkeit* than to any word in English. In any language it means contentment.

# Danish Pickled Oysters

1 pint shucked medium oysters with their
    liquor
½ onion, sliced thin
½ lemon, sliced thin

½ cup white wine vinegar
1 teaspoon pickling spice
Salt and pepper
1 tablespoon minced parsley

In the morning or the night before you plan to serve them, put the oysters and their liquor (add water if there isn't enough liquid to cover them) in a saucepan and poach until the edges curl. Drain, saving the broth, and plunge them into ice water. Drain again and arrange in a flat serving bowl. Cover with onion and lemon slices.

Add the vinegar and pickling spice to the broth and bring to a boil. Reduce heat and simmer for 10 minutes. Strain the mixture and pour it over the oysters. Sprinkle with salt, pepper, and parsley. Cover the bowl with plastic wrap and refrigerate for at least 12 hours. Serve with thin slices of dark rye bread.

# Viking Meat Patties

¼ pound boneless veal
¼ pound boneless pork
2 tablespoons grated onion
1½ tablespoons flour
¾ cup club soda
2 tablespoons beaten egg (beat one egg,
    measure the amount you need, and
    reserve the rest—or feed it to the cat,
    which is what happens around our
    house)

Salt and pepper
1 tablespoon butter
1 tablespoon oil

Grind the veal, pork, and onion together twice through the finest blade of a meat grinder (or have the butcher grind the meats for you and mix in the finely grated onion yourself).

In a mixing bowl, beat the flour into the meat mixture with a wooden spoon. Beat in the club soda, a tablespoon at a time, until the mixture is light and fluffy. Add the egg and salt and pepper to taste. Cover the bowl and refrigerate for an hour to make the mixture easier to handle.

Shape the meat into two oblong patties. Heat the butter and the oil in a skillet over medium heat and sauté the patties for 6 to 8 minutes on each side until they are a rich brown color and the juices run clear, signifying that the meats are completely cooked.

# Dilled Potatoes

4–6 small new potatoes
2 tablespoons butter
Salt

Dill weed (fresh is best, naturally, but
   dried will do)

Scrub potatoes well, leaving skins on. Drop them into a pan of boiling water and cook until just tender, about 15 to 25 minutes.

  Melt butter in a skillet and add cooked potatoes, shaking gently over low heat until well coated. Serve sprinkled with salt and minced dill weed to taste.

# Scandinavian Red Cabbage

1 pound red cabbage
2 tablespoons butter
3 tablespoons water

2 teaspoons red wine vinegar
2 tablespoons red currant jelly
Salt and pepper

Wash and shred cabbage, discarding any tough portions. Melt butter in a skillet over medium heat, add cabbage and cook, stirring for 3 to 4 minutes. Add water, vinegar and sugar and stir until sugar is dissolved. Cover, reduce heat, and simmer 45 minutes or until tender. Stir in currant jelly and salt and pepper to taste. This is equally good made a day in advance, refrigerated, and reheated.

# Garnet Fruit Pudding

½ pound fresh strawberries, raspberries,
   or a combination of both
2 teaspoons sugar
2 teaspoons arrowroot

4 teaspoons cold water
Sweetened whipped cream
Toasted slivered almonds

In the morning or night before you plan to serve, wash and hull the berries. Drain and pat dry with paper towels. Put the fruit in the container of a blender or food processor and purée completely. Place the purée and the sugar in a saucepan and, stirring constantly, bring to a boil. Remove pan from heat. Mix the arrowroot with the water to make a smooth paste and whisk into the purée. Return the pan to low heat and simmer, stirring constantly and taking care not to let the mixture boil, until slightly thickened. Pour the pudding into individual dessert bowls. Chill thoroughly and serve topped with whipped cream and toasted almonds.

# PLAN OF ATTACK

## Cook Number One

*ahead of time*
Prepare and chill pickled oysters.
*1 hour 30 minutes before*
Prepare meat patty mixture and refrigerate.
*15 minutes before*
Begin sautéeing meat patties.

## Cook Number Two

*ahead of time*
Prepare and chill dessert.
*1 hour before*
1. Wash and shred cabbage.  2. Scrub potatoes.
*50 minutes before*
Start cooking cabbage.
*30 minutes before*
1. Start cooking potatoes.  2. Chill wine.
*just before*
1. Shake potatoes in butter, sprinkle with salt and dill.  2. Stir currant jelly and salt into cabbage.

# IRELAND

# MENU

*Salmon Mousse*
*Gaelic Stuffed Pork Tenderloin*
*Mountain of the Woman Carrots*
*Dublin Brown Bread or Emerald Isle Bread*
*Irish Mist Soufflé*

There's a truly Irish pub near our home called the Kerry House. St. Patrick's Day usually finds us there, sipping Guinness and watching the earnest faces of the children from St. Leo's Parish demonstrating their skill at Irish step dancing. This is the one night of the year Bill Denehy's saloon becomes a place for the whole family. The scarred tables that usually serve as battlegrounds for gin rummy or heated debate are pushed back against the walls, and parents cheer encouragement to quartets of their costumed offspring as they trace the intricate steps of the *ceili*. It's always a memorable evening, with much singing and outrageous lying going on between boisterous dart games. We've found it's wise to ballast ourselves against the rigors of this celebration with a hearty dinner beforehand.

For many years we stuck pretty close to tradition with corned beef and cabbage, regarding that as the apex of Irish ingenuity in the kitchen. It took a trip to Ireland for us to discover that cooking there goes far beyond the boiling pot. We once considered Irish cuisine much like English cooking, only not so spicy. That was before we visited the countryside.

It is true that for the most part Irish food is straightforward and generally innocent of any seasoning more extraordinary than salt and pepper. Restaurant meals, in fact, can be downright depressing. But in private homes and on the farms where one can taste the real flavor of the land, meals are showcases for the fresh products of the dairy, henhouse, field, and garden. Plump trout and salmon, delicious locally made sausages, and newborn vegetables intrigue even the most sophisticated palate. And what emerges from Irish ovens is sheer poetry. The fragrance of baking bread, cakes, and pies permeates every kitchen. Our favorite was the rustic brown bread we were served at every meal. Its crisp crust and dense texture were so delightful that once home, we spent hours trying to recapture our memory of it using American ingredients. We think the two alternate recipes in this menu are the next best thing to the original.

If you want to carry authenticity to the extreme, you can wash down this meal with a bottle of bitter stout served at room temperature. We believe, however, that a chilled California White Riesling is a good accompaniment for both the Salmon Mousse and the pork.

## Salmon Mousse

1 tablespoon unflavored gelatin
3 tablespoons white wine
⅓ pound cooked boned salmon
⅓ cup mayonnaise (see p. 221)
⅓ cup sour cream
1 teaspoon tarragon wine vinegar
1 teaspoon lemon juice

1 tablespoon prepared horseradish
1 dash Tabasco sauce
1 dash Worcestershire sauce
1 teaspoon grated onion
Salt and pepper
⅓ cup minced parsley

Dissolve the gelatin in white wine in the top of a small double boiler or in a custard cup in a shallow pan of simmering water. Cool.

Flake the salmon with a fork and remove any bones. Mix together the salmon, mayonnaise, and sour cream and stir in the cooled gelatin. Add the vinegar, lemon juice, horseradish, Tabasco, Worcestershire sauce, onion, and salt and pepper to taste. Fold in the parsley and spoon the mixture into two small molds that have been rinsed in cold water. Chill until firm and unmold on beds of crisp ruffled lettuce leaves. Serve with warm slices of brown bread.

# Gaelic Stuffed Pork Tenderloin

The pig is a respected citizen in Ireland, and in this specialty of County Cork its most succulent portion has the added dividend of a delicious stuffing.

*1 pork tenderloin (1 pound)*
**DRESSING**
*½ cup chopped onion*
*2 tablespoons butter*
*1 cup fresh bread crumbs*
*¼ cup minced parsley*

*¼ teaspoon sage*
*¼ teaspoon rosemary*
*Salt and pepper*
*1 egg, lightly beaten*
*1 thick slice bacon, cut in half*

*Preheat oven to 350 degrees F.* Split the tenderloin lengthwise partway through to butterfly. Open out and pound to flatten.

Sauté onions in butter until translucent. Add bread crumbs to the pan and continue cooking, stirring, until the crumbs are slightly crisp. Add the parsley, herbs, and salt and pepper to taste. Cool and add just enough of the beaten egg to moisten. Spread the stuffing on half of the butterflied pork, leaving about ¼ inch around the edges. Close up the tenderloin, placing the two pieces of bacon on top, and tie it up with string. Place on a rack in a baking pan and roast for 1 to 1½ hours, or until the pork reaches 170 degrees F. on a meat thermometer.

# Mountain of the Woman Carrots

This dish takes its unusual name (which in Gaelic, a language nearly as unprint-able as it is unspeakable, is *Slieve na mBan*) from a ruddy mountain that peeks out above a veil of milk-white mist. A very poetic name for a vegetable dish, we admit, but we think it lives up to it.

*4 carrots*
*4 teaspoons butter*
*¼ cup milk*
*¼ cup cream*

*1 egg yolk*
*Salt and pepper*
*1 teaspoon minced parsley*

Trim the carrots so they are a similar length and peel. Cut each one into quarters lengthwise and then cut the quarters into 3-inch strips. Melt the butter in a saucepan over low heat and add the milk. Add the carrots and simmer gently, not allowing the milk to boil, until the carrots are tender. Beat the cream with the egg yolk. Remove the pan from the heat and stir in the cream mixture. Reheat but don't boil, stirring until the sauce thickens. Season to taste with salt and pep-per. Just before serving, sprinkle with fresh minced parsley.

# Dublin Brown Bread

The most important ingredient in Irish bread is the flour, which in Ireland is coarse, like gritty sand. It is this roughly crushed grain that gives the distinctive texture of Irish brown bread. Since our whole-wheat flour seems to have a finer texture than that available in Eire, the oatmeal is included to help make a rougher loaf.

| | |
|---|---|
| 2 cups stone-ground whole-wheat flour | ¾ teaspoon salt |
| 1 cup all-purpose flour | ¾ teaspoon baking soda |
| ¼ cup oatmeal | 1½ cups buttermilk |

*Preheat oven to 425 degrees F.* Mix together the flours, oatmeal, salt, and baking soda in a large bowl. Make a well in the center and blend in the buttermilk. At this point you'll have to use your own judgment, for some flour is more absorbent than others. Add as much buttermilk as it takes to make a soft, yet easily handled dough. It will be between 1¼ and 1½ cups.

Dust your hands with flour and knead the bread dough into a ball. Place it on a greased baking sheet and, using your hands, flatten it into a circle 1½ to 2 inches high. Dip a sharp knife in flour and cut a cross in the center of the bread (this helps it rise and allows the loaf to be broken into quarters, or *farls,* after it's baked).

Bake for 25 minutes, then reduce heat to 350 degrees F. and bake 15 minutes longer. Allow the bread to set for several hours before cutting. Dublin Brown Bread may be reheated just before serving, and it makes memorable toast.

# Emerald Isle Bread

Because the stone-ground flour called for in the preceding recipe is not universally available, this version uses home-ground oatmeal. This recipe makes three small loaves, which should disappear rapidly.

| | |
|---|---|
| 1¼ cups rolled oats | ¼ cup honey |
| 3 cups flour | ¼ cup minced fresh parsley |
| 1½ tablespoons baking powder | 1 egg |
| 2 teaspoons salt | 1 tablespoon melted butter |
| 1 cup milk | |

*Preheat oven to 350 degrees F.* Generously grease three 6×3×2¼-inch loaf pans.

Grind the oats in a food processor or blender until fine. Transfer to a mixing bowl and add the flour, baking powder, and salt and mix well. In another bowl whisk together the milk, honey, parsley, and egg. Add to the dry ingredients and mix well. Divide equally among the three pans and bake until loaves test done, about 50 minutes. Turn out onto a rack and brush tops with melted butter.

## Irish Mist Soufflé

1 egg, separated
2 tablespoons superfine sugar
1 tablespoon Irish Mist liqueur

1 teaspoon unflavored gelatin
1 tablespoon slivered toasted almonds
¼ cup heavy cream, whipped

Place the egg yolk in a bowl with the sugar and beat until light and fluffy. Melt the gelatin with the liqueur in a small cup over simmering water or in the top of a small double boiler. Cool. Sir the gelatin mixture and the almonds into the yolk mixture. In another bowl beat the egg white until stiff and fold the egg white and whipped cream into the other ingredients. Spoon into individual dessert dishes or wine glasses and chill for several hours.

# PLAN OF ATTACK

## Cook Number One

### ahead of time
1. Make and chill salmon mousse.   2. Make and chill Irish Mist soufflé.
### 2 hours before
Butterfly and pound pork loin.
### 30 minutes before
1 trim and peel carrots.   2. Simmer carrots in milk until tender.   3. Chill wine.
### 15 minutes before
Make sauce for carrots; keep warm.
### dinnertime
Serve carrots.

## Cook Number Two

### ahead of time
Make and bake bread.
### 2 hours before
1. Prepare dressing for pork.   2. Stuff and tie roast.
### 1 hour, 15 minutes before
Put loin in oven.
### 15 minutes before
1. Unmold salmon mousse.   2. Warm bread.
### dinnertime
1. Remove pork from oven and let set during first course.   2. After serving salmon mousse, carve and serve pork.

# SPAIN

## MENU

*Sopa de Ajo*
(Garlic Soup)

*Riñones de Cordero Andaluz*
(Lamb Kidneys in Sherry)

*Menestra de Legumbres*
(Vegetable Stew)

*Plátanos al Ron*
(Bananas in Rum Sauce)

OK, let's hear it for kidneys! Before you rush to throw this book in the trash compactor, hear us out.

The fact is that, properly prepared, kidneys are tender, juicy, and delicately flavored. The secret is in the cooking time. It must be very short to prevent them from becoming tough. Otherwise they must be braised forever to get them tender again. Unfortunately, too often in this country we encounter gray and tasteless kidneys the consistency of typewriter erasers, which probably explains their popularity as cat food. But we were reminded again on a trip to Spain what a delicacy this form of, you should pardon the expression, offal, can be.

Anyone who thinks of Spain as a single, homogeneous nation hasn't been paying attention. The lighthearted denizens of Andalusia are as different from the Catalans around Barcelona as the Italians are from the Dutch. The Basques bear little resemblance to their eastern neighbors in Galicia, some of whom have red hair and blue eyes and, for some reason, play the bagpipes. None of the foregoing are similar to the Guanches, who originally inhabited the Canary Islands.

Each of these colorful and ruggedly individualistic peoples has its own language and, inevitably, its own native cooking based not only on tradition but also on the best ingredients available locally.

With the exception of Sherry, the wines of Spain have been largely (and mistakenly) overlooked, and yet the technology, skill, and dedication to quality in many of the *bodegas* of the Rioja, for instance, are equal to those of any winery. In the Penedés region of Catalonia, immense wineries produce some remarkable sparkling wines using the *méthode champenoise* of France. As we've said before, the beauty of this enological ignorance on our part is that Spanish wines, especially some of the finer reds of the Rioja, can be great bargains.

But we were talking about kidneys.

Variety meats have been staples in the human diet since man first clambered out of the trees and began preying on his fellow creatures. We have no real explanation for the fact they often have been ignored or abused on this side of the Atlantic, but maybe it has something to do with those putty-colored slabs of overcooked liver a lot of us endured as children. Whatever the reason, the comparative lack of demand, as in the case of Spanish wines, has given kidneys the added bonus of being relatively inexpensive. They're also good for you, but you shouldn't hold that against them.

Kidneys are generally available from four different animals: cows, calves, lambs, and pigs. The largest, beef, weigh in at something over a pound and feed three to four people. Lamb kidneys, the smallest, are about two ounces apiece, and it takes two or three to make a serving.

Beef and pork kidneys have stronger flavors, need to be soaked in water with lemon juice or vinegar for at least an hour, and are most often used in dishes that require long cooking. Veal and lamb kidneys are smaller and, as far as we're concerned, are best grilled or sautéed briefly. If anybody tries to sell you something called "baby beef" kidneys by telling you they are veal, call the Better Business Bureau and then treat them as beef kidneys in cooking.

Since different types of kidneys require different preparation, don't try to substitute one for another in recipes, including the one below. If you can't find a nice bottle of Rioja to accompany this entrée, by the way, we suggest a California Pinot Noir.

## *Sopa de Ajo*
### (GARLIC SOUP)

This spartan list of ingredients produces a truly remarkable soup. The garlic flavor is not overwhelming, but it's best to eat it with someone you love. Or someone you hate.

| | |
|---|---|
| 2 tablespoons plus 1 teaspoon olive oil | 1 tablespoon minced parsley |
| 3 teaspoons finely minced garlic | 2 cups chicken broth (see p. 220) |
| 2 slices cubed French or Italian bread, crusts trimmed | 1 egg, lightly beaten |
| 2 tablespoons minced green onion | Salt and pepper |

Heat 2 tablespoons olive oil in a heavy 1-quart saucepan. Add 1 teaspoon of the garlic and the bread cubes and cook over low heat, stirring, until the bread is golden brown. Remove the croutons and set aside.

Add the remaining garlic and olive oil, green onion and parsley to the same pan and cook, stirring, for about a minute. Stir in the broth, bring the soup to a boil, then reduce the heat and simmer, covered, for 30 minutes. Remove the pan from the heat and slowly stir in the beaten egg (the soup must be below the boiling point or the egg will curdle). Season to taste with salt and pepper, top with croutons, and serve.

(In other variations of this soup, the egg is poached first and then placed in the soup, or it is poached in the broth as the soup cooks.)

## Riñones de Cordero Andaluz
### (LAMB KIDNEYS IN SHERRY)

5 lamb kidneys
3 tablespoons butter
1 tablespoon olive oil
1 tablespoon fresh or 1 teaspoon marjoram
1 teaspoon salt
½ teaspoon pepper

10 small whole button mushrooms
1¼ cups finely minced onion
½ cup medium dry Sherry
¼ cup red wine
2 slices toast cut in triangles
Minced parsley

First, if the butcher hasn't already done it, pull away all the fat from the kidneys and, using a pair of kitchen scissors, cut away the fat and tubing on the underside. Cut them crosswise into slices between ⅛ and ¼ inch thick.

Melt 2 tablespoons of the butter with the oil over high heat. Add the kidneys, marjoram, ½ teaspoon of the salt, and ¼ teaspoon of the pepper and sauté for 2 to 3 minutes, or until the kidneys have "seized" (browned and the blood has ceased to run). Remove from the pan and set aside.

Add the remaining butter to the pan and sauté mushrooms and onions over medium heat until the mushrooms are slightly browned. Add the remaining salt and pepper and the wines and cook rapidly over high heat until the sauce is reduced and thickened. Lower the heat, add the kidneys and continue cooking just until slices are heated through, about 1 minute. Serve immediately on toast triangles and garnish with minced parsley.

## Menestra de Legumbres
### (VEGETABLE STEW)

In Spain vegetables are treated with great respect. Cooks there respond to the seasons, preparing whatever is fresh in the market with great imagination and finesse, often flavoring them with fruity olive oil and garlic. One of our favorite vegetable dishes is this stew from the Penedés.

¼ pound fresh green beans
2 tablespoons olive oil
1 clove garlic, minced
¼ cup chopped onion
1 slice boiled ham, diced

¼ cup dry white wine
1 bay leaf
1 can whole small artichoke hearts (7 ounces)
Salt and pepper

Remove the ends and string the beans. Break them in half and parboil for 12 minutes. Rinse in cold water and drain.

Heat the oil in a skillet, add the garlic, onion, and ham and cook over very low heat until the onion is soft but not brown. Add the wine, bay leaf, artichoke hearts, and parboiled beans and simmer for about 10 minutes until the vegetables are tender and the wine somewhat reduced. Add salt and pepper to taste and serve at once.

## Plátanos al Ron
### (BANANAS IN RUM SAUCE)

In Spain most of the bananas come from the Canary Islands. The idea of flaming them with rum is a heritage of the former Spanish colonies in the Caribbean.

¼ cup brown sugar
¼ teaspoon cinnamon
Dash powdered clove
Dash powdered ginger

2 small bananas, cut in half lengthwise
3 tablespoons butter
2 tablespoons dark rum

Preheat oven to 375 degrees F. Blend the brown sugar and spices and roll the banana halves in the mixture. Melt the butter in a skillet and sauté the bananas until the sugar on them begins to caramelize. Place the bananas in a shallow heatproof dish and sprinkle over them the remaining sugar mixture. Bake in the oven until the bananas are hot and the sugar is melted. Heat the rum, flame it, and spoon it over the bananas. Carry with appropriate flourish to the table.

# PLAN OF ATTACK

## Cook Number One

*1 hour, 15 minutes before*
Begin making soup.
*1 hour before*
Make dessert to the point it goes into the oven, cover, and set aside.
*45 minutes before*
1. Remove soup from heat and set aside until ready to serve.  2. Sauté onions, garlic, and ham for *Menestra* and set aside.
*15 minutes before*
1. Add remaining ingredients for *Menestra* and simmer while kidneys are cooking.  2. Make toast triangles for kidneys.  3. Preheat oven for dessert.
*after main course*
Heat, flame, and serve dessert.

## Cook Number Two

*1 hour, 15 minutes before*
Prepare and parboil beans for *Menestra* and refresh them in cold water.
*1 hour before*
1. Prepare kidneys for cooking by removing fat and tubing if the butcher hasn't (don't slice until just before cooking).  2. Prepare all other ingredients for kidneys.
*1/2 hour before*
1. Reheat soup, stir in eggs, and serve.  2. Open wine.
*15 minutes before*
1. Slice kidneys and sauté.  2. Finish sauce and serve kidneys along with partner's *Menestra*.

# ITALY

# MENU

*Tomato Ice*
*Fritto Misto*
*Fennel Salad with Gorgonzola Dressing*
*Cassata al Cioccolato*

This menu often has been our ticket to the seacoast of Italy. As we plunge a fork into crisp golden bits of fried fish, we can fancy ourselves sitting on a balcony overlooking the sun-dappled waters of the Bay of Naples. Since our imagination is more acute than our eyesight, we can see from our terrace the ruins of Herculaneum and, beyond, Pompeii and the nervous slopes of Vesuvius. It's a delightful evening's vacation, and our Italian dinner speeds us across oceans and continents almost as fast as and a lot cheaper than the Concorde.

The main course, *Fritto Misto,* is popular everywhere along Italy's lengthy coastline, where it usually is composed of a combination of crisply fried local fish. But in the north and the interior, *Fritto Misto* (which means simply "mixed fried") might include sweetbreads, veal, chicken, and vegetables. For our version we have combined fish and vegetables. The result should be a light and delicate dish, worlds away from the greasy fried food dear to the hearts of those stalwarts who wheel their big rigs from coast to coast sustained only by truck-stop chow and the wisecracks of waitresses along the way. Like any properly cooked deep-fried food which hasn't absorbed excess oil and has been well drained, this dish isn't exorbitantly high in calories, especially since it started with fish and vegetables.

There are a few rules about deep frying that will help guarantee successful results. First, the oil must be fresh and of good quality. An electric deep-fat fryer or electric frying pan is convenient because it has a built-in thermostat, but a heavy saucepan or skillet and a fat thermometer also will do the trick. Never fill any container more than half full of fat, to allow room for the food and for a certain amount of bubbling as any moisture in the ingredients evaporates. And don't be tempted to start cooking until the fat has reached the proper temperature for, as Alexandre Dumas said, deep-fried food should be "surprised" by the heat so it will develop a golden crust and seal itself against the intrusion of fat.

The food should be dry before it is battered, and then it should rest awhile before frying. Introduce the food into the fat gently, using a slotted spoon that has been warmed first in the hot fat. Don't overcrowd the pan; fry a small amount at a time if necessary, keeping the cooked portions warm in a low oven.

This menu begins with a sparkling tomato ice. The entrée needs only the salad and crusty bread for companions. Dessert is splendidly sinful and keeps in the refrigerator for about a week, which is a good thing since slender slices definitely are in order. In Italy *fritto misto* would likely be accompanied by a light white wine such as a dry Frascati from the hills just south of Rome, or a Soave from the Veneto region near Verona. Although Italy has become the largest exporter of wine to the United States, the whites, which represent some interesting bargains, still tend to be overlooked.

## *Tomato Ice*

3 large tomatoes, peeled, seeded, and
   chopped
1 small clove garlic, pressed
¼ cup chopped onion
¼ cup chopped celery
¼ teaspoon salt
1 tablespoon sugar

1 tablespoon lemon juice
2 sprigs fresh mint (or ¹/₄ teaspoon dried
   mint)
½ teaspoon Worcestershire sauce
2–3 drops Tabasco sauce
**GARNISH**
Mint sprigs (if available)

Purée all ingredients in the container of a blender or a food processor. Taste and adjust seasoning (the mixture should be fairly highly seasoned, as freezing diminishes flavor). Pour into a shallow container and freeze just until solid. Return to the blender or food processor and whirl, or place in a bowl and beat with an electric mixer until lightly whipped. Return to the freezing container, cover, and refreeze until firm. To serve, divide between two wine glasses and garnish with mint sprigs.

## Fritto Misto

½ cup instant-blending flour
1 tablespoon dry white Vermouth
1 egg, separated
¼ cup water
Salt and pepper
Oil for deep frying
6 large shrimp, shelled and deveined
¼ pound firm-fleshed fish fillets, cut in
   chunks

**USE ANY TWO OF THE FOLLOWING**
1 medium zucchini, cut into ½-inch
   chunks or 6 medium mushrooms,
   cleaned and trimmed or 6 frozen
   artichokes hearts, thawed or 1
   Japanese eggplant, trimmed and sliced
   into ½-inch chunks
**GARNISH**
Lemon wedges

To make the batter, place the flour, Vermouth, egg yolk, water, pinch of salt, and a few grindings of pepper into a bowl. Stir until smooth. Beat the egg white until stiff and fold into the batter mixture.

*Heat the oil to 370 degrees F.* Dip the seafood and vegetables into the batter and let rest on a cake rack while the oil heats. When the oil is ready, fry until golden brown, turning often. Sprinkle with salt and pepper and garnish with lemon wedges.

## Fennel Salad with Gorgonzola Dressing

1 fennel bulb
2 radishes
4 raw mushrooms
1 tablespoon minced red onion
2 tablespoons minced chives
2 tablespoons minced fresh parsley

**DRESSING**
2 tablespoons olive oil
½ teaspoon Dijon mustard
1½ teaspoons fresh lemon juice
Salt and pepper
2 tablespoons crumbled Gorgonzola cheese
Lettuce
Ripe olives
Lemon wedges

Trim fennel, cut in slices and place in a bowl. Slice radishes and mushrooms and add to the bowl. Stir in onion, chives, and parsley. Mix together the olive oil, mustard, and lemon juice and season to taste with salt and pepper. Stir in the Gorgonzola. Toss the salad with the dressing, arrange on lettuce leaves, and garnish with a few ripe olives and lemon wedges.

## *Cassata al Cioccolato*

**CAKE**
*⅓ cup butter*
*¾ cup sugar*
*2 eggs*
*¾ cup cake flour*
*Pinch salt*
*¼ teaspoon vanilla*

**FROSTING**
*4 ounces semi-sweet chocolate (chocolate chips may be used)*
*¼ cup strong coffee*
*5 tablespoons chilled sweet butter*

**FILLING**
*⅓ pound ricotta cheese*
*4 teaspoons sugar*
*2 ounces heavy cream or sour cream*
*1 tablespoon Amaretto*
*2 tablespoons chocolate chips (or 1 tablespoon chocolate chips and 1 tablespoon glacéed fruit)*

**GARNISH**
*Finely chopped nuts*

*Preheat oven to 325 degrees F.* Butter and lightly flour a 6×3×2¼-inch loaf pan.

To make the cake, cream butter and sugar together and continue beating until light. Add eggs one at a time, beating well after each addition (this much can be done in a food processor). Stir in flour, salt, and vanilla and mix until smooth. Spoon into pan and bake for about 1 hour or until an inserted toothpick comes out clean. Cool in pan for 5 minutes before turning out to finish cooling on a rack. When the cake is completely cool, cut a slice off the top and even the edges to make a perfect rectangle. Cut the cake horizontally into ½-inch layers.

To make the frosting, melt chocolate and coffee together in a heavy-bottomed pan over very low heat. Remove the pan from the heat and beat in the chilled butter a bit at a time. Continue beating until the mixture is smooth. Chill until the frosting thickens to spreading consistency.

To make the filling, put into a blender or food processor the ricotta cheese, sugar, cream or sour cream, and Amaretto and blend until smooth. Spoon into a bowl and fold in the chocolate chips or chips and glacéed fruit. Spread between layers of the cake, ending with a plain slice on top. Gently press the cake to make it as firm as possible (it will become completely firm as it chills later). Spread the frosting evenly over the top, sides, and ends of the cake and sprinkle the top with finely chopped nuts. Put the frosted cake in the freezer for ½ hour or chill thoroughly in the refrigerator before covering loosely with plastic wrap or foil. This cake is best refrigerated 24 hours before serving.

# PLAN OF ATTACK

This plan of attack is hardly worth the name, because it's obvious from reading the recipes that two parts of the meal, the beginning and the end, have to be made far in advance. Since one cook should make the cake the night before to let it chill for 24 hours, we suggest that as a good time for the other to prepare the tomato ice.

### Cook Number One

*ahead of time*
Make and refrigerate dessert.
*10 minutes before*
Assemble and dress salad.

### Cook Number Two

*ahead of time*
Make tomato ice.
*20 minutes before*
Make batter and dip ingredients for *Fritto Misto.*
*10 minutes before*
Start frying *Fritto Misto.*

# NORTH AFRICA

# MENU

*Lamb Couscous*
*Roasted Pepper and Tomato Salad*
*Oranges Casablanca*

Say "couscous," and to some the word evokes an image of Charles Boyer skulking around Algiers as Pepe LeMoko, breathing into Hedy Lamarr's perfumed nape an invitation to taste the forbidden delights of the Casbah.

To others, "couscous" sounds like a mourning dove with a speech impediment.

A third group, made up of people who know it's the ubiquitous dish of Mediterranean Africa north of the Atlas Mountains, regards couscous as one of the world's delicacies, usually requiring hours of preparation, which can be tasted only in restaurants in a handful of cosmopolitan cities with large Arab populations.

Far too few realize that this exotic mélange can be as easy to prepare at the end of a busy day as, say, spaghetti and meatballs.

For those who have not yet ventured into the seductive world of North African cuisine, couscous consists of a luxurious mound of fluffy grains (from which the dish gets its name) that have been cooked in the spicy steam of a meat or vegetable stew. Since most of the recipes for it could satisfy the appetites of a regiment of Legionnaires, it isn't something most people would consider appropriate for a dinner for two.

Yet couscous can be made to serve any number and, with a little planning, can appear at the table an hour after its final preparation has begun. The trick is to do the preliminary cooking of the stew in the morning, or the evening before. Since it is the simplest of processes—simmering meat with spices in water—one scarcely need be awake to undertake this first step. If you're afraid to trust yourself with even this elementary task in the early hours, the lamb can simmer away in a slow cooker all day and then be finished with the couscous in the evening.

The couscous itself is made up of tiny golden pellets similar to pasta and usually made of semolina, although it may also be made of other whole grains. These days it can be found packaged in most supermarkets or, wanting that, in health food stores or gourmet shops.

Traditionally it's cooked in a special pot called a *couscoussier* consisting of two sections. The lower portion holds the simmering stew. The upper section, which holds the couscous, has a perforated bottom that allows the steam from the stew to penetrate the grains. Since our own *Batterie de cuisine* didn't include a *couscoussier* when we started fooling around with this, we were forced to improvise just as you may have to do. A sieve or colander fitted into a similar-sized saucepan works well (be sure the couscous doesn't touch the stew below it). We found our own solution by using the sieve from our KitchenAid mixer, fitted into a 4½-quart Calphalon saucepan. Invention may produce some odd-looking rigs, but the result is what counts. If your couscous grains come out light and separate and almost breathtakingly fragile, you will have succeeded, no matter what contraption you have used.

To contrast with the vibrant character of the couscous, we suggest a refreshing mint-flavored salad of tomatoes and roasted green peppers and a chilled orange dessert. Although alcohol is not commonly served in Moslem countries (mint tea is consumed in prodigious quantities), you might want to accompany this meal with a California or Alsatian Gewürztraminer, or perhaps chilled lager. At its best, Gewürztraminer is a pungent, spicy white wine with a distinctive flavor and sturdy enough character to stand up to heavily seasoned foods.

# Lamb Couscous

½ dried red chili pepper
¼ cup butter
¾ pound boneless lamb cut into
    1-inch cubes (shoulder is a good
    cut for this)
¾ teaspoon ground ginger
¾ teaspoon ground turmeric
1 pinch saffron, ground and
    dissolved in 1 tablespoon water

Dash cayenne pepper
½ teaspoon salt
¼ teaspoon pepper
1 onion, sliced
¾ cup couscous
1 cup canned garbanzo beans
1 zucchini, cut in chunks
¼ cup raisins

To make it easier to retrieve it later, put the dried red pepper in a tea ball. Melt 2 tablespoons of the butter in the bottom of a couscoussier or in a saucepan if you have improvised your equipment. Add the lamb and the spices, including the tea ball containing the dried red pepper, and toss in the hot butter until the meat is heated but not brown. Pour on water to cover, bring to a boil, reduce the heat and simmer, covered, for 45 minutes. If you do this the night before or early in the morning, cool and refrigerate.

For final preparation, skim the fat from the top of the liquid (if it has been chilled this will be easier) and remove the dried red pepper. Add the sliced onion and return to the heat.

Rinse the couscous grains in a strainer under cold water and rub the granules between the palms of your hands so they crumble and don't stick together. When the lamb mixture comes to a boil, reduce the heat to a simmer and place the upper part of the couscoussier on top. If the holes in the upper part are large, line it with cheesecloth that has been rinsed in warm water and squeezed dry. If you are using some sort of homemade lash-up, check the seal between the top and bottom; you may want to wrap the juncture between the two with foil to assure that the steam from the stew below escapes only through the couscous.

Add the couscous to the top of the cooker a little at a time, allowing steam to rise between each addition. After the grains are all in, simmer uncovered for 30 minutes, fluffing the grains occasionally with a fork so they cook evenly. Turn the heat off under the stew and turn the couscous grains out onto a baking sheet, breaking up any lumps, and allow them to sit 10–15 minutes to dry. Sprinkle with 1–2 tablespoons of water, season lightly with salt and pepper, and stir the remaining 2 tablespoons of butter, cut in small pieces, into the grains. Return the couscous to the top of the cooker.

Add the garbanzos, zucchini, and raisins to the lamb stew, reheat it until it's simmering, replace the top of the cooker, and steam the couscous for another 15 minutes, adding more water to the stew if necessary.

To serve, heap the fluffy grains on a warm platter, make a well in the center, and fill with lamb stew.

# Roasted Pepper and Tomato Salad

1 green bell pepper
2 tomatoes, peeled, seeded, and cut into
   small cubes
1 clove of garlic, pressed
1 pinch ground cumin
2 teaspoons olive oil

1 teaspoon lemon juice
½ teaspoon grated lemon peel
2 tablespoons chopped fresh mint or a
   pinch of dried mint flakes
Salt and pepper

Either grill the pepper over a gas flame at the end of a fork until it begins to char or place it in a preheated 450-degree F. oven on a baking sheet for 10 minutes, turn, and bake another 10 minutes until the skin begins to char and blister. Place the pepper in a closed plastic bag for a few minutes to cool and further loosen the skin. Slip off the skin and core, seed, and cut the pepper into the same-sized pieces as the tomatoes.

Put the tomatoes and pepper into a serving bowl. Add the remaining ingredients except the salt and pepper and mix thoroughly. Season to taste with salt and pepper and chill thoroughly before serving.

# Oranges Casablanca

2 large oranges
⅓ cup water
⅓ cup Marsala or orange liqueur

½ cup sugar
⅛ teaspoon cream of tartar
Juice of ½ lemon

Remove very thin strips of peel (the zest) from the oranges, using a sharp knife or a lemon zester, taking care not to include any of the bitter white pith. Set the strips and the oranges aside.

Combine the remaining ingredients in a small, heavy saucepan, bring slowly to a boil, stirring occasionally, add the orange peel strips, and simmer until the syrup is reduced by about a third. Cool.

With a sharp knife remove all the remaining peel and pith from the oranges. Holding the fruit over a plate or bowl to catch the juices, cut each orange into slices crosswise. Put each one back together again by placing a long wooden pick through the center to hold the slices in their original alignment. Add any juice accumulated during slicing to the syrup.

Arrange the oranges in two small serving bowls, preferably glass, and spoon the syrup and peel over each one. Refrigerate, basting occasionally with the syrup, and serve chilled.

# PLAN OF ATTACK

In every household where two people abide there is always one who jets out of bed with the dawn and is the soul of efficiency, brewing coffee, popping toast, and scrambling the newspaper. This individual will be able to handle the responsibilities of Cook Number One without missing a beat. Cook Number Two, on the other hand, can continue to feign unconsciousness while trying valiantly to ignore the din issuing from the kitchen.

## Cook Number One

*morning*
Prepare the lamb stew, or *tagine* as it is known in Morocco.
*1 hour, 15 minutes before*
Rinse couscous.
*1 hour before*
Steam couscous for 30 minutes.
*30 minutes before*
1. Spread couscous to dry for 10 to 15 minutes.   2. Chill wine.
*15 minutes before*
Season and butter couscous and return to steamer for final cooking before serving.

## Cook Number Two

*morning*
Pull covers smartly over your head and try not to feel guilty while Cook Number One makes the stew.
*1 hour, 15 minutes before*
Prepare syrup for oranges and cool.
*1 hour before*
Prepare salad and chill.
*45 minutes before*
1. Slice and reassemble oranges for dessert.   2. Begin chilling and basting dessert in refrigerator.
*15 minutes before*
Set table and warm plates and serving platter.
*after dinner*
Wash dishes (fair's fair).

(If you can persuade your partner to eat the couscous in the Moroccon way with just the first three fingers of the right hand—a real challenge for unschooled fingers—there won't be any forks to wash.)

# NEW ORLEANS

## MENU

*Daube Glacé*
(Beef in Aspic)

*Poireaux Acadiens*
(Marinated Leeks)

*Jambalaya*
(Shrimp and Ham with Rice)

*Bourbon Street Pudding*

Mardi Gras, the aptly named "Fat Tuesday" that immediately precedes Ash Wednesday and the beginning of Lent, has for centuries provided an excuse for bacchanalian excesses all over the world. But for most of us Mardi Gras means New Orleans and the climax of a thoroughly secular winter carnival devoted to marvelous nonsense and eating and drinking.

If, like us, you are among the 4.5 billion or so humans who *won't* find themselves billeted in the French Quarter when Shrove Tuesday rolls around next time, that doesn't mean you can't join the festivities, at least vicariously.

The cooking of Louisiana is unique. A lot of people who haven't been there think it's simply Americanized French cuisine, a notion that would startle the *chaussettes* off any tourists from Paris wandering around the Crescent City. Some of the terms are the same, but just as the language has evolved into a patois that few Parisians can understand, the dishes that developed into Creole and Cajun classics bear little resemblance to food in the old country. The recipes grew up from local ingredients leavened by the tastes and cultural influences of immigrants who came willingly from other parts of Europe and unwillingly from Africa. Thus, if those Gallic visitors we mentioned happened into a restaurant near the French Market and ordered *boudin blanc* expecting the light, delicately seasoned sausages of chicken and veal they were used to back home, their palates would likely be incinerated by the fiery mixture of coarsely ground pork, rice, and red peppers that masquerades innocently under that name in New Orleans. In the final analysis the city and country cooking of Louisiana is like New Orleans itself: exciting, boisterous, and not a little raffish.

To begin with, if you don't already own any, go out and buy a couple of Dixieland albums recorded at Preservation Hall. That will get you in the mood for preparing this menu, which definitely is not designed to be whipped up quickly after a hard day at the millrace. Fortunately the first course, *Daube Glacé*, should be made the day before. It's followed by one of our favorite jambalayas, of which there are as many versions as there are cooks in the Gulf states, accompanied by leeks marinated in a spicy dressing flavored with vinegar and mustard. Dessert is a down-home bread pudding with an uptown Bourbon Street sauce.

Although this dinner is served in courses, we suggest staying with a single wine throughout, a sturdy red such as one from the Rhône Valley or a Petite Sirah from California.

# Daube Glacé
## (BEEF IN ASPIC)

½ pound stewing beef
1 tablespoon cooking oil
¼ onion, chopped
½ stalk celery, chopped
¼ cup chopped carrots
1 sprig parsley
1 whole clove
¼ teaspoon thyme
½ carrot, peeled and coarsely grated

1 clove garlic, minced fine
1 pinch cayenne pepper
Salt and pepper
1 can jellied consommé (10$^1$/$_2$ ounces)
¼ cup dry Sherry
1 envelope (1 tablespoon) unflavored
    gelatin dissolved in ¼ cup water
2 thin slices lemon
Watercress

Dry the beef chunks with paper towels. Heat the oil in a heavy pot and brown the meat, turning frequently so the pieces achieve a rich color without burning. Remove the meat from the pot and add the onion, celery, and carrots. Cook gently until the vegetables are limp but not brown. Return the meat to the pot, cover with water and add the parsley, clove, and thyme. Cover the pot and simmer for 3 to 3½ hours or until the meat shreds easily with a fork. Remove the meat and cool. Shred the beef and toss in a bowl with the grated carrot, garlic, cayenne pepper, and salt and pepper to taste. Refrigerate until ready to finish the dish.

Warm the consommé, Sherry, and dissolved gelatin together. Pour a ¼-inch layer of the mixture into the bottom of a 6×3×2¼-inch loaf pan. Refrigerate until the aspic has jelled and is firm to the touch. Dip the lemon slices in the unchilled aspic and arrange them over the firm aspic in the bottom of the pan. Chill the pan again until the lemon slices are firmly anchored in the jelled base.

Pour the remaining aspic mixture (if it has begun to set, warm slightly to liquefy) over the beef and mix well. Spoon the mixture into the loaf pan and refrigerate for at least 12 hours.

To unmold, dip the pan in hot water for a moment, run a knife around the edges and turn out onto a platter. Garnish with watercress.

# Poireaux Acadiens
## (MARINATED LEEKS)

4 leeks
1 cup white wine
1 tablespoon tarragon vinegar
½ teaspoon paprika
½ teaspoon Dijon mustard

⅛ teaspoon Tabasco sauce
¼ teaspoon salt
3–4 tablespoons olive oil
Lemon wedges
½ carrot, sliced thinly into curls

Clean the leeks carefully under running water, cutting away any roots at the base and the broad leaves at the top. Place the leeks in a skillet and add the white wine and enough water to cover them. Bring the liquid to a boil, then partially cover the skillet, reduce the heat, and simmer the leeks for 10 to 15 minutes or until tender. Drain and arrange them on a serving plate.

In a small bowl whisk together the vinegar, paprika, mustard, Tabasco sauce, salt, and olive oil. Pour the mixture over the leeks and let them cool to room temperature, turning them occasionally in the marinade. Chill in the refrigerator and serve cold, garnished with lemon wedges and curled strips of carrot.


# Jambalaya
## (SHRIMP AND HAM WITH RICE)

1 tablespoon cooking oil
¼ pound ham, cut into ¼- to ½-inch
  cubes
1 small (or ½ large) green pepper,
  coarsely chopped
½ onion, chopped
¼ pound medium shrimp, cleaned and
  deveined, with tails on
¾ cup canned tomatoes, drained and
  chopped

¾ cup water
1 clove garlic, minced fine
1 teaspoon Worcestershire sauce
¼ teaspoon dried red pepper flakes
Salt and pepper
½ cup long-grain rice
Chopped parsley

Heat the oil in a medium skillet or an electric frying pan. Add the ham, green pepper, and onion and sauté until the meat is brown and the vegetables have softened. Add the shrimp, tomatoes, water, garlic, Worcestershire sauce, red pepper flakes, and salt and pepper to taste. Bring the mixture to a boil, then add the rice, stir once, cover the pan, reduce the heat, and simmer without lifting the lid for 20 minutes or until all the liquid is absorbed. Serve sprinkled with chopped parsley.

# Bourbon Street Pudding

4–6 thick slices day-old French or Italian
  bread
1 cup milk
1 egg
⅓ cup sugar
2 teaspoons vanilla
¼ cup raisins

**SAUCE**
2 tablespoons butter
½ cup brown sugar, packed
½ cup warm cream
2 tablespoons Bourbon

*Preheat oven to 350 degrees F.* Break the bread into small pieces in a bowl. Add milk and stir with a fork until the bread is thoroughly soaked and all the milk is absorbed. In a separate small bowl beat the egg, sugar, and vanilla until smooth. Pour the mixture into the bowl with the bread and mix with a spoon until all the ingredients are well combined. Stir in the raisins.

Liberally butter the bottom and sides of an 8×8-inch baking pan and spread the mixture in a shallow layer. Place the pan in a larger pan, pour boiling water into the larger pan to a depth of about ¾ inch, put into the oven, and bake 45 minutes.

To make the sauce, cream the butter and sugar together in a small bowl. Gradually beat in the warm cream. Transfer the mixture to a small saucepan and stir over medium heat until it reaches the boiling point. Remove from the heat, add the Bourbon, and beat the sauce with a rotary beater until it is smooth.

Spoon the pudding from the baking pan into bowls and serve warm, topped with the hot sauce.

# PLAN OF ATTACK

## *Both Cooks*

**night before**   Prepare the *Daube Glacé* and put in to chill overnight.

## *Cook Number One*

*1 hour, 30 minutes before*
Clean, cook, marinate, and chill leeks.
*1 hour before*
Make bread pudding.
*45 minutes before*
1. Put pudding in to bake (it will be ready just at dinnertime; keep it warm until ready to serve).   2. Make pudding sauce (reheat and beat it just before serving).

## *Cook Number Two*

*1 hour before*
Prepare and assemble all ingredients for Jambalaya.
*30 minutes before*
1. Begin cooking Jambalaya.   2. Open wine.

# NEW MEXICO

# MENU

*Gazpacho Blanco*
(Cold Soup)

*Chuletas de Cordero con Piñones*
(Lamb Chops with Pine Nuts)

*Rellenos de Calabacines*
(Stuffed Zucchini)

*Sopaipillas*
(Fried Puffed Bread)

*Avocado Ice Cream*

We have already made note of the inevitable diversity between members of any duet. To the list of incompatibilities we have already confessed, you may add the fact that one of us is a lover of fiery food and the other is a thoroughbred with a very tender mouth. This menu, from the Southwest part of the United States and distinct from the Mexican dinner that follows it, is our version of détente.

It begins with a cooling white gazpacho to soothe the delicate taste buds of the cautious, and then moves on to broiled or barbecued lamb chops with a torrid sauce redolent of chili, garlic, and pine nuts. If the budget is a consideration, we've found the same sauce works wonders for inexpensive lamb patties. Accompaniments are whole zucchinis that hold a hidden treasure of melted cheese, tomatoes, and a whisper of chili, and the crisp contrast of *sopaipillas,* the unusual puffed fried bread of New Mexico. Dessert is a suave avocado ice cream with the tang of lime juice and yogurt to offset the richness of the cream and avocado. As you can see, a little something for everybody.

The pivotal seasoning for most Southwest cooking is the chili, a feisty flavoring that can kick its way out of most corrals. In the fall anyone driving along the upper Rio Grande toward Taos will see *ristras*—ropes—of pepper pods hanging against sienna adobe walls. These peppers, which will dry until they're the color of hot coals, are the essence of the New Mexican cuisine that has drawn equally on its Spanish, Indian, and Anglo heritages.

Our lamb sauce, with its subtle interaction of lusty flavors and the resinous hint of New Mexico's native pine nut, or *piñon,* is typical of the fascinating food found close to the slopes of the Sangre de Cristo Mountains.

Although only one small chili is used in this recipe, it's important to know how to handle this form of legal dynamite. It's always wise to wear rubber gloves when working with them, and be particularly careful not to rub your face or eyes after touching chilies until you have thoroughly washed and dried your hands. The best kind of rubber gloves is not the cumbersome gauntlets advertised as a means of keeping debutantes from getting dishpan hands, but the thin kind you can buy in most paint stores and which resemble disposable surgical gloves.

Rinse chilies in cold water and remove the stems. Partially slit each one and brush out the seeds with your fingers. If you want the flavor without the blaze, removing the veins also will lessen the bite. Tear dried chilies into small pieces, cover with boiling water, and soak them for 10 minutes to an hour before using. Fresh ones can be used immediately after being skinned, a task that is easily accomplished by blistering them on all sides in a broiler, plunging them in ice water, and then peeling them from the stem downward. Fresh chilies also can be blistered over an outdoor grill (which lends them a wonderful flavor) or over a gas flame.

Naturally, you can adjust the chili in the lamb sauce to suit yourselves, but the amount we call for is the compromise that satisfied our disparate palates. On one subject, though, we are in complete agreement. With this menu most wines would be a waste of time, so quench the fire with long quaffs of cold beer.

# Gazpacho Blanco
## (COLD SOUP)

1 cucumber, peeled, seeded, and cut into
   chunks
1 cup chicken broth (see p. 220)
1 cup sour cream
1 clove garlic, chopped

1 tablespoon white wine vinegar
Salt and pepper
Chopped tomatoes
Chopped green onions

Place the cucumber, broth, sour cream, garlic, and vinegar in the container of a blender or food processor and blend until well mixed but the cucumber retains some texture and is not puréed. Season to taste with salt and pepper. Chill and serve sprinkled with chopped tomatoes and green onions.


# Chuletas de Cordero con Piñones
## (LAMB CHOPS WITH PINE NUTS)

¼ cup pine nuts
2 cloves garlic, peeled and chopped
1 dried hot red chili pepper about 1 inch
   long, stemmed, seeded, soaked, and
   chopped (dried chilies do not need to be
   skinned)
¼ teaspoon salt

1 tablespoon white vinegar
½ teaspoon sugar
¼ cup tomato paste
6 tablespoons olive oil
4 small loin lamb chops or 2 half-pound
   ground lamb patties

Heat the pine nuts in an ungreased skillet over moderate heat, shaking occasionally, until pale golden brown. Reserve 2 tablespoonfuls of the nuts and place the remaining 2 tablespoonfuls in the container of a blender or food processor. Add the garlic, chili pepper, salt, vinegar, sugar, and tomato paste and blend well. With the machine on, slowly add the olive oil in a thin stream and continue processing until the mixture is thick and well blended. This sauce can be made early in the day and refrigerated (you may have to blend it again to recombine the ingredients just before using). It can also be made by pounding together the dry ingredients (in this case don't soak the dried chili) in a mortar and pestle, then adding the vinegar and tomato paste before slowly beating in the oil. This method, though picturesque, isn't recommended for those suffering from tendonitis.

    If the lamb chops are to be broiled, place them on an oiled broiler pan and spread each one with about 1 tablespoon of the sauce. Broil about 5 minutes, then turn, coat the other side with sauce, and continue broiling until done. If you grill the lamb on an outdoor barbecue, baste the chops with the sauce as they cook. The same process should be used for lamb patties. When ready to serve, place the lamb on warm plates and sprinkle with pine nuts. The remaining sauce can be warmed over low heat or in a double boiler and served as an accompaniment. If the sauce separates as it is heated, reconstitute it quickly with a brief whirl in a blender or food processor or by using a strong arm and a whisk.

## Rellenos de Calabacines
### (STUFFED ZUCCHINI)

2 zucchini
½ cup grated Cheddar cheese
1 tablespoon chopped green chilies
   (canned)
½ tomato, peeled, seeded, and diced

¼ teaspoon salt
Flour
1–2 eggs, lightly beaten
Oil for deep frying

Place the whole zucchinis in boiling salted water and cook for 5 minutes. Plunge immediately into cold water. Using a small sharp knife or apple corer, hollow out the middle of each squash. Mix together the cheese, chilies, tomato, and salt and fill the insides of each zucchini with the mixture. Roll them in flour and then in the beaten egg. Heat oil to 365 degrees F. and fry the zucchinis until the coating is crisp and the cheese has begun to melt. They may be held in a 200-degree F. oven 15–20 minutes before serving.

## Sopaipillas
### (NEW MEXICO FRIED BREAD)

These lighter-than-air poufs of bread are universally loved in New Mexico. They're often served hot with honey or syrup, but we also like them cold the next day, cut open and stuffed with salad or some savory filling. If you fry them first and keep them warm, the same oil can be used to fry the zucchini in this menu.

1 cup flour
½ teaspoon salt
½ teaspoon baking powder

1½ teaspoons nonfat dry milk
1 teaspoon shortening or lard
½ cup water

Sift together the flour, salt, baking powder, and nonfat dry milk. Work in the shortening and enough water to make a soft dough. Roll dough out on a floured surface into a circle ⅛ inch thick. Cut the dough into pie-shaped wedges.

Heat at least 2 inches of oil in a heavy skillet, deep fryer, or electric frying pan to 380 degrees F. Fry 2 or 3 sopaipillas at a time. When the bread begins to puff, push the area where the air bubble develops back down into the oil to help it puff evenly. Turn several times and cook until golden brown. Keep them warm in the oven until time to serve.

# Avocado Ice Cream

½ cup heavy cream
3 tablespoons sugar
¼ teaspoon salt
1½ teaspoons gelatin
2 tablespoons water

1 egg, separated
1 large avocado, peeled and seeded
½ cup plain yogurt
2 tablespoons fresh lime juice
Raspberry sauce (optional)

Combine the cream, 1 tablespoon of the sugar, and salt in a saucepan. Heat gently just until bubbles form on the rim. Soften gelatin in the water. Beat egg yolk and stir into gelatin, then stir the gelatin mixture into the cream and cool.

Purée the avocado in a blender or food processor. Stir avocado, yogurt, and lime juice into the cooled cream mixture. Beat egg white until it forms soft peaks. Gradually add the remaining 2 tablespoons of sugar and continue beating until stiff. Fold avocado mixture into the egg white. Spoon into refrigerator tray, cover with foil, and place in freezer until firm. For a lighter texture, beat the mixture two or three times during the freezing process (about every 20–30 minutes).

**RASPBERRY SAUCE**
1 package (10 ounces) frozen raspberries
¼ cup sugar
1 tablespoon dark rum

Purée all ingredients in a blender or food processor. Strain to remove the seeds and spoon over ice cream.

# PLAN OF ATTACK

## Cook Number One

*ahead of time*
1. Make and freeze ice cream.   2. If you want raspberry sauce, make and refrigerate it.
*30 minutes ahead*
Make and fry *sopaipillas*. Keep warm.
*10 minutes ahead*
Broil lamb chops.

## Cook Number Two

*ahead of time*
1. Make chili sauce for lamb chops. Refrigerate.   2. Chill beer.
*1 hour ahead*
Make and chill gazpacho.
*30 minutes ahead*
Prepare zucchini for frying.
*10 minutes ahead*
Fry zucchini.

# OLD MEXICO

## MENU

*Shrimp Salad*
*Creamy Chicken Enchiladas*
*Lemon-Pepper Green Beans*
*Café Mexicano*
*Wedding Cookies*

Concha didn't exactly look like our idea of a cook. She was slim and wiry with the darting motions of a fragile bird. But when we rented the house on the coast of Mexico, Concha agreed to stay on to prepare our meals.

On the first evening, as we sat sipping margaritas on the bougainvillea-shaded patio, we tantalized ourselves by imagining the good stuff being conjured up in the kitchen. By the time dinner was announced we had worked ourselves into a frenzy of anticipation. Would it be a rich, dark mole, perhaps some freshly made tamales, or maybe some dish prepared with one of the fish we had seen being brought to the beach in nets that afternoon?

We sat down and Concha shyly presented her *pièce de résistance*—meat loaf.

It was actually quite a good meat loaf, but something of a letdown after our dreams of glorious Mexican dishes. Following dinner we haltingly explained in our fractured Spanish that we hoped she would cook some local specialties, real *cocina típica,* for us during our visit. She protested, telling us politely that the American alimentary system was too underdeveloped to handle anything but toy food. No, we insisted, we knew Mexican cooking and wanted to sample any typical dishes she would make for us. It was a struggle, but we finally convinced her we were sincere. From that moment on, Concha took us under her wing to introduce us to some delightful nuances of Mexican cuisine.

We accompanied her in the early morning to the market where we watched in awe as this tiny and modest woman bargained fiercely, rejecting anything that didn't meet her standards of excellence. We sat on stools in her immaculate kitchen as she stirred sauces and peeled chilies to re-create for us a dish she had learned from her grandmother. We brought back windfall avocados from afternoon walks that she turned into bowls of irresistible guacamole.

This menu, in memory of those sunlit days, is selected from the delicate end of the spectrum. The filling for the creamy enchiladas with chicken and just a gentle persuasion of chilies works splendidly in crêpes if you can't find tortillas.

Although the main dish is benign enough to go well with a chilled, young white wine, it almost seems a shame to pass up the opportunity to knock back one of the excellent Mexican beers. Brewing, a legacy of German and Swiss immigrants, has been a going business in Mexico for 140 years, and an awful lot of suds disappear in that hot nation. Some marvelous local beers aren't available outside their districts of origin, but about a dozen national brands are exported. Our particular favorites are *Superior, Tres Equis, Tecate,* and *Bohemia*—all light, clean, and refreshing.

## Shrimp Salad

Serve this appetizer salad mounded in 2 crisp corn tortilla cups or arranged on a few bright green lettuce leaves.

*2 teaspoons fresh lemon juice*
*¼ cup olive oil*
*Salt and pepper*
*1 cup cooked, shelled, and deveined*
  *shrimp, coarsely chopped*
*2 tablespoons minced onion*
*1 small tomato, peeled, seeded, and cubed*
  *(or use cherry tomatoes, halved)*

*½ small avocado, peeled, seeded, and*
  *cubed (leave the seed in the remaining*
  *half, brush with lemon juice, wrap and*
  *refrigerate for later use)*
*2 teaspoons finely chopped fresh*
  *coriander or parsley*

Place the lemon juice in a small bowl. Whisk in the olive oil and season to taste with salt and pepper. Stir in the shrimp and onion and allow to marinate while you prepare the remaining ingredients. Add the tomato, avocado, and chopped coriander or parsley and toss lightly to coat with the dressing.

To make tortilla cups, press a corn tortilla into a large ladle and hold in place with a slightly smaller spoon (a wire bird's nest potato maker works very well for this). Fry in deep fat until the tortilla is crisp. These can be held in a turned-off oven overnight if you like. Tortilla cups are pretty containers for guacamole or sauces as well as salads.

## Creamy Chicken Enchiladas

*2 tablespoons butter*
*1 onion, thinly sliced*
*¾ cup shredded cooked chicken (about ½*
  *large breast)*
*2 tablespoons diced canned green chilies*
  *(or more to taste)*
*3 ounces cream cheese, diced*

*Salt*
*Oil for frying*
*4 flour tortillas*
*⅓ cup heavy cream*
*1 cup grated Monterey Jack or other mild*
  *white cheese*

GARNISH

Chopped green onion

Sliced black olives

Lime wedges

Heat the butter in a skillet and add the onion. Cook over very low heat, stirring occasionally, for 20 minutes or until limp but not brown. Remove from heat and add the shredded chicken, chilies, and diced cream cheese. Mix lightly with a fork to blend and add salt to taste.

Preheat oven to 375 degrees F.

In another small skillet, heat about ¼ inch oil. Place tortillas one at a time in the hot oil and fry a few seconds until they blister and become limp. Don't let them crisp. Remove with tongs and drain on paper towels.

Spoon ¼ of the filling down the center of each tortilla and roll. Set the rolled enchiladas, seam side down, in a baking dish and moisten the tops with cream. Sprinkle with grated cheese and bake, uncovered, for 20 minutes. Garnish and serve.

## Lemon-Pepper Green Beans

½ pound fresh green beans cut in 2-inch
  lengths
1 tablespoon butter
1 tablespoon minced parsley

1 tablespoon fresh lemon juice
¼ cup diced sweet red pepper or drained
  canned pimiento
Salt and pepper

Cook the beans, uncovered, in rapidly boiling salted water just until tender crisp, about 7 minutes. Drain. Add the butter, parsley, and lemon juice and toss with the beans. Stir in the red pepper or pimiento and season to taste with salt and pepper.

## Café Mexicano

1 ½ ounces (1 ½ squares) semi-sweet
  chocolate
1 cup milk
¼ teaspoon almond extract
¼ teaspoon cinnamon

1 tablespoon sugar
1 cup hot, strong coffee
2 ounces brandy
2 cinnamon sticks (optional)

Break the chocolate into pieces and put it in a small saucepan with the milk. Heat gently, stirring, just until the chocolate melts and the milk is hot but not boiling. Put the mixture in the container of a blender with the almond extract, cinnamon, and sugar and blend at medium speed for 15 seconds. Fill two large mugs half full with the chocolate mixture. Pour hot coffee into each mug almost to the rim and stir 1 ounce of brandy into each. Serve with a cinnamon stick in each mug if you like.

# Wedding Cookies

Buttery and rich, these beloved Mexican sweets are thickly coated with powdered sugar while still warm. This recipe makes about a dozen.

*½ cup sweet butter, softened*
*1 cup flour*
*¼ cup sifted confectioners' sugar*
*Pinch of salt*

*½ cup finely chopped pecans or almonds*
*½ teaspoon vanilla*
*Additional confectioners' sugar*

*Preheat oven to 350 degrees F.* Beat the butter until light and fluffy. Beat in the flour, confectioners' sugar, salt, nuts and vanilla to make a soft dough. Pinch off pieces of dough the size of large walnuts and roll between your palms to form round balls, or form into half-moon shapes. Place about 1½ inches apart on an ungreased baking sheet and bake in the center of the oven for 20 minutes or until cookies are pale golden. Cool slightly on wire racks and dust thickly with confectioners' sugar while still warm.

# PLAN OF ATTACK

## Cook Number One

***ahead of time***
1. Make and bake wedding cookies.
2. Chill beer.

***1 hour before***
1. Cook, peel, devein, and coarsely chop shrimp.  2. Wash and cut string beans.  3. Prepare garnishes for enchiladas.  4. Prepare salad dressing.

***20 minutes before***
1. Prepare rest of salad ingredients and make salad.  2. Set out ingredients to make and serve Café Mexicano after dinner.

## Cook Number Two

***ahead of time***
1. Make tortilla cups for salad.  2. Cook and shred chicken.

***1 hour before***
1. Prepare filling for enchiladas.  2. Fry flour tortillas, fill, place in baking dish, moisten with cream, and sprinkle with grated cheese.

***20 minutes before***
1. Place enchiladas in preheated oven.  2. Prepare lemon-pepper beans.

# POLYNESIA

# MENU

*Lahaina Sunset*
*I'a Ota*
(Marinated Raw Fish)
*Curried Coconut Chicken in Pineapple*
*Sugar Snap Peas with Mushrooms*
*Macadamia Chiffon Tarts*

This is the sort of dinner we like to have in the dead of winter, a time that forever divides travelers and stay-at-homes. While our friends flash cruise brochures or exhibit obscenely bronzed hides, we are usually found huddled by the fire getting crosser by the minute. If you, too, find it irritating to be nursing snow-shovel elbow while all around you people are packing bikinis and heading for warmer climes, even one evening in paradise (a reference to neither a new perfume nor an X-rated movie) can lift your spirits. Turn up the heat past the federal guidelines for a couple of hours, take that awful aloha shirt out of mothballs, and settle down for a luau for two.

There was a time when the ingredients required for such self-indulgence were hard to find on the mainland any time of year, but it happens that everything needed for this menu is available in midwinter, especially pineapple, which is at the height of its season.

No dinner in the tropics would be complete without one of those insidious rum drinks that have come to symbolize raffish saloons on Polynesian waterfronts. The cocktail we suggest for this equatorial fantasy is not as lethal as some of those explosive mixtures, and it works perfectly for two people.

The first course, *I'a Ota,* is a traditional Tahitian delicacy in which the fish is "cooked" as it marinates in lime juice (in the tropics, any dish that allows you to stay out of the kitchen is as popular with cooks as a ninth wave is with surfers). The fish is followed by chicken and fresh pineapple in a creamy curry sauce served in a pineapple shell. Crisp sugar snap peas or Chinese pea pods sautéed with mushrooms add color and texture, and a light chiffon tart studded with macadamia nuts closes this escapist menu. In keeping with the spirit of this vicarious tropical holiday, pour a light, refreshing summer wine such as a dry Chenin Blanc.

# Lahaina Sunset

2 ounces light rum
2 ounces dark rum
1 tablespoon grenadine
1 ounce curaçao
Juice of 1 medium orange

Juice of 1 lime
Juice of 1 lemon
1 tablespoon confectioners' sugar
1 cup chopped ice

Combine all the ingredients in a blender and blend at high speed 15–20 seconds. Divide the drink between two large (at least 12-ounce) glasses filled with ice cubes, and garnish with pineapple and cocktail cherries on toothpicks.

# I'a Ota
### (MARINATED RAW FISH)

The important thing about marinated raw fish is that it should be made with *very fresh* ocean fish, not fish that has ever lived in fresh water. The latter are subject to parasites. The coconut milk called for in this recipe and the following one is now available frozen in many markets, but we have included a way of making it at home in a pinch. It has nothing to do with the liquid found inside fresh coconuts, by the way. That's called coconut water.

½ pound fresh skinned and boned fish
    such as halibut, white sea bass, tuna, or
    shark
3–4 large limes
2 green onions, chopped with some of the
    green tops

1 small tomato, peeled, seeded, and
    chopped
¼ cup coconut milk

Cut the fish into ½-inch chunks and place in a glass or stainless steel bowl. Cover with cold salted water and allow to stand for 30 minutes. Drain thoroughly. Squeeze enough lime juice to cover the fish and marinate for at least 2 hours at room temperature or at least 4 hours in the refrigerator. When ready to serve, drain off the lime juice, add the rest of the ingredients, and stir gently until well mixed.

**COCONUT MILK**
Pour *2 cups boiling water* over *4 cups grated fresh coconut meat* and allow it to stand for 30 minutes. Strain through a double layer of cheesecloth that has been rinsed and squeezed dry, squeezing to remove all the milk. If you use dried coconut, substitute milk for the water.

# Curried Coconut Chicken in Pineapple

This is best served with freshly cooked rice and chutney passed on the side.

1 small pineapple (about 2 to 2¹/₂
    pounds)
3 tablespoons butter
1 clove garlic, minced
½ cup chopped onion
1 piece (¹/₂ inch) of fresh gingerroot,
    peeled and chopped
2 teaspoons curry powder or more to taste
2 tablespoons flour
1¹/₂ cups coconut milk (see above)
½ teaspoon salt

1 tablespoon butter
1 large whole chicken breast, boned,
    skinned and cut into bite-sized pieces
½ cup water
¼ teaspoon Chinese 5-spice seasoning or
    ¹/₄ teaspoon ground anise seed
GARNISH
Fresh mint or watercress
Toasted coconut or slivered toasted
    almonds

Halve the pineapple lengthwise and carefully remove the fruit, leaving a shell about ½ inch thick. Discard the core and cut the fruit into chunks. Place the pineapple shells upside down on paper towels to drain.

In a saucepan melt 2 tablespoons of the butter, add the garlic, onion, and ginger and cook gently over low heat for about 20 minutes or until onion is limp and golden. Mix together the curry powder and flour and stir into onion mixture. Cook, stirring constantly, for about 5 minutes. Add coconut milk and cook over low heat, stirring occasionally, until mixture thickens (5–10 minutes). Strain.

Heat the remaining 1 tablespoon butter in a skillet and sauté chicken pieces over moderate heat until golden brown. Add water and 5-spice powder or anise, cover, and simmer 5 minutes. Remove chicken with slotted spoon and drain on paper towels. Add chicken and pineapple to curry sauce and reheat. Spoon into pineapple shells, garnish as you like, and serve.

# Sugar Snap Peas with Mushrooms

It's not often that an entirely new vegetable appears on the scene, but the sugar snap pea is just such a debutante. Its availability will increase as time goes by, but meanwhile the more widely known Chinese pea pods, fresh or frozen, can be used in this recipe.

⅛ pound sugar snap peas or fresh or
    thawed frozen Chinese pea pods
1 teaspoon cooking oil

3 mushrooms, cleaned and sliced
1 teaspoon soy sauce
Toasted sesame seeds

To prepare sugar snap peas for cooking, pinch the very tip to get a grip on the string. Pull the string up the straight side of the pea toward the stem. Pinch off the stem and continue pulling the string down the other side until it is removed on both sides. Sugar snap peas must be strung before they are cooked. Cut the peas or pea pods in half crosswise.

Heat the oil in a skillet or a wok over medium heat. Add the sliced mushrooms and sauté until slightly browned. Cover and simmer 3 minutes. Uncover and add the peas or pea pods and cook, stirring, for 2 minutes. Stir in the soy sauce, cover, and cook 1 minute longer. Serve sprinkled with toasted sesame seeds.

# *Macadamia Chiffon Tarts*

**CRUST**
½ cup vanilla wafer crumbs
2 tablespoons sugar
2 tablespoons melted butter
**FILLING**
⅓ cup unsalted macadamia nuts,
   toasted*
½ teaspoon unflavored gelatin

1 tablespoon cold water
1 egg, separated
2 tablespoons sugar
2 tablespoons boiling water
2 tablespoons dark rum
½ teaspoon finely grated lemon zest
Sweetened whipped cream (optional)

*Preheat oven to 350 degrees F.* To make the tart shell, mix together the crumbs, sugar, and melted butter and press into two 3-inch tart pans. Bake 8 minutes. Cool.

NOTE   If the macadamia nuts are salted, spread on a towel and rub to remove as much salt as possible. Chop nuts and place in a single layer on a baking sheet. Toast 5 minutes in a 350-degree F. oven, or until golden brown.

To make the filling, put the cold water in a heatproof glass cup, sprinkle the gelatin into it, and let soften 2–3 minutes. Set the cup in simmering water and stir over low heat until the gelatin dissolves.

Beat the egg yolk until lemon-colored, then add 1 tablespoon of the sugar and continue beating until mixture is thick enough to fall from the beater in a ribbon. Continue beating and add the boiling water slowly. Pour the mixture into a small saucepan and stir over low heat until it thickens enough to coat a spoon. Remove the pan from the heat and stir in the gelatin. Strain into a bowl. Stir in the rum and lemon zest and cool the mixture to room temperature, stirring occasionally.

Beat the egg white until frothy and then gradually add the remaining 1 table-spoon of sugar while continuing to beat until soft peaks form. Fold the chopped nuts and egg white into the custard and pour the mixture into the tart shells. Refrigerate. Serve chilled, topped with whipped cream and/or additional toasted nuts.

# PLAN OF ATTACK

Since both the marinated raw fish and the tarts must be done ahead of time, the actual preparation time for dinner is only about an hour. That's about how long it should take to consume the Lahaina Sunset if you're prudent.

## Cook Number One

**ahead of time**
Make *I'a Ota*.
**1 hour before**
1. Begin sautéeing onions for curried chicken.   2. Prepare pineapple shells and reserve fruit.
**40 minutes before**
Add flour and curry powder to onion, cook, and add coconut cream.
**20 minutes before**
1. Sauté and simmer chicken pieces. 2. Finish making main dish and serve.

## Cook Number Two

**ahead of time**
Make tarts.
**1 hour before**
String sugar snap peas and slice mushrooms.
**30 minutes before**
1. Cook rice to accompany curried chicken.   2. Chill wine.
**10 minutes before**
Cook sugar snap peas.

# CHINA

# MENU

*Egg Flower Corn Soup*
*Vegetable Beef*
*Tomato Salad in Papaya Sampans*
*Beijing Glazed Apples*
*or*
*Gingered Ice Cream*

Much of Chinese cuisine is, in a way, the original fast food, requiring only a brief flirtation with the fire to reach its perfect stage of doneness. The drawbacks are all that chopping ahead of time, and the fact that often the cooking chores must be performed at the last minute. But Chinese recipes should be in the repertoire of every busy cook.

While the thought of stir frying may seem intimidating to some, the technique is really quite simple. A wok looks nice hanging in your kitchen, but a good electric frying pan or a skillet will do the trick almost as well. The key to success is organization, so before you turn on the heat be sure to have everything you need on hand, cut up, and ready to go. Line up your ingredients in their logical order and half the battle's won.

Place the wok or skillet over high heat. When it's hot enough to cause a drop of water to sizzle, add a necklace of oil around the top rim of the pan so it will slither down the sides and coat the surface (if you're using a skillet, just film the bottom with oil). In a few seconds the oil will begin to smoke. At that instant add any flavoring ingredients such as garlic, ginger, or chili peppers, stirring continuously so they don't burn. Now add the remaining ingredients according to their cooking times. Finally, add the liquids and any thickening and stir well.

The term "stir frying" can be misleading since the process is really a folding action, using a spatula to slide under the food and turn it. The idea is to keep the mass in constant motion.

A classic Chinese menu would consist of several dishes of contrasting flavors and textures, but since that can be an awesome undertaking even for experts, we prefer to serve things in the occidental fashion: soup, a single main course, rice, salad, and dessert.

The conventional wisdom when it comes to Chinese food is that wines of European origin (or persuasion) are inappropriate, that tea or the traditional white or yellow rice wines should be served. So much for conventional wisdom. For this particular entrée we like a Beaujolais or California Gamay served at cellar temperature (about 55 degrees F.).

## Egg Flower Corn Soup

2 cups chicken broth (see p. 220)
1 teaspoon Sherry
Salt
½ cup fresh corn scraped from the cob or creamed corn

1 egg, beaten
1 tablespoon cornstarch
3 tablespoons water
1 tablespoon minced toasted almonds

Combine the broth and Sherry in a saucepan and add salt to taste. Bring to a boil. Add the corn and return the soup to a boil. Cook for 2 minutes, stirring constantly. Lower the heat until the liquid is just simmering.

Dribble the beaten egg into the soup to form "flowers." Combine the cornstarch and water and stir into the soup. Cook for 1 minute, stirring gently. Serve at once, garnished with minced toasted almonds.

# Vegetable Beef

Part of the genius of Chinese cooking (and all great cuisines) is that menus are planned around what's freshest in the market. Follow their example and select for this dish whatever vegetable is at its seasonal best. Broccoli flowers, asparagus cut Chinese fashion on the diagonal, fresh green beans, even sliced zucchini are good choices.

½ pound flank steak
1 tablespoon cornstarch
2 tablespoons soy sauce
3 tablespoons peanut oil
1 small clove garlic, minced
½ teaspoon sugar

1 cup vegetables, blanched in boiling
   water 1–2 minutes and cut up
2 tablespoons Sherry
2 tablespoons chicken broth (see p. 220)
Cooked rice

Cut the flank steak across the grain into very thin slices. Then cut the slices into ½-inch strips. This is easy to do if the meat is partially frozen and if your knife is saber-sharp.

    Combine the cornstarch, soy sauce, and 1 tablespoon of the oil. Pour over the beef in a bowl and stir to coat all sides. Allow the beef to marinate while you enjoy the soup.

    Heat the remaining 2 tablespoons of oil until sizzling. Add the garlic and stir-fry just until golden. Sprinkle on the sugar and add the vegetables and stir-fry for 1 minute. Add the beef strips and stir-fry 1 minute longer. Add the Sherry and chicken broth and stir-fry for another ½ minute. Serve at once over cooked rice.

# Tomato Salad in Papaya Sampans

DRESSING
3 tablespoons oil
1 teaspoon fresh lime or lemon juice
½ teaspoon chopped fresh basil or ⅛ teaspoon dried
Salt and pepper
SALAD
1 papaya

1 teaspoon lime juice
1 tomato, peeled, seeded, and diced
1 stalk celery, diced
1 green onion, chopped with some of the
   green top
¼ cup bean sprouts
Lettuce
2 tablespoons chopped walnuts

Combine dressing ingredients, including salt and pepper to taste.

    Cut papaya in half lengthwise and scoop out the seeds. Sprinkle the cut halves with lime juice. Combine the tomato, celery, chopped green onion and bean sprouts in a bowl. Toss with the dressing and spoon into the papaya halves. Place each half on a crisp lettuce leaf on salad plates and serve topped with a sprinkling of chopped walnuts.

## Beijing Glazed Apples

Although the Chinese aren't devoted to dessert, this one provides a dramatic grand finale for many sumptuous restaurant meals. Since it requires careful timing and coordination, we've also offered a simple alternative dessert for those who've had a hard day and don't feel steady enough to cope with a pan of boiling sugar.

| | |
|---|---|
| *1 tablespoon oil* | *3 tablespoons cornstarch* |
| *¾ cup sugar* | *Oil for deep frying* |
| *1 tart apple* | *1 tablespoon toasted sesame seeds* |
| *1 egg* | *Bowl of ice water with ice cubes* |

Lightly oil the surface of a serving plate so the glazed apples won't stick.

Combine 1 tablespoon of oil with the sugar in a heavy-bottomed saucepan. Stir and gently bring to a boil, then reduce heat and simmer for 4 minutes. Keep syrup hot.

Peel and core the apple and cut it into six wedges. Dip in beaten egg and then sprinkle on all sides with cornstarch. Heat the oil for deep frying to 375 degrees F. Cook the coated apple wedges, a few at a time, until golden (5–8 minutes). Remove with a slotted spoon to the oiled serving plate. Pour the hot syrup over the fruit, coating each piece of apple thoroughly. Sprinkle with toasted sesame seeds.

Place the bowl of ice water in the center of the table and immediately bring in the hot candied apples. With forks dip the sugar-coated fruit into the ice water and hold there until the syrup hardens and forms a crackly glaze over the deep-fried apples. Biting through the shimmering syrup coating and into the apple with its melting soft center is truly a memorable experience.

Or, you may prefer to say the heck with it and serve the following.

## Gingered Ice Cream

Spoon some rich vanilla ice cream into the bottom of parfait or sundae glasses. Top with chopped sweet preserved ginger with a little of its syrup. Add more ice cream and top with some more ginger and syrup.

# PLAN OF ATTACK

## Cook Number One

*30 minutes before soup*
Slice and marinate beef.
*20 minutes before soup*
Cut and blanch vegetables.
*5 minutes before soup*
Start cooking rice.
*15 minutes after soup*
Stir-fry Vegetable Beef and serve with rice.

## Cook Number Two

*30 minutes before soup*
Make and refrigerate salad.
*15 minutes before soup*
1. Make soup.  2. If wine has not been in a cellar, refrigerate briefly.
*15 minutes after soup*
1. Clear soup bowls.  2. Put salads on table.  3. Take rice off stove and spoon onto plates.

## Both Cooks

*after main course*   Make dessert together. You work it out.

# JAPAN

# MENU

*Shrimp-and-Cucumber Sunomono*
*Sukiyaki*
*Japanese Steamed Rice*
*Fresh Fruit*

The differences between Chinese and Japanese cooking are at once subtle and substantial, and help to define their differences in character. Although both cultures enjoy food with great gusto, the Japanese learned a long time ago that dinner can be a soothing oasis at the end of a trying day. The calm ceremony of preparation and the artistic challenge of presentation are age-old rituals designed to settle jangled nerves.

While many Japanese dishes are unfamiliar to Westerners, one that is widely known and appreciated is sukiyaki (pronounced *skee-yah-kee*). The name, which means "broiled on the blade of a plow," reveals something about the dish's origins. Generations ago farmers and hunters cooked just-killed animals over an open fire on whatever utensil might be handy. In most Japanese households today the plow has been replaced by an electric frying pan, and sukiyaki has evolved into a much more sophisticated modern version. It combines two styles of Japanese cooking: *nabemono,* which describes food cooked at the table, and *nimono,* which refers to boiling in seasoned liquids.

Although the ingredients in this menu are somewhat similar to those in the Chinese one that preceded it, the effect is quite different. As with all Japanese foods, the presentation of the sukiyaki is as important as the flavor. Tender beef, sliced to almost transparent thinness, and colorful vegetables are arranged artfully on a platter until the time comes for them to be cooked. The platter can be arranged well ahead of time and covered with plastic wrap and refrigerated.

The Rolls-Royce of beef in Japan, and the choice for sukiyaki by those who can afford it, is grown in Kobe. Pampered cattle are curried each day and massaged to distribute their fat. For some reason this is done with gin, which seems to us a criminal waste but they appear to like it. The chosen steers grow plump and content on a diet of beans, rice, and bran and on their third birthdays they get ID cards that say they're of legal age to drink beer. During the twilight of their short lives, Kobe cattle slosh down enough beer to sustain the American college fraternity system. The result of all this excess is an exquisitely flavored, well-marbled beef called *shimofuri* or "fallen frost," treasured by connoisseurs. It should be, for it costs the earth. Although the beef available in your market may not have enjoyed as much of *la dolce vita,* if you choose a good piece of sirloin or fillet your sukiyaki should be delicious.

Before the main course we suggest a shrimp-and-cucumber salad, one of the type known in Japan as *sunomono,* or vinegared. The sukiyaki will, of course, be accompanied by rice. But dessert for a menu such as this is a challenge. The Japanese, like the Chinese, generally don't go in for sweets at the end of a meal. A good solution is to serve fresh fruit. We usually follow sukiyaki with wedges of melon sprinkled with grated orange rind and grated fresh ginger.

The orthodox accompaniment for this meal would be sake, the traditional rice wine that has been drunk in Japan since antiquity. A colorless, slightly sweet fermentation ranging between about 12 and 18 percent alcohol, sake is an acquired taste for most Occidentals, although its popularity in America has increased fast enough that there are a couple of rice wineries producing domestic versions. Most of it, however, is still made in Japan.

The Japanese serve sake warm, pouring it from earthenware flagons into small porcelain cups. An insidious game played on late evenings in geisha houses involves two players alternately pouring small amounts of sake into a tiny cup until one of them can't add any more without causing it to overflow. The hapless loser has to drink one tall cup for every person at the table, which means that after large gatherings he might have to be taken home on a shutter.

For those who wish to confine sake to cooking, we recommend a sturdy red wine to go with sukiyaki, perhaps a California Petite Sirah or a Côtes du Rhône.

## Shrimp-and-Cucumber Sunomono

*2–3 ounces tiny cooked shrimp*
*1 cucumber*
*½ teaspoon salt*
*1 tablespoon toasted sesame seeds*
**DRESSING**
*1 tablespoon rice vinegar*

*½ teaspoon sugar*
*Pinch salt*
*¼ teaspoon Mirin (Japanese sweet sake)*
    *or dry Sherry*
*½ teaspoon soy sauce*

Drain the shrimp. Place in a bowl and chill. Peel the cucumber and, using a very sharp knife, cut about 12 thin slices from it. Wrap the remaining cucumber in plastic wrap and refrigerate it for later. Place the cucumber slices in a colander and sprinkle with ½ teaspoon salt. Allow them to stand for 30 minutes. Drain on paper towels and toss lightly into the bowl with the chilled shrimp.

To make the dressing, combine all the dressing ingredients in a small jar, put the top on, and shake well to blend. Just before serving, toss the shrimp and the cucumbers with the dressing and sprinkle the top of each serving with toasted sesame seeds.

## Sukiyaki

The ingredients for this can be as exotic or as simple as you like. If you have an international grocery or oriental market nearby, you'll be able to make a totally authentic version. If not, we've offered ideas for substitutions.

*1 small piece of beef suet (or 2 tablespoons cooking oil)*
*½ pound fillet or sirloin steak, cut in paper-thin slices*
*2 green onions, split lengthwise and cut into 1½-inch lengths including the green tops*
*½ cup thinly sliced white onion*
*2 ribs of celery, sliced on the diagonal*
*2 ounces mushrooms, thinly sliced*

*¼ pound spinach, stemmed and cut crosswise into 1-inch strips*
*2 ounces drained shirataki (noodlelike yam threads, available in cans), or substitute 2 ounces thin spaghetti, cooked and drained*
*2 ounces tofu (bean curd) cut in ½-inch cubes, or substitute a 1-egg omelet, cooled and cut into ½-inch strips*

**COOKING SAUCE**

2 tablespoons soy sauce
1 teaspoon sugar
1 tablespoon sake or dry Sherry
2 tablespoons beef broth (see p. 266)
1 tablespoon water

**FOR DIPPING**

2 raw eggs (extremely optional), slightly
  beaten

Arrange the platter of ingredients with all the artistry you can muster, noticing the shapes and colors of the foods and how they relate to one another. Mix together the sauce ingredients in a small pitcher and have it waiting near the scene of the action. Bring the electric frying pan to the table and set it at medium high. (If you don't have an electric frying pan, sukiyaki can be cooked in a skillet in the kitchen, but if your Japanese neighbors find out about it they're likely to laugh you out of the neighborhood.)

Using chopsticks if you have them, place the suet in the hot skillet, rub it around until it melts, and then discard it. Otherwise, film the pan with the cooking oil. When the pan is hot, add the beef slices and stir until they lose any pink color, but don't brown them. Push the beef to one side of the pan and add the vegetables except the spinach in sequence, beginning with the green onions and keeping each in separate little piles. Add the cooking sauce and simmer uncovered for about 4 minutes.

Push each of the piles of vegetables to the edges of the pan and add the spinach, pushing it down into the liquid and turning frequently. When it has wilted, push it into a mound at the edge of the pan. Add the noodles and the bean curd, turning gently to allow them to absorb the flavors of the broth. If you use omelet strips, add them just before serving.

You don't have to be a virtuoso with chopsticks to show off with them making sukiyaki. Use them to transfer the ingredients from the pan to two plates, dividing them evenly. Purists insist on dipping each bite into slightly beaten egg before consuming it. We don't.

## *Japanese Steamed Rice*

1 cup short-grained rice (or long-grained
  if that's all you can find)

1⅛ cups water (if using long-grained
  rice, increase the water to 2 cups)

Wash the rice thoroughly if using short-grained rice. Cover it with water and let it soak 30 minutes. Drain.

Place the rice in a heavy saucepan with the water and bring it to a boil over high heat. Reduce the heat to medium and cook 5 minutes. Reduce the heat to low, cover, and continue cooking for 15 minutes more. Turn off the heat and allow the rice to steam with the cover on for another 10 minutes before serving.

This will produce two bowls of rice in the Japanese style, which is fluffy but still sticky enough to allow you to get a purchase on it with chopsticks.

# PLAN OF ATTACK

## Cook Number One

*1 hour before*
1. Chill the shrimp for the salad.   2. Peel and slice cucumber and place in a colander.   3. Make the dressing.
*30 minutes before*
Arrange platter of Sukiyaki ingredients.
*just before*
Toss salad with dressing and serve.

## Cook Number Two

*1 hour before*
1. Wash rice thoroughly and begin soaking it.   2. Prepare cooking sauce for Sukiyaki.   3. Ready fresh fruit for dessert and chill.
*30 minutes before*
Drain and begin cooking rice. If serving sake, warm the opened bottle in a pan of gently simmering water.
*10 minutes before*
Turn the heat off under the rice for final steaming.
*just before*
Heat electric frying pan during salad course.

# SIX

# INSTANT ELEGANCE

In the best of all possible worlds, everyone would have time to make a perfect little dinner every night. There would be candles on the table and no cork in the wine. But we all know this is seldom the case.

More often the scenario runs something like this:

You arrive home tired and hungry, anticipating a savory *Gigot de pré-salé roti*, but can't find the leg of lamb you took out of the freezer that morning. The dog, on the other hand, is belching guiltily and there's evidence of freshly dug earth in the begonia bed.

Or, you left the house in the morning full of self-confidence, knowing that a ragout was bubbling in your slow cooker. That evening you find in the mailbox a cheery announcement from the power company that the electricity was off all afternoon.

Or, at 5:30 P.M. you realize that the veal chops you planned for dinner are still residing in the freezer, as cold and unyielding as the Arctic tundra.

Or, you have just returned from vacation with a suitcase full of damp bathing suits, a raging case of poison oak, and no desire to be seen in any restaurant where you might be recognized.

We could go on with this tragic litany, but you get the idea. These are the nights when only a well-stocked cupboard and a ration of ingenuity can save the situation.

Most cooks have a few swift improvisations they turn to when disaster strikes, but it's easy to become dependent on just one reliable dish in every emergency. The following share several characteristics: they are made from ingredients one is likely to have on hand or that keep well; they are simple enough not to confound you if your biorhythms are out of whack, and yet, for those of us who believe eating well is the best revenge, none sacrifices flavor for the sake of speed.

To make things as simple as possible, we've listed each dish under the heading of its main ingredients so if you find yourself staring piteously at a single can of shrimp or a few eggs, you can instantly check your options.

But before we get to the main course, why not pause for a moment, pour yourself a pacifier, and put together something to nibble on while you contemplate the next step.

# APPETIZERS

- Spread crackers or toast rounds with cream cheese or brie and hot-pepper jelly.
- Put peanuts in a single layer on a cookie sheet and sprinkle with curry powder. Stir gently to coat nuts and bake in a 350-degree F. oven 5–10 minutes.
- Wrap saltines in thinly sliced bacon strips and bake in a 350-degree F. oven for 10 minutes or until the bacon is crisp.

- Arrange cucumber slices on a serving plate and top each with a slice of lox. Serve with lemon wedges and cracked black pepper.
- Blend a 7-ounce can of drained tuna with a cup of mayonnaise (see p. 000) and season with capers, basil, and chopped green onions to taste. Serve with cherry tomatoes, raw mushrooms, and sliced cucumbers for dipping.
- Slice raw beef paper-thin and drizzle with olive oil mixed with parsley, lemon juice, and capers. Roll in cylinders and garnish with lemon wedges and watercress.
- Blend canned garbanzo beans with garlic, parsley, and olive oil and serve with crisp raw vegetables and triangles of toasted pita bread.
- Combine mayonnaise (see p. 000) with any of the following:
  - grated Cheddar cheese, chopped green onions, minced olives, and Tabasco.
  - grated Parmesan cheese and chopped green onions.
  - chopped mushrooms and tarragon.

  Spread on toast rounds and slip under the broiler until puffed and bubbly.
- Spread *tahini* (sesame seed paste) on puffed-rice cakes and top with crumbled bacon or sliced green onions.
- Toast one side of dark whole-grain bread and drizzle the other side with olive oil. Top with crumbled Kasseri cheese (available in cheese shops and Greek markets) and dried oregano. Broil until golden.
- Fry shrimp chips (available at oriental markets) in deep oil just until they rise to the surface and puff. Serve with a dip of sour cream mixed with chopped chutney and curry.
- Sprinkle drained and dried oysters with lemon juice and Tabasco and wrap in bacon. Broil until bacon is crisp.
- Combine Gorgonzola cheese, a little sour cream, and brandy to taste. Use to fill raw mushroom caps.

And now, without further ado, we'll trot out some of our favorite save-the-day dishes to pass in brief review.

# MAIN COURSES

## *Eggs*

Even the most frivolous cook usually has a few *oeufs* tucked in the refrigerator. There was a time, to be sure, when eggs retired after breakfast and didn't come out of their shell again until the next morning, but that day is long past.

The omelet is the perfect package to hold any number of intriguing fillings, and with a salad, some crusty bread, and a glass of wine is a perfectly respectable and often memorable meal. There are those, however, who feel they don't have the knack for omelet making. Often they believe there is some mystique to it and one must be born with the gift. Phooey. Omelets are not much harder to prepare than scrambled eggs, and it's well worth the practice it takes to learn the skill. If you promise not to spread it around, we'll admit we're heretics when it comes to omelets—we like them firm. If you do too, just cook them slightly longer over lower heat and all will be well. And remember, if your first attempts don't work, scramble things up, stir in the filling you have chosen, and only you will know the difference.

**Basic Omelet**   For each omelet, stir together with a fork 2 large eggs (at room temperature), 1 tablespoon water, and salt and pepper to taste. Heat an omelet pan (a 9-inch pan that slopes down to a 6-inch center is a good size for 2 eggs) over high heat until a drop of water sprinkled on the surface bounces around. Add 1 tablespoon butter to the pan and swirl until it foams but doesn't brown. Pour in the eggs. Using your left hand, shake the pan so the eggs slide back and forth over the pan bottom. With a fork or a wooden spatula, lift the cooked edges to allow the uncooked egg to flow underneath. Add the filling and then reverse your grip on the handle, holding it in the palm of your hand. Tip the pan forward so the omelet rolls onto itself and slide it onto a plate, using a fork or spatula to guide it so the smooth surface is on top.

*Omelet or Scrambled Egg Additions* Each omelet will hold about ⅓ cup filling, so judge proportions accordingly.

- Sour cream, chopped green chilies, and grated Monterey Jack or Cheddar cheese.
- Sautéed chopped green onions, minced gingerroot, bean sprouts, sliced celery, shredded cooked pork or ham or chicken seasoned lightly with soy sauce.
- Cottage cheese, chopped peeled tomatoes, and fresh basil.
- Flaked canned salmon moistened with sour cream and seasoned with dill.
- Chopped red and/or green peppers, onions, ham, and peeled tomato sautéed first in olive oil with some minced garlic. Add a tablespoon of chopped anchovy fillets just before spooning filling into the omelet.
- Chopped cooked potato, diced bacon, and green pepper sautéed together until bacon is cooked. Top hot omelet with grated Cheddar cheese.
- Chopped chicken livers and sliced mushrooms sautéed in butter. Pour in a little heavy cream and reduce until syrupy before filling omelets.
- Diced avocado, shredded Havarti, Tybo, Samsoe, or Swiss cheese, and diced cooked turkey or chicken.
- Chopped ripe olives mixed with softened cream cheese or whipped cottage cheese, Sherry and green onion.
- Crab or lobster chunks (canned is fine), sautéed in butter and bound with a thick béchamel or sour cream. Season with a touch of Sherry, paprika, and parsley.
- Sliced zucchini and chopped onions sautéed in butter and mixed with grated Cheddar cheese, basil, and oregano.

- Cooked diced potatoes, onions, and minced clams heated in butter and mixed with heavy cream.
- Cooked grated carrot heated with heavy cream or crème fraîche and seasoned with powdered allspice.
- Fresh sliced mushrooms cooked in cream and tarragon until cream is reduced to a silky sauce.

# *Pasta*

Whether it's vermicelli, linguini, or spaghetti, pasta is a good friend to a frantic cook. Cook the pasta of your choice (8 ounces is about right as a main course for two) in a large amount of rapidly boiling salted water to which you have added a couple of good glugs of olive oil. Boil it until it is just tender but still retains some "bite." Drain, toss lightly with butter, and dress with one of these easy sauces.

- Combine *½ cup sour cream, ¼ cup heavy cream, the juice of ½ lemon,* and *3 table-spoons butter* in the top of a double boiler and warm over hot water, stirring occasionally. Toss hot pasta with sauce and as much *caviar* as the budget will allow, working carefully to avoid bruising.
- Put a *2-ounce can drained anchovy fillets, ¼ cup chopped walnuts, 1 clove garlic, 2 tablespoons olive oil, ⅓ cup heavy cream,* and *¼ teaspoon pepper* in a blender or food processor. Whirl until smooth and warm gently over low heat. Toss with hot pasta.
- Sauté *1 cup of fresh sliced mushrooms* in *2 tablespoons butter.* When they are golden, add *4 ounces of foie gras* and stir until it combines with butter. If necessary, thin with a little cream and toss with cooked pasta.
- Cook *½ cup chopped onions* and *¼ pound sliced mushrooms* in *2 tablespoons butter.* Stir in *2 teaspoons flour* and cook over low heat for 2 minutes. Add *½ cup crumbled Roquefort cheese, ½ cup chicken broth,* a dash of *nutmeg,* and *2 tablespoons cream.* Simmer, stirring constantly, until the sauce has thickened. Toss with cooked pasta and top with additional crumbled Roquefort cheese if you like.
- Dice *4 slices of bacon* and cook until transparent but not crisp. Add *½ pound peeled, seeded, and chopped tomatoes, ½ cup white wine, ¼ teaspoon oregano, ¼ teaspoon basil,* and *salt and pepper.* Simmer for 15 minutes, stirring occasionally, and serve on hot buttered pasta.
- Boil *2 cups chopped broccoli* with the pasta (it will be cooked but still crunchy when the pasta is ready). Drain it all together. Heat *¼ cup olive oil* with *1 clove minced garlic* and *1 teaspoon crumbled dried red peppers* or more to taste. Toss with the pasta and broccoli. Sprinkle with *grated cheese.*

And for those with a bit more time, here are some slightly more elaborate sauces:

***Harlot's Sauce***   The story goes that this sauce received its racy name because it was a favorite of the ladies of the evening in Naples who could whip it up in short order between assignments. We can't speak for their other talents, but they must have been excellent cooks.

Heat *2 tablespoons olive oil* in a large skillet. Sauté *2 cloves minced garlic, 1 minced celery rib,* and *1 minced sweet red pepper* (optional) until soft. Press a *2-pound, 3-ounce can Italian plum tomatoes* through a food mill and add to the skillet along with *8 chopped anchovies*. Simmer for 10 minutes. Stir in *8 sliced pitted ripe olives, 1 teaspoon capers, 1 teaspoon basil,* and *¼ teaspoon dried red pepper*. Simmer, uncovered, for 20 minutes and serve with hot pasta that has been tossed with butter.

***Parsley-Clam Sauce***   Sauté *1 chopped onion* in *1 tablespoon butter* and *¼ cup olive oil* very slowly until soft and transparent. Add *½ teaspoon sweet basil* and *½ teaspoon oregano*. Stir and cook slowly for 5 minutes. Add *2 cups minced parsley*. Cover and simmer slowly for 5 minutes. Add a *7-ounce can minced clams (drained)*, cover and simmer for 5 minutes. Serve on pasta and top with grated Parmesan cheese.

# Cheese

Even the barest refrigerator usually has a bit of cheese secreted somewhere. If you can find it, transform it into a handsome main course in one of these ways.

***Welsh Rarebit***   Place *2 tablespoons butter* in a saucepan and heat. Add *¼ cup ale or beer, salt and pepper, ½ teaspoon dry English mustard,* and *1 teaspoon Worcestershire sauce*. Bring the mixture almost to the boil and stir in *1 cup grated Cheddar cheese*. Stir just until cheese has melted and serve on buttered toast or toasted English muffins.

***Feta Fondue***   Melt *3 tablespoons butter* in a shallow, heatproof dish. Layer *1 pound Feta cheese* crumbled or cut in slices in the dish. Sprinkle with *pepper*. Warm over low heat until the cheese softens and begins to bubble. Add *3 tablespoons fresh lemon juice* and garnish with *poppy seeds*. Serve very hot with French or Italian bread cubes for dipping.

***Swiss Fondue***   Rub the inside of a crockery fondue dish with a *cut clove of garlic*. Put *¾ pound grated Swiss cheese* and a dash of *salt and pepper* into the dish. Add enough *dry white wine* to barely cover the cheese. Cook over medium heat, stirring constantly, just until cheese melts. Make a smooth paste of *3 tablespoons cornstarch, 1 tablespoon kirsch,* and *1 tablespoon water*. Stir cornstarch mixture into cheese and wine and cook until thickened. Serve with French or Italian bread cubes.

***Tomato-Cheese Strata*** Soak *6 slices bread* in ⅔ *cup milk* for 15 minutes. Drain off excess milk. Line the bottom of a buttered casserole with the bread slices. Add a layer of *tomato sauce* (see p. 000), sprinkle with *Italian herbs,* and cover with a layer of sliced *Mozzarella, Bel Paese, or Fontina cheese.* Continue making layers, ending with a layer of bread, tomato sauce, and herbs. Beat *3 eggs* with *2 tablespoons Parmesan cheese* and pour over the casserole. Dot the top with *butter* and bake in a preheated 350-degree oven for 1 hour or until the top is puffed and browned. If you happen to have any on hand, you can include some cooked crumbled *Italian sausage* or some slices of *pepperoni* or *salami.*

# Seafood

While we always prefer fresh fish, there are times when a can of seafood on the shelf can save the day and the dinner.

***Seafood Soufflé*** Melt *3 tablespoons butter* in a saucepan, stir in *3 tablespoons flour,* and cook over low heat for 2 to 3 minutes without browning. Blend in *1 cup milk* and stir until thickened. Remove from the heat and add *3 egg yolks,* one at a time, stirring after each addition. Fold in a *7¹/₂-ounce can drained seafood (shrimp, tuna, salmon, or crab), 2 tablespoons mayonnaise,* and *2 tablespoons grated Swiss cheese.* Beat *4 egg whites* until stiff but not dry and fold them into the egg-yolk mixture. Pour the soufflé into a buttered 1-quart soufflé dish. Bake 30–40 minutes in preheated 375-degree oven.

***Deviled Crab*** Drain a *7¹/₂-ounce can of crabmeat.* Melt *1 tablespoon butter* in a skillet, add *¼ cup cracker crumbs* and *¾ cup milk* and bring to a boil. Remove from the heat and beat in *2 eggs, ¾ teaspoon powdered mustard, 1 teaspoon prepared horseradish,* a dash of *Tabasco sauce,* and *salt and pepper* to taste. Add the crabmeat and spoon the mixture into ramekins or a baking dish. Brush with melted butter and bake in a 375-degree oven for about 20 minutes.

***Crab with Green Peppercorns*** Green peppercorns may not be a staple in your cupboard, but they do add punch to an otherwise plain dish, and you can keep them in the freezer and defrost them quickly under running water. Rinse *1 tablespoon green peppercorns* under cold water to remove the outer membranes. Mash with the back of a spoon. Boil *1 cup cream* until reduced by half, stirring occasionally. Add the peppercorns and *salt* to taste. Heat *1 tablespoon butter* in a skillet and warm the *crab meat from a 7¹/₂-ounce can.* Stir the crab into the cream sauce and serve on *hot buttered rice.*

***Scalloped Oysters*** Using *1 cup of fresh cracker crumbs* and an *8-ounce can or jar of oysters,* alternate layers of the two in a buttered baking dish, dotting each layer with *butter* and sprinkling with *salt and pepper.* Pour on ½ *cup cream* and bake for 20 minutes in a 425-degree oven.

# *Chicken Breasts*

With a supply of boned chicken breasts on hand, you are just minutes away from a number of delicious main courses. Thin slices of turkey breast or veal scallops can be used in the same fashion. For most of the following dishes, pound the cutlets, lightly dredge in seasoned flour, and sauté in about ¼ cup clarified butter (see p. 225). Keep warm in a low oven while you make the sauce.

Unless you're in a big hurry, there's no reason to pay the butcher to bone chicken breasts.

First, pick up the whole breast with the skin side against the palm of your hand and the pointed end of the breast down. If you gently pull the skin back from the V formed by the meaty end of the breast, you can almost see the two sides of the wishbone just below the surface of the meat. With a sharp knife, scrape the thin layer of meat from those two small bones. Then work your fingers behind the bones and gently work them up to the apex of the wishbone. Free the knob at the apex of the wishbone with your fingers and pull the wishbone out. (NOTE: This first step is not essential to bone a chicken breast, but it makes for a cleaner job.)

Second, place the whole breast skin side down on a cutting board with the point away from you. In the middle you will notice the flat side of the keel bone. With the point of a boning knife, cut through the white cartilage above the keel bone on the end toward you. Pick up the whole breast, bend back the keel bone and it will come loose. Work your fingers down both sides of the keel bone to loosen the meat all the way to the cartilage at the tip of the breast and pull the bone and cartilage away. Now you know why it's called a keel bone: it's shaped like the keel of a sailboat.

Third, place the whole breast back on the cutting board skin side down with the point away from you. With the point of the knife, cut through the membrane holding one side of the rib cage. Scraping against the bones with the knife, free the meat on that side, working around the flat shoulder blades. Repeat on the other side and lift out the rib cage.

If you intend to use the whole breast, to stuff it for instance, be careful during the whole process not to break the skin. For the following recipes, pull the skin off and cut the whole breast in two pieces lengthwise through the middle.

**Chicken Piccata**   Drain off all but 2 tablespoons of the butter in which chicken was cooked. Stir into the pan *2 tablespoons Madeira, 1 tablespoon lemon juice, 2 tablespoons capers,* and *2 tablespoons minced fresh parsley*. Simmer until sauce thickens.

**Ginger Cream Chicken**   Add *1 chopped green onion* to the pan in which the chicken was cooked and sauté briefly. Stir in *1 tablespoon flour* and cook gently for 3 minutes. Blend in *¼ cup chicken broth, 3 tablespoons Madeira, ¼ cup cream,* and *1 tablespoon minced crystallized ginger*.

**Chicken Normandy**    Pour off all but 2 tablespoons of the butter in the pan. Stir in *1 peeled, cored, and sliced apple.* Sauté until tender. Sprinkle on *1 table-spoon flour* and cook for 2 minutes. Add *½ cup cream* and *¼ cup apple brandy.* Cook until sauce thickens.

**Chicken Scandia**    Dip cutlets in *beaten egg* and then in *rye bread or cracker crumbs.* Sauté in *butter.* Remove cutlets from the pan and pour off all but *1 table-spoon butter.* Stir in *1 tablespoon flour* and cook for 2 minutes. Add *½ cup sour cream, 1 tablespoon fresh dill* or *1 teaspoon dried, 1 teaspoon grated lemon rind,* and *salt and pepper* to taste.

**Fresh Lemon Chicken**    Pour off but 2 tablespoons of the butter. Sauté *1 teaspoon minced fresh ginger* and *1 clove garlic* briefly in the pan. Deglaze the pan with *½ cup Sherry.* Stir in *1 teaspoon fresh lemon juice* and reduce until sauce is thick and glossy. Season to taste with *salt and pepper* and garnish with *thin slices of lemon* and *fresh minced parsley.*

**Chicken Marsala**    Pour off the fat from the pan in which the breasts were cooked. Add *½ cup Marsala* and *½ cup chicken broth* and reduce, scraping up the brown bits in the pan, until the liquid is syrupy. Remove the pan from the heat, season to taste with *salt and pepper,* and whisk in *2 tablespoons softened butter.* Spoon the sauce over the chicken breasts.

# DESSERTS

Here is a selection of speedy finales designed to satisfy those who consider a meal without dessert as unsatisfactory as a movie without popcorn.

# *Fruits*

- One of the easiest and most elegant desserts in the world is the simple combination of fruit and cheese. Be sure the fruit is perfectly ripe and the cheese is at room temperature.
- Place peeled, sliced fresh peaches in a baking dish. Spread with a layer of sour cream and cover completely with brown sugar. Broil just until sugar is caramelized.
- Cut small melons in half and remove the seeds. Fill the cavities with Port wine and chill.
- Poach pears or peaches in red wine spiced with a cinnamon stick and some cloves and sweetened to taste with honey or sugar.

- Serve poached or canned pears with warm chocolate sauce and toasted almonds.
- Top chilled mandarin oranges with warm orange marmalade and a dollop of sour cream.
- Sauté halved bananas with brown sugar, butter, and dark rum and serve warm.
- Soak poached or drained canned apricots in Southern Comfort and serve with vanilla ice cream and a sprinkling of pistachio nuts.
- Sweeten sour cream with brown sugar and combine with fresh stemmed strawberries or seedless grapes.
- Bathe fresh sliced oranges in Curaçao and scatter with toasted coconut.
- Beat vanilla ice cream with anise-flavored liqueur. Serve over fresh poached peaches and garnish with chocolate curls.
- Marinate peeled, halved, and pitted peaches in honey-flavored orange liqueur. When ready to serve, place peach halves in wine glasses and add Champagne to cover. Garnish each portion with one perfect strawberry.
- Top papaya slices with vanilla yogurt and sprinkle with chopped macadamia nuts.

# *Ice Creams*

Keep the freezer stocked with at least one kind of ice cream and you need never wonder where your next dessert is coming from:

- Drizzle dark rum over lemon or lime sherbet.
- Whirl vanilla ice cream in the blender with a little brandy or Kahlúa and serve with chocolate shavings.
- Top raspberry sherbet with a spoonful of Crème de Cassis.
- Layer vanilla ice cream, maple syrup, and nut brittle in a parfait glass.
- Spike warm mincemeat with dark rum and spoon over vanilla ice cream.
- Soak candied fruit in brandy and layer with eggnog ice cream for a quick holiday dessert.
- Smother strawberry ice cream with raspberry sauce (see p. 186).
- Spoon chocolate-almond ice cream into parfait or wine glasses and layer with marshmallow cream and chocolate sauce.
- Melt chocolate-covered peppermints in a double boiler over simmering water and pour over pistachio ice cream. Thin with cream or milk if desired.
- Chop a few dates and moisten with honey and brandy. Serve over burnt almond ice cream.

# *Fresh Fruit Tarts*

Fresh fruit tarts are one of the priceless gifts of the French pastry maker. Some also are wonderfully quick and easy to prepare. In this version, the cookie-like crust forms a base that is painted with jam to prevent any seepage of juices. Uncooked fruit is then arranged in the crust and painted with warm melted preserves to give the tart a beautiful glaze.

**CRUST** Sift together *½ cup flour, 1 tablespoon ground blanched almonds,* and *1 tablespoon confectioners' sugar.* Cut in *¼ cup butter* until mixture resembles coarse meal. This also can be done in a food processor, but don't overmix. Chill for 15 minutes. Press dough into the bottom and sides of two 3-inch loose-bottomed tart pans. Bake at 425 degrees F. for 8 to 10 minutes or until golden. Cool.

**FILLING** Spread *2 tablespoons melted jam* in each tart shell. Rinse fruit of your choice and pat dry. Peel or slice if necessary. Divide fruit between tart shells and gently spoon melted jelly over it. Sprinkle with appropriate garnish.

Here are some luscious combinations to try:

| BASE | FRUIT | GLAZE | GARNISH |
|---|---|---|---|
| Apricot-Pineapple Jam | Blanched Apricots | Strawberry Jelly | Ground Almonds |
| Strawberry Jam | Whole Strawberries | Raspberry Jelly | Ground Pistachios |
| Orange Marmalade | Stewed Rhubarb | Strawberry Jelly | Grated Orange Peel |
| Peach Jam | Sliced Pears | Apple Jelly | Ground Walnuts |
| Plum Jam | Sliced Plums | Red Currant Jelly | Grated Lime Zest |
| Cherry Jam | Cherries | Red Currant Jelly | Ground Hazelnuts |
| Peach Jam | Sliced Peaches | Orange Marmalade | Praline Powder *or* Ground Peanut Brittle |
| Apricot Jam | Green Grapes | Quince Jelly | Ground Walnuts |

# Coffees

For some people, the perfect end to a meal is the simplicity of a steaming cup of well-made coffee. Others like to tart up their coffee so they can drink their dessert.

**Irish Coffee**    For each serving, place *3 cocktail-size sugar cubes* in a warm stemmed heatproof glass and fill ¾ full with *hot, black coffee.* Pour in a *generous ounce of Irish whisky* and top with half an inch of *slightly whipped cream.*

**Dutch Treat**    For each serving, place *5 ounces of hot black coffee* in a mug and stir in *1 teaspoon sugar.* Add *1 ounce brandy* and *1 ounce chocolate liqueur.* Garnish with a *twisted strip of lemon zest.*

**Spiced Coffee**    Combine *2 cocktail-size sugar cubes, 2 whole cloves,* and *2 ounces Bourbon* in a heatproof mug. Fill with *hot coffee* and stir with a *cinnamon stick.*

**Café Orange**    Place *1 teaspoon grated fresh lemon zest* in a coffee cup, add *coffee* until it is about ⅔ full, and stir in *1 jigger (2 tablespoons)* orange liqueur.

**Gnome of Zurich**    For 2 servings, combine *1 tablespoon unsweetened cocoa, 1 tablespoon sugar, 1 tablespoon water,* and a *dash of salt* in a small saucepan and heat just to boiling. Stir in *1 cup hot milk, 1 cup hot coffee,* and *3 ounces Crème de Noyaux or almond liqueur.* Serve in heated cups.

# SEVEN

# BACK TO BASICS

I n every kitchen in this country one finds The Drawer. Sometimes it has an adjective assigned to it, but basically it's the place where everything goes that otherwise would be homeless. It contains string, matchbooks with one match left, rubber bands, tools that the most recent users were too lazy to take back to the basement, thumbtacks, almost used tubes of glue, friction tape, and a host of other dross that only gets rescued or thrown away when the householder moves.

This chapter is the junk drawer of this book.

The title describes what most of it is about, recipes for basic preparations such as broths, sauces, pastry, and pasta called for in other chapters. We also discuss preserving techniques and how to make your own vinegar, and we throw in a recipe for a dynamite stew that just wouldn't fit anywhere else but which, if you keep it going like a good sourdough starter, is something you might want to leave to your grandchildren.

The fundamental message of this chapter is that cooking by and/or for two people can be made easier, less expensive, and better all around with a little foresight—and advance preparation.

# TAKING STOCK

Buying canned beef or chicken broth is a mug's game. Not only are they expensive, considering the fact their essential ingredients are things most American cooks erroneously discard, but they also tend to be oversalted.

There's no secret to making basic stocks. It takes time but very little effort, and the results are inevitably better than anything you can buy. The thing to remember is, never throw away those beef or chicken bones. Collect them in a plastic bag in the freezer, and when you have enough, whomp up a mess of stock. A good stockpot is very handy for this, although any large kettle will get the job done. All of these recipes yield between 2 and 3 quarts, and all stock can be stored frozen for several months.

## *Beef Broth*

2 pounds beef bones
2 pounds cheap beef (shank, oxtails, etc.)
1 veal shank, cracked or sawed in half
3 carrots, cleaned and cut up
2 onions, peeled
2 celery stalks, cut up, including tops

2 leeks, carefully washed to remove any grit
Bouquet garni consisting of 1 bay leaf, 4 parsley sprigs, 2 garlic cloves, and 2 whole cloves
2 teaspoons salt

*Preheat oven to 450 degrees F.* Put the beef bones in a roasting pan and roast, uncovered, for about 30 minutes until they are brown. Place them in a large stockpot along with the beef and the veal shank and cover with about 4 quarts of cold water. Bring the pot to a boil over moderate heat, skimming off the gray scum that comes to the surface as the water heats. Continue skimming until it stops accumulating. Add the other ingredients, reduce the heat, and simmmer the stock for 5 hours, skimming occasionally if need be.

Strain the stock by pouring it into a large bowl or another pot through a colander that has been lined with several thicknesses of cheesecloth that has been rinsed in cold water and wrung out. Allow to cool and then refrigerate it for several hours until the fat that has risen to the surface hardens and can be removed. If the stock is not to be frozen, refrigerate it and use within 3 days.

# Veal Broth

Veal stock or basic white stock is made the same way, substituting veal bones and meat, except the bones are not browned in the oven and the stock should be ready after about 4 hours of simmering.

# Meat Glaze

Meat glaze, or *Glace de Viande,* is called for in several recipes in this book and is always nice to have around. Since the only thing removed is water, it can be easily reconstituted whenever you need stock in a hurry, and it takes little room to store. It will keep for weeks in a tightly sealed jar in the refrigerator, but we have learned that our ice cube trays freeze it in precisely 2-tablespoon amounts, which is exactly how much is needed to make 1 cup of stock.

To make meat glaze, boil beef or veal stock until it has been reduced to ⅛ its original volume. Thus, every quart will produce half a cup or 8 tablespoons. Carefully measure what you have at the beginning, and keep an eye on the stuff after it has been reduced by half. After that, the reduction accelerates. Don't wander off to answer the phone or you'll end up with a scorched pot. To measure how much you have left, pour it into a heatproof measuring cup as you near the end of the boiling period. If it is more than ⅛ of the original, pour it back in the pot and continue boiling until you have the right amount.

# Chicken Broth

4 pounds chicken bones, necks, wings,
    backs, etc.
4 carrots, cleaned and cut up
2 onions, peeled
2 stalks celery, chopped including the
    leaves

1 leek, cleaned and cut up
1 teaspoon salt
Bouquet garni *as for beef stock*

Follow the directions for basic beef stock, but don't brown the chicken and simmer for only 2 hours. Chicken stock may be refrigerated for 3 days, frozen for several months, or concentrated as a glaze in the same way as beef or veal stock.

# Fish Stock

Fish stock is useful for making soups such as chowders, for poaching fish, and as the basis for sauces for seafood. Since it loses its freshness after a couple of days in the refrigerator, we freeze it. It doesn't concentrate very well.

4 pounds fresh *fish, fish heads, bones,*
    *etc.*
1 onion, peeled and quartered
1 bay leaf

1 teaspoon salt
2 cups dry white wine
6 cups water

Place all the ingredients in an enamel or stainless steel pot, bring to a simmer (do not boil), and cook for 1 hour, skimming occasionally as needed. Strain through a fine strainer lined with several thicknesses of cheesecloth that has been rinsed in cold water and wrung out.

***Notes on degreasing and clarifying stock:*** The simplest method of degreasing stocks is explained in the basic beef recipe. If you're in a hurry to use it, however, there are a number of degreasing cups on the market that work very well. The strained stock is poured in, the fat accumulates at the top, and the degreased broth is drawn off at the bottom. Most of them come in 1- to 2-cup sizes, although one company manufactures a quart size.

As far as we're concerned, the only reason to clarify a stock is to use it in an aspic, for which there are recipes in this book. It can be tricky if you're not careful.

Begin with cold stock. For 2 quarts, stir 3 slightly beaten egg whites and the broken egg shells (make sure there is no trace of yolk) into the stock. Bring it *very slowly* to a simmer, taking great care to see that it doesn't boil. If it does you've blown it and have to start all over.

As the stock heats up, the free particles floating in it adhere to the egg white, which rises to the top and forms an ugly layer of foam. Barely simmer for 15 minutes, carefully pushing the foam aside with a spoon now and then to look in and make sure the stock isn't bubbling. Turn off the heat and let the stock stand for 15 minutes.

Line a fine strainer with several thicknesses of cheesecloth that has been rinsed in cold water and wrung out. Carefully skim off the foam on top of the pot and discard, then gently ladle the stock through the strainer into a bowl.

# A FEW BASIC SAUCES

## *Mayonnaise*

To put it bluntly, there is no excuse in the world for anyone to use store-bought mayonnaise. That may sound like heresy in a country where kids grow up thinking the mayo that binds their tuna-fish sandwiches has to come with a label on it to be genuine. But since Fred Waring stepped down from the bandstand long enough to invent the blender, making mayonnaise at home has been so easy and the results so much better that it just doesn't make sense to buy it.

Other than the fact we all agree it's French, the origin of what is probably the best-known cold sauce in the world is uncertain. Some say it was first named *mahonnaise* after the battle of Mahón on Minorca in the eighteenth century. Others insist it came from *moyeu*, the Old French word for egg yolk.

No matter who invented it, he or she would doubtless not recognize the stuff we buy in the supermarket. According to law, anything that contains salad oil and eggs can be called mayonnaise, and it may contain gelatin, starch, or gum emulsifiers and all sorts of additives such as MSG.

Not only is homemade mayonnaise fresher, you can alter the ingredients to match your own tastes. Classically it is made with egg yolks, olive oil, mustard, and lemon juice. We usually use the whole egg, which makes the finished sauce somewhat lighter, and often substitute an oil with a less overpowering flavor. Experiment with the basic recipe to come up with the mayonnaise you like best.

*1 whole egg (or 2 egg yolks)*
*1 tablespoon Dijon mustard*
*1 tablespoon lemon juice*

*½ teaspoon salt*
*1½ cups oil*

Put the egg or egg yolks, the mustard, lemon juice, and salt in a blender or food processor and turn it on. Very gradually add the oil, a drop at a time in the beginning and working up to a thin stream. After about a cup has been absorbed by the eggs, turn off the machine and check the consistency of the mayonnaise. If it is too thin, turn the machine back on and add up to another ½ cup. Store in a jar in the refrigerator.

## *Basic Mustard*

Jinx has not always been a baseball fan. "It can't be baseball season yet," she would mutter crossly. "They're still playing basketball. And hockey. Besides, the Super Bowl was only the day before yesterday."

Then, by an accident of history, we happened to find ourselves living a reasonable distance from the home ball park of a team that regularly found itself in the World Series. Her attitude seemed to change, and from time to time Jeff could entice her to a game. But we both knew the reason she went was the hot dogs. Give her a nice warm day, a not too dull contest, two or three hot dogs and enough beer to wash them down, and she cares not who makes this nation's laws.

The one ingredient that neither of us cherishes at these events is the mustard. Mustard is a deeply personal matter, but neither of us has ever developed a taste for the thin stuff that squirts out of those dispensers at hot-dog stands. Although we occasionally spring for high-quality foreign mustards, especially those from Burgundy, this basic recipe has a nice bite. The recipe yields a little over a cup. By doubling it, you come up with a couple of 8-ounce jars as gifts for other frankophiles (forgive us) with about half a jar left over for yourself. Also, don't overlook the equally simple recipe for sweet-hot Mustard Maison (see p. xxx) in Chapter Four. The secret to that one is the malt vinegar. Don't try it with any other kind. Between the two, you shouldn't have to go to the mustard store very often.

| | |
|---|---|
| ½ cup chopped onion | 1 tablespoon honey |
| 1 clove garlic, minced | 1½ teaspoons cooking oil |
| 1 cup dry white wine | ½ teaspoon salt |
| 1 can (2 ounces) Colman's dry mustard | Dash Tabasco sauce |

Combine onion, garlic, and wine in a small saucepan and bring to a boil. Reduce the heat and simmer 5 minutes. Strain into another small saucepan and cool. Add the mustard to the wine and, using a whisk, stir until all the lumps are gone. Add all the other ingredients and cook over medium heat, stirring constantly, until the mustard thickens. Store in tightly sealed jars in the refrigerator.

# The Kansas City Connection

As it happens, what we laughingly call our wedding reception was catered by Arthur Bryant's barbecue joint in Kansas City, which is probably the least significant piece of information brought to your attention so far this week. What makes it unusual is that this party was held in Santa Monica, which was also strange because we were married on a ship in San Francisco Bay.

What happened was we found ourselves in Southern California shortly after our wedding, among a group of alumni of the Kansas City *Star* and other degenerates of the newspaper trade. One of their number, a gentleman lofty in the precincts of the Los Angeles *Times,* had journeyed back to Missouri and was to return that day with a couple of thermal bags full of barbecued ribs, beef, and ham from Bryant's. This was in the days before airport X-ray machines, so it was possible for him to do this without getting arrested (we can imagine what it would be like today if a security guard saw all those bones in his screen: "My God, that man is carrying a chopped-up body!").

For years we had been putting up with obvious exaggerations about the splendid barbecue available at Bryant's from Gene Ayres, a newspaperman of parts who worked with Jeff on the West Coast after decamping from Kansas City. After orchestrating our wedding on the bridge of the old *S.S. President Wilson* (don't ask), Ayres arranged for us to be present in Santa Monica when the bags were opened and a keg of beer was tapped. Although everyone played lip service to our recent change in estate, it would be inaccurate to say we were the guests of honor. The ribs, beef, and ham were.

As any of you who may have read the sterling prose of Calvin Trillin probably expected, the barbecue was a poem. We ate for hours. Ever since then we have been attempting to divine the secret of Bryant's barbecue sauce. We know that, like searching for fragments of the True Cross, this is a fool's errand, but still we try. What we have developed over the years is a basic barbecue sauce that has received a certain modest acclaim among our friends. It is not Bryant's. Nothing else is.

## Not Remotely Bryant's Barbecue Sauce

2 cloves garlic, minced
1 onion, minced
1 1/2 teaspoons dry mustard
1 tablespoon prepared horseradish
1 1/2 cups water
1/4 cup vinegar
1/4 cup sugar

2 teaspoons salt
1 tablespoon lemon juice
1/4 cup butter
1 cup ketchup
3 tablespoons Worcestershire sauce
1/2 teaspoon liquid smoke
Tabasco sauce

Combine all ingredients except Tabasco sauce in a saucepan and bring to a boil. Reduce heat and simmer slowly, uncovered, for 45 minutes. Remove from the heat and season to taste with Tabasco sauce. Place the sauce in the container of a blender and whirl until smooth. Can be stored for several days in the refrigerator in a tightly sealed jar and reheated. Makes about 3 cups.

Use this sauce to baste ribs, beef, ham, or sausage as you grill it, or use it to dip hot cooked meats.

# *The Saucy Tomato*

We have never found a commercial tomato sauce that set us free. There are a number of pretty good ones on the market, but somehow we find it more satisfying to make it ourselves. Besides, then we know exactly what is—and isn't—in it. What follows are two basic recipes, one of Italianate bent to make when vine-ripened tomatoes aren't available, the other to use when they are. Both yield about 2 cups.

While we're on the subject, a word about tomato paste. As we all know, virtually no recipe in the world, certainly none in this book, calls for a whole can of it. For years we kept leftover tomato paste in the freezer, digging out what we needed from time to time and bending all of our measuring spoons in the process. Then we found that the Italians, who do so many things well, put up a super tomato paste in tubes, just like toothpaste. It keeps in the refrigerator indefinitely, and you only have to squeeze out what you need. No cooking couple should be without it.

## *Richard Paoli's Tomato Sauce*

Paoli is another journalist (you can see we need to get a better class of friends), a man who specializes in writing about travel and other things sybaritic. He is also one of the best cooks in the world. He says that's because he's Italian, and likes to point out that the Italians civilized the French barbarians by teaching them how to cook. Mr. Paoli has been thrown out of a number of Paris restaurants.

*3 tablespoons olive oil*
*1 clove garlic, peeled*
*½ cup onion, finely chopped*
*2 cups canned tomatoes*

*1 teaspoon dried basil*
*1 teaspoon sugar*
*½ teaspoon salt*

Heat the olive oil in a large skillet. Add the garlic clove, fry it until it is golden, and discard it. Add the onions to the pan and sauté slowly until they are translucent. Add all of the other ingredients and simmer uncovered for about an hour. Purée in a blender or food processor.

## Fresh Tomato Sauce

2 tablespoons cooking oil
2 onions, diced
12 medium tomatoes, peeled, seeded, and
   chopped
2 tablespoons sugar

1 tablespoon minced parsley
½ teaspoon thyme
½ teaspoon marjoram
½ teaspoon dried basil
Salt and pepper

Heat the oil in a large skillet and slowly sauté the onions until they are soft but not brown. Add the other ingredients except the salt and pepper. Mash the tomatoes with a potato masher and simmer the whole mess, stirring occasionally, for 30 minutes. Work the mixture through a sieve, using the back of a spoon to extract as much pulp as possible. Put the sauce back in the pan and continue simmering it until it has reduced to the consistency you want. Season to taste with salt and pepper.

# THE DAIRY

## Clarified Butter

There are some recipes in this book that call for clarified butter. The reason is that it takes a much higher temperature before it begins to burn. Cooking oil, which has a much higher browning point, can be substituted but the flavor is not the same.

    There is no mystery to making clarified butter, and since it keeps well we like to do it a pound at a time so as to have it on hand. Both sweet and salted butter can be clarified, but the latter will not be quite as clear as the former.

    Cut a pound of butter into pieces, put in a saucepan over low heat, and allow it to melt completely. Remove the pan from the heat and let it stand for a few minutes to allow the white milk solids to settle to the bottom. Carefully skim the foam from the top and gently pour the clear yellow liquid off, leaving the milk solids in the pan. Allow the liquid to cool, strain it through several layers of cheesecloth, and store it tightly covered in a pint jar in the refrigerator. It will keep in this form longer than regular butter, and although it may become cloudy as does refrigerated oil, it will clear again when it's heated in cooking.

## *Crème Fraiche*

Several recipes in this book call for or suggest the use of *crème fraîche,* which is French for fresh cream, which in turn is a little silly because it isn't. In France *crème fraîche* is actually cream that has been allowed to ferment slightly, which thickens it and gives it its slightly tangy flavor. It is not sour cream by any means. Commercial *crème fraîche* is available in some parts of the United States, but the last time we looked it was $5 a pint and that was before the economy went berserk.

To make a much cheaper substitute, combine one tablespoon of buttermilk with each cup of heavy cream. Heat to lukewarm and pour into a glass jar. Loosely cover and allow to stand at room temperature overnight or until the cream has thickened. Stir, cover tightly, and chill. The cream will keep for about two weeks in the refrigerator and won't curdle in cooking. It's also handy to have to spoon over fresh fruit or other desserts.

# WINE VINEGAR

At one time or another we've all had a bottle of wine that didn't quite live up to its notices. Whether through poor storage (your own or the wine merchant's), a faulty cork, or plain bad luck, a good bottle of wine can go bad. When this unfortunate event takes place there's only one thing left to do—beat nature to the punch and make vinegar.

Many years ago Sam Sebastiani, who oversees California's Sebastiani Vineyards, gave us his recipe for making vinegar. He said one should always start with a decent wine to make a decent vinegar. Poor wine can make vinegar, but its flavor won't improve in the transition. A lot of cheaper wines are pasteurized and can't be made into vinegar.

Take a clean crock or wine bottle (the 3-liter size is ideal) and pour in whatever leftover wine you have lurking about. Don't fill the container more than halfway up—leave plenty of air space at the top. Cover the top with a bit of cheesecloth secured with a rubber band. To start the vinegar working, you need about the same temperature it takes to make dough rise (somewhere in the neighborhood of 75 degrees), so put your vinegar near the kitchen stove or tuck it into a corner near the water heater. Try to pick a place where you can leave it undisturbed for a long time.

In about a month or two you should see a light film forming on the surface of the wine. Taste the vinegar and, if it is as acetic as you want it to be, filter it though several thicknesses of washed cheesecloth or, better yet, a coffee filter and decant it. If you want to keep your vinegar production going, leave one third of the vinegar in the jug and add two thirds fresh wine and repeat the process.

Occasionally the first batch doesn't quite make it, but don't be discouraged. The tiny airborne organisms that make vinegar aren't always dependable, but they'll come around in time. If they absolutely refuse to cooperate, combine one-third commercial wine vinegar between 4 and 6 percent acidity (expressed as "grain"; thus vinegar of 5 percent acid is called "5-grain") with the first batch of wine. Naturally, if you're starting with red wine use red wine vinegar. The same with white.

Once you've succeeded in producing a batch, you may want to expand your repertoire to include herbed and spiced vinegars. This is where the basic vinegar you make at home becomes uniquely yours, and it saves a ton. Flavored vinegars make great gifts and give a certain look of authority to the kitchen, not to mention the taste they'll add to your cooking.

Find some handsome jars, wine bottles, or cruets and make sure they're sparkling clean. Place whatever combination of herbs and spices you like into the jar and fill with wine vinegar. Allow the vinegar to stand in a cool, dark place tightly covered for about a month without disturbing it. When ready to use, strain out the herbs and spices and rebottle.

- Sweet basil, oregano, a whole peeled clove of garlic, and a few whole black peppercorns.
- Fresh mint, a spiral of lemon peel, and a few Thompson seedless grapes with white wine vinegar.
- Fresh thyme, whole strands of chives, and a few mustard seeds.
- Sprigs of tarragon, a whole clove of peeled garlic, and a few whole cloves.
- A twig of rosemary, a sprig of chervil, several sliced shallots, and a few whole peppercorns.
- For a spicy vinegar, wonderful to use in fruit salad dressings or marinades for poultry, add a couple of whole cinnamon sticks, half a dozen cloves, a few currants, and a spiral of orange peel to a pint of white wine vinegar.

# PRESERVATION

## *The Joys and Perils of Home Canning*

Both of us, you will be pleased to know, had mothers. And both of us were born shortly before World War II (you had to read this far to find that out), so that we passed our early childhoods during an era of shortages and rationing. We both remember our mothers hitting the produce markets like one-woman plagues of locusts every fall to gather the harvest bounty and rush home to "put a little something up" for the winter. For weeks our houses, which were a couple of thousand miles apart from each other at the time, were redolent of the smells of spices and cooking fruits and vegetables. Unless we could think of some logical excuse for disappearing, we both had chores to perform during these bouts of patriotic thrift, usually involving hauling water or scrubbing jars. When it was all over, the shelves in our basements were lined with glistening glass containers of corn, tomatoes, pickles, and who knows what else, each neatly labeled and ready for use. The problem was that sometime around January, both of our mothers would get panicky over the possibility of botulism, and most of the products of their autumn labors ended up in the garbage. *Sic transit gloria piccalilli.*

Admittedly, the preservation of certain kinds of foods is tricky and involves some fairly heavy-duty equipment. So-called "low acid" foods such as vegetables, meat, poultry, and fish must be processed with a sustained heat of at least 240 degrees F., so the only practical way to can them at home is with a large steam canner similar to but much more costly than a pressure cooker. Unless you have a small farm or a large vegetable garden, we don't recommend going into this hobby. If you do, buy a good book on canning.

"High-acid" foods—virtually all fruits, fruit juices, fruit purées, and jellies as well as most tomatoes and pickles (a high proportion of vinegar is essential)— can be safely processed in boiling water because the combination of acidity and a processing temperature of 212 degrees F. discourages the growth of bacteria.

Heatproof canning jars come in a variety of sizes, from 1 cup on up. They may be reused, as long as they don't have any nicks around the rims that would prevent a perfect seal. The flat lids and the threaded bands that hold them on are sold separately, and the lids should never be reused.

The watchword when is comes to canning is cleanliness. Thoroughly wash and rinse the jars and then put them with the lids and bands in a large kettle of boiling water. There is a gadget called a canning jar lifter, a set of tongs that looks sort of like the ones icemen used to use, that is ideal for fishing things out of hot water. After scalding the jars, lids, and bands let them dry on a cake rack over paper towels.

After preparing the food to be canned, fill the hot jars to within ¼ inch of the top, making sure there are no air bubbles in the food. Carefully wipe any spills from the rims, place the tops on them and screw the bands down as tight as you can. Using the can lifter, immerse the jars in the kettle of boiling water, the surface of which must be at least an inch above the tops. Boil for the time called for in each recipe. Remove the jars and let them cool completely. The way to test for a good seal is to press down on the center of the lid after cooling. If it stays down and doesn't pop back up like those cricket clickers we played with as kids, you've got it made. If the top does pop back, follow the example of our mothers and throw the jar away.

# A Tale of Two Chutneys

Serving curry is like marrying an aging movie queen—it isn't the original cost, it's the upkeep. In India the wealth of a maharaja was judged by the number of servants he had. At a palace dinner where curry was the main course, each condiment or *sambal* was carried to the table by a different bearer, which is why curry condiments are still often called "boys." The list sometimes seemed endless, but everyone agreed on one thing: a curry was naked without chutney.

During their tenure as custodians of India, the British adopted chutney as if they had invented it in the first place, and some of the best commercial versions are still made in England. The English found that chutney is a wonderful relish with all kinds of meat, savory stews, fish, and even vegetables, and it became a staple in British pantries. We agree that it should be, but the problem is that even American brands are expensive enough to discourage its use very often. Thus, we offer two good basic chutney recipes.

## Major Morgan's Mango Chutney

¾ cup brown sugar
1½ cups white wine vinegar
1 large onion, chopped
1 green pepper, seeded and chopped
1 clove garlic, minced
1 lime, thinly sliced
1½ teaspoons cinnamon
½ teaspoon ground cloves

½ teaspoon ground ginger
½ teaspoon chili powder
½ teaspoon ground coriander
Pinch of saffron (optional)
½ teaspoon ground allspice
¾ cup raisins
3 large ripe mangoes
2 pounds ripe peaches

In a large pot combine all the ingredients except the mangoes and peaches and bring to a boil, stirring occasionally. Reduce the heat and simmer uncovered for an hour.

While the mixture is cooking climb into the bathtub or pull on a wet suit and peel and slice the mangoes (they are messy). Peel, pit, and slice the peaches. After an hour add the fruit to the pot and continue simmering until the fruit is tender, about 30 minutes. Pour the mixture into hot sterilized canning jars and follow the preceding directions for processing high-acid foods, boiling the jars for 5 minutes.

## Tomato Chutney

4 cups tomatoes, peeled, seeded, and
  roughly chopped
2 onions peeled and chopped
1 lime, thinly sliced
1¹/₂ cups cider vinegar
1¹/₂ cups sugar
1 tablespoon salt
1 tablespoon ground ginger

3 cloves garlic, pressed
2 teaspoons chili powder
¹/₂ teaspoon ground mace
2 tablespoons fresh gingerroot, minced
1 tablespoon white mustard seed
3 tablespoons chopped canned green chili
  peppers

Place all ingredients in a large pot and simmer gently over low heat for 1½ hours or until thick and syrupy. Pour into hot sterilized canning jars and follow the preceding directions for processing high-acid foods, boiling the jars for 5 minutes.

# Freezing

A freezer, once regarded as necessary only for big families, can be the salvation of cooking couples. We have mentioned the subject at many points along the way in this little seminar, suggesting artful ways two people can use one of these marvelous inventions to save time and money. The response from some of you will be, "We have a perfectly good freezer on top of the refrigerator, and besides, there's no room to put one of those behemoths in our apartment." Wrong on both counts, guys.

To begin with, the freezer section of a refrigerator is designed to do two things well: make ice cubes and keep ice cream at serving temperature for short periods. Beyond that it's inadequate for anything other than the short-term storage of already frozen food. The temperature in it can vary from 20 degrees F. up to 32 degrees F., which is the point at which ice begins to melt. All authorities agree that 0 degrees F. is the best temperature for long storage.

Second, virtually every freezer manufacturer has at least one small model ideal for use in cramped quarters. And show us where it's written that a freezer has to be in the kitchen in the first place. Ours is in the garage, and one couple we know has a perfectly adequate little job about 3½ feet high and 2 feet wide hidden in a hall closet. It has a capacity of 10 cubic feet, about half the size of a regular freezer.

The value of a freezer is obvious. If you follow our advice and periodically spend a Saturday or Sunday making a couple of gallons of stock or some *glace de viande* or a pint or two of tomato sauce, it's almost essential. There are a few things to remember, however.

Don't ever try to freeze anything with gelatin or mayonnaise in it. The former will get as weepy as a teenage romantic seeing *Casablanca* for the first time, and the latter will curdle. Hard-cooked eggs become rubbery, lettuce and other greens wilt, and freezing any kind of poultry or meat stuffing is an invitation to salmonella. And in most cases it's a bad idea to freeze cooked leftovers of any kind. The temperature necessary to reheat them will likely cause them to dry out and become overcooked (one exception to this is leftover chili).

Most meats, fruits, and vegetables do freeze well if they are in sturdy, airtight containers and all the extraneous air and moisture are pushed out to avoid freezer burn. We have had the best luck with freezer foil, reusable cardboard containers with plastic bag inserts, and a device that seals food of various amounts in heavy-duty plastic. The latter, marketed under a number of brand names by several manufacturers, is a very welcome addition in any kitchen that specializes in meals for two. Among other things, we use ours to package unconcentrated stocks in cup and pint sizes, which is usually perfect for most recipes for two.

Herbs and spices keep well in tightly closed jars in a cool, dark place. But if you don't think you'll use up a green herb or spice in three months or so, freeze half of it in a sealed plastic bag.

The useful life of frozen foods varies widely, from about two weeks for unbaked breads and rolls to up to a year for most meat and poultry. A good rule of thumb is to label everything with the date it went into the freezer and rotate the contents frequently.

# PASTRY AND PASTA

## *Basic Pastry*

There exist a number of recipes for basic pastry made in a food processor, but we tend to favor the old-fashioned method. If you overprocess the dough it makes the pastry tough as nails. Also, it is necessary to freeze the fat, which takes time. This formula will make enough dough for use in any of the recipes in this book calling simply for basic pastry.

*1 cup flour*
*Pinch salt*

*½ cup shortening, lard or butter*
*1–3 tablespoons ice water*

Put flour and salt in a bowl. Cut in the shortening, lard, or butter thoroughly. Sprinkle in water, a little at a time, mixing until the flour is moistened and mixture almost cleans the sides of the bowl. Form into a ball, wrap, and chill.

For a little variety in savory pastry, try adding one of the following:
- ½ teaspoon celery, poppy, or fennel seeds
- ¼ cup grated sharp Cheddar cheese (we like this with pork or apple pie)
- 2 teaspoons toasted sesame seeds
- 1 teaspoon grated lemon zest

Or substitute ½ cup whole-wheat flour for ½ cup of the white flour.

# Basic Pasta and Variations

No home should be without a formula for making pasta. No matter how good the ingredients are, the kind you get in the supermarket is not as good as that which is fresh. There is really no trick to it, and contrary to what the catalogs say, there is no need to rob a bank to buy one of those doomsday pasta makers with all the bells and whistles known to science. Wonderful homemade noodles can simply be rolled out and cut with a knife. If you make a lot of pasta, however— and we believe all civilized people should—a relatively inexpensive pasta-rolling machine with blades to make tagliarini, fettucini, and lasagne shapes is a real help. Their other advantage is that you don't have to knead the dough. This basic recipe gives directions for making it with or without a food processor.

*2 eggs*                                    *⅛ teaspoon salt*
*1 tablespoon olive oil*                     *1½–2 cups flour*

To make pasta without a processor, beat eggs, oil, and salt together. Mound 1½ cups of flour on a work surface. Make a well in the center and pour in the egg mixture. Using one hand, gradually incorporate the flour from around the edge of the well into the eggs, stirring with your fingers to form a batter. Continue working until the dough forms a stiff paste. If the dough is too soft, add more flour. Knead for 5 to 10 minutes if dough will be rolled and cut by hand.

To make the pasta in a food processor, place eggs, oil, and salt in the work bowl and process until the eggs are beaten. Add flour and continue processing until the dough forms a ball.

Dough made by either process should be covered and allowed to rest for 1 hour. If using a pasta machine, follow the directions and cut the pasta on the desired-size rollers. If cutting by hand, divide the dough into sections, each about as big as an orange, and roll on a lightly floured surface until almost translucent. Sprinkle with cornmeal to prevent it from sticking, and fold the sheet into a loose roll. Cut crosswise into strips as wide as you want. Unroll noodles and place them to dry on a lightly floured surface.

Boil the noodles in a large pot of salted water with a few tablespoons of olive oil until tender but still firm. Drain.

**HERB PASTA**

For a long time we tried to create one of those summer gardens full of exotic fruits, sixteen types of lettuce, and corn at least as high as a Shetland pony's eye, but the only beneficiary of our effort was the man who sold manure. Finally we realized it was time to accept our limitations and concentrate on the single crop that seemed to thrive on our haphazard ministrations: herbs. Being inordinately proud of this meager horticultural accomplishment, we tend to throw herbs about the kitchen with great abandon. One of the more successful landings was in this pasta.

*2 eggs*
*1 tablespoon olive oil*
*⅛ teaspoon salt*
*1 tablespoon fresh oregano, minced*

*1 tablespoon fresh rosemary, minced*
*¼ cup fresh sorrel, stemmed and minced*
*1½–2 cups flour*

Put the eggs, oil, salt, and herbs in a blender or food processor and whirl until the herbs are puréed. Follow the directions above for making and cooking the pasta.

**GREEN PASTA**

The coloring and flavoring ingredient in this version is spinach. Blend ¼ pound of cooked spinach that has been pressed dry in a sieve with the eggs, oil, and salt. Follow the directions above for making and cooking the pasta.

**RED PASTA**

This, in combination with Basic Pasta and Green Pasta, is nice if you want to make a lasagne with the colors of the Italian flag. Blend 2 tablespoons of tomato paste with the eggs, oil, and salt. Follow the directions above for making and cooking the pasta.

# The World's Greatest Perpetual Stew

According to legend, any Frenchwoman can take a carrot, two mushrooms, and some unspeakable portion of an animal and transform them into a glamorous concoction worthy of the centerfold in a glossy food magazine. Although we all know that's something of a hyperbole, it is true that the French have made an art of making do.

One of the most delicious products of the French aptitude for thrift and inventiveness is a succulent stew prepared for centuries by farm wives in the Médoc region of Bordeaux. Strictly family fare, this ragout uses odd bits and pieces of meat that might otherwise be tossed to the *chien*. Our basic recipe calls for beef and pork at the beginning, and we suggest you use the cheapest cuts you can find—chuck, neck, etc.

Two ingredients give this stew its character: wine and time. While the Médoc is one of the world's greatest wine-growing regions, the wine used in the farmhouses is far from the lofty vintages that command ridiculous prices in the marketplace. When we first made this we had very good luck with an inexpensive California Zinfandel. The rich, earthy flavor comes from the manner in which it is cooked. The Médoc farm wife keeps her stew going sometimes for years, always leaving some at the bottom of the pot to form the base for new additions. Once it has attained maturity it becomes, as Anatole France described it, "this antique and precious base that gives the dish a quality comparable to the unique amber skin tones characterized in the works of the old Venetian masters." Old Anatole often got carried away writing about food.

It takes about five days to get the stew started properly, including three days in the refrigerator before serving it the first time. We have listed the ingredients needed on each of the first two days. Following the initial meal, fill the pot again with layers of the same ingredients, or substitute whatever's available—ham, lamb, sausages, chicken, or turkey—for the beef and pork. Pour on wine to cover and cook again until the wine is reduced by half. The flavor improves and matures each time new ingredients are added.

When serving remember that the new ingredients are on the top and that the flavorful, concentrated sauce is at the bottom, so be sure to dig down with the serving spoon.

In France, the pot stays on the back of the stove, and the stew is served and revamped about once a week. We have found that after making it the first time, the base freezes well for use later. This recipe makes enough for six hearty appetites with enough left over to start again.

# Ragoût de Bordeaux

**DAY 1**

½ pound salt pork, cut in ⅛-inch slices

3 carrots, thinly sliced

1 small bunch parsley

¼ cup snipped fresh thyme or 2 teaspoons
   dried

2 cloves garlic, minced

8 figs, cut in half (fresh is best, but dried
   will do)

4 onions, sliced

1 pound beef, cut in 1-inch cubes

Salt and pepper

1 pound pork, cut in 1-inch cubes

½ pound mushrooms

3 bay leaves

½ cup brandy

Dry red wine (at least 1 bottle)

*Preheat oven to 325 degrees F.* In a large greased casserole, Dutch oven, or *cocotte*, place the slices of salt pork to cover the bottom. Add the carrots in a layer. Add the parsley, thyme, garlic, and figs, distributing them evenly, and cover with a layer of 2 of the sliced onions. Add the beef in a layer and sprinkle with salt and pepper. Cover with a layer of the other 2 sliced onions. Add the pork in a layer and sprinkle again with salt and pepper. Clean and stem the mushrooms and add, pushing the caps and stems down into the mixture. Add the bay leaves. Warm the brandy in a small pan, ignite it, and pour it flaming over the mixture. When the flames die out, pour in enough red wine to cover all the ingredients. Place the pot, tightly covered, in the oven and allow it to burble gently until the wine is reduced by half, 2 to 3 hours (longer if need be). Allow the pot to cool and refrigerate it overnight.

**DAY 2**

3 carrots, thinly sliced

1 pound beef, cut in 1-inch cubes

2 onions, sliced

1 pound pork, cut in 1-inch cubes

½ pound mushrooms

Salt and pepper

Dry red wine

*Preheat oven to 325 degrees F.* Remove any fat that has risen to the top and bring the pot back to room temperature. Layer in the carrots, beef, onions, pork, and mushrooms, lightly salting and peppering each layer. Add enough red wine to cover the ingredients and return the pot to the oven until the wine is reduced by half. Cool, find and discard the bay leaves, and refrigerate the stew for three days. Reheat before serving.

# INDEX